The Breaking Point

10 Transformation Lessons on How to Master Adversity and Craft a Life of Excellence

JONO GILARDI

The Breaking Point: 10 Transformation Lessons on
How to Master Adversity and Craft a Life of Excellence
Copyright © 2025 by Jono Gilardi
All photos courtesy the author unless otherwise noted.

No part of this publication may be reproduced or transmitted in any form or by any means without the prior written permission of the author, except in the case of brief quotations embodied in critical reviews and certain other noncommercial uses permitted by copyright law.

www.jonogilardi.com

Hardcover ISBN: 979-8-9997029-1-3
Paperback ISBN: 979-8-9997029-0-6
Ebook ISBN: 979-8-9997029-2-0

Printed in the United States of America
on acid-free paper.

Cover design by Vanessa Mendozzi
www.vanessamendozzidesign.com

Editorial and design services provided by Kent Sorsky.
Editorial and writing support services provided by Jordan Ring.

Contents

Introduction vii

PART I: MY STORY

1. "Those Guys Aren't Your Friends". 3
2. Dreams Die 15
3. The Ghosted Advisor. 25
4. "Right Between the Eyes" 35
5. So You Wanna Be a Gangster .43
6. Pay Your Dues. 55
7. There's Good in All Adversity .67
8. One Bad Decision from Disaster 77
9. Change Hurts 89
10. A Message from Hell 97
11. Bottomed Out. 111
12. An Angel Emerges 121
13. Hello, Grim Reaper, My Name Is Jono 131

PART II: THE 10 TRANSFORMATION LESSONS

14. Transformation Lesson 1. Master Self-Image........151

15. Transformation Lesson 2. Conquer the Victim Mentality..163

16. Transformation Lesson 3. Guard Your Environment...175

17. Transformation Lesson 4. Develop Self-Control, the Ultimate Adversity-Busting Superpower 191

18. Transformation Lesson 5. Master Your Fears........205

19. Transformation Lesson 6. The Art of Failure........217

20. Transformation Lesson 7. Fight Your Way Out of the Gloom 231

21. Transformation Lesson 8. Treat Your Mind Like a Sanctuary 247

22. Transformation Lesson 9. Habit of Hard!...........263

23. Transformation Lesson 10. Fuck Average! 279

Conclusion: From the Depths We Shall Rise 295

Transformation Steps Quick Reference................299

About Jono Gilardi..................................319

To my wife, Ali Gilardi, whose unwavering support, encouragement, and belief in me made every word of this book possible. And to my children, Gio and Olivia, who inspire me to reach for greatness even in the darkest moments. You guys are my everything. I could never love you enough.

Introduction

> *"When we are no longer able to change a situation,
> we are challenged to change ourselves."*
> —*Victor Frankl*

The year was 2001. I tiptoed to the front window of my apartment, pinching the curtain with my thumb and index finger, careful not to let anyone see I was looking out. My gut had been right—something was wrong. Heat surged through my body, my heart sinking in my chest as my stomach turned over a dozen times. I was simultaneously stunned by fear and sadness, all these emotions rushing through me in seconds. Time was running out. *So this is it*, I thought. *This is how it's going down.* What I feared all along was winding its way up my rickety metal staircase. *I suppose it's time to face the music.*

Walking to the door, I took a deep breath to compose myself, though I knew nothing could truly prepare me for what waited outside. I grabbed the knob and swung the door wide open, standing there in my pajama bottoms and worn moccasin slippers. The sun was shining low through the trees, creating a beautiful cascade of sunshine across my doorstep. I squinted at the wonderful morning, thinking, *A shame it has to go away.* Taking my gaze off nature and the blue sky, I looked down at the mess I had created. The county's task force had strategically placed themselves behind cars and trees, their fully automatic ARs pointed directly at me. *What the fuck! How the hell did I get here? How did I so completely screw up my life?*

Have you ever wondered this same thing during your darkest moments? If so, you're in the right place.

How this standoff ended, and the series of choices that led to it, is a story I'll share later in these pages. For now, let me mention my life didn't start out this way. In fact, I had a great childhood, filled with the kind of memories most people look back on and smile at: family dinners, Little League games, summer adventures. My parents were good people who did the best they could with what they knew. However, sometimes, that foundation just isn't enough to keep you on the straight and narrow.

Sometimes in life, we have to learn things the hard way. Not because we weren't taught better, but because something inside us refuses to accept the easier path. Sometimes our pride whispers that we know better, our stubbornness convinces us to push boundaries, or our lack of confidence drives us to prove ourselves in all the wrong ways. And for some of us, the only way to truly learn life's most important lessons is to walk straight through the damn fires of hell. I'm one of those people.

That moment, standing in my doorway facing armed agents, was just one stop on my journey through those hell fires. One point that tried to break me. My life reads like a crazy script written by a bad screenwriter who stuffed in everything that could possibly go wrong. Time behind bars in my early years. A brush with suicide that brought me face-to-face with my own mortality. A business venture that swallowed my life savings whole. And now, a battle with blood cancer that reminds me daily how precious and uncertain life truly is.

But here's the thing about walking through fire: if you survive, you emerge transformed. Each of these experiences, as painful as they were, taught me something invaluable. My time incarcerated showed me the raw power of consequences and choices. My dance with death revealed what truly matters in life. That failed business? It taught me humility, patience, and wisdom. And my ongoing battle with an incurable blood cancer? It drives me to put every damn ounce of energy into this beautiful life, because I know death is always there. As they say, you only get one shot, so you better give it your all.

This is what *The Breaking Point* is all about. It's not just about surviving adversity; it's about using it as a catalyst for transformation. It's about developing the inner strength to rebound from your personal hell. Struggles, setbacks, failures, disease, heartbreak, misfortune, trouble with the law, drugs, distress, they can either whittle you down to nothing, leaving you paralyzed with fear, or give you an opportunity to grow, emerging stronger than before.

The Breaking Point starts with accepting what we cannot control while taking full responsibility for how we respond to it. It means listening to life's greatest teacher, adversity itself. Those of us who have been through real adversity with an attitude of learning from it have gained resilience. It has fortified us well for this journey called life.

I wrote this book for us, the ones who have gone through struggles and pains, disease and disaster. For those who, like me, fucked up their lives almost beyond repair, who dismantled what once seemed like a fair hand into one with the odds stacked against us. For those who finally realized they were ready to depart the self-destructive path and seek a new way into a life worth living.

You see, the setbacks we've faced were placed before us for a reason. They were opportunities disguised as obstacles. The purpose behind your pain might not be clear right now, but eventually, that purpose will reveal itself when you're ready to see it.

You, who have been through such disasters, are someone extraordinary. The lessons you've learned aren't taught in any classroom or online course. They're yours and only yours. Nobody can take them from you, and nobody can teach what you yourself have been through, because everyone's life adversities are unique.

We don't have to remain down just because it feels good, or because it's the easy choice. We, the defeated, shall rise to the top because we, unlike most, have gone through struggles that will fuel us to our ultimate victory. We've learned things like patience, persistence, failure, and defeat firsthand. We've lost money, time, and health. We've seen things most cannot imagine, and we survived. We now view the world through a different lens, one that most cannot comprehend because they made the "right" choices and lived "safe" lives.

It's time to use your scars as a map to find your buried treasure. Time to rebuild from what once broke you. Time for you to reach beyond your breaking point and discover what lies ahead.

Part I

My Story

Life isn't a neat, tidy story with a beginning, middle, and end. It's a messy, chaotic jumble of moments, some beautiful, some ugly, and a whirlwind in between. We're all writing our own stories, day by day, decision by decision. Some chapters are filled with triumph and joy, others with pain, regret and moments that try to break us. We're not just the authors of our tales, we're also the main characters. Sometimes, we're our own worst enemies.

My story? It's a twisted roller coaster ride through the heights of success and the depths of despair. I've been the villain, the victim, and occasionally, the hero. I've made bad choices that would make your skin crawl and good-but-difficult decisions that might inspire you. I've danced with death, flirted with disaster, and somehow managed to crawl my way back to something resembling redemption.

But this isn't just about me. It's about you, too. It's about all of us stumbling through this crazy voyage called life, trying to make sense of it all. Maybe you've never dealt drugs or faced down cancer, but I bet you've felt lost or scared, or like you're royally fucking up your one shot at existence. We are all in this together, and it's our stories, shared vulnerably, that inspire the way forward.

In part 1 of this book, I'm going to share my story, so you can see how you can get knocked on your ass, time after time, yet still end up standing tall. You'll find hard-earned wisdom on everything from the power of decision-making to the power of facing your own mortality. You'll learn how to turn adversity into fuel for personal growth, how to find meaning in life's darkest moments, and why self-discipline might just be your ticket to beating the odds. But most importantly, you'll discover that no matter how far you've fallen, there's always a way to climb back up, if you're willing to do the work.

So, are you ready to face your fears, confront your demons, and maybe, just maybe, come out the other side a little stronger, a little wiser, and a whole lot more alive? Then let's get started. This is your wake-up call, your invitation to live a life you can look back on, be proud of, and say, "I lived," with a smile on your face.

1

"Those Guys Aren't Your Friends"

"Always be yourself, have faith in yourself, do not go out and look for a successful personality and duplicate it."
—*Bruce Lee*

It was the first day of middle school and I was excited. I was ready for the change, to grow up a little and have more responsibilities. The carefree days of the 1980s were fading into memory as we stepped into a new decade. And in middle school, that's where it all begins to happen. Our voices begin to crack, acne pops up, the girls we used to play with now have boobs. We become more serious. What you do and who you roll with begins to matter. The innocent sleepovers filled with Nintendo games and mountains of candy were giving way to something entirely different: smoking weed behind the school and endless conversations about which girls had gotten hot over the summer.

After-school dances, playing on the youth sports teams, and cheerleaders. Such a shift from grade school. Simplicity quickly switches over to complexity. We were getting lockers to keep our stuff in, and if that wasn't enough to make you feel like a big boy or girl, finally reaching the age of changing your clothes for physical education class certainly would. Locker rooms and showers signaled we were growing up, and I was ready. Well, not for the showers. Unless of course you possessed confidence, and confidence was something that consistently eluded me in those early years.

Despite my excitement about middle school, social challenges quickly emerged. I had two friends who came with me from grade school, two friends who helped hold together the foundation of who I was. As time went on and the pressure of being "cool" grew heavy on me, those two friends and I had a serious falling out one day after school. We were riding our bikes over to a buddy's house in the middle of a hot September day. It was a long ride, and they were starting to pull away and get far ahead of me, not bothering to wait for me to catch up. I was getting more and more frustrated. I saw this as a total slap in the face, for whatever reason, so I turned my bike around and went home and, just like that, we never spoke again. It wasn't the first time my sensitivity had ruined something important.

The next day of school, I found myself in a bit of a predicament. When that lunch bell rang, I had nowhere to go, nothing to do, no friends to lean on. Suddenly, I had become a loner, a loser, and I felt it. There was this song by Whodini called "Friends" and it sang, "Friends, how many of us have them?" That song haunted me for years afterward, playing in my head like a taunting reminder every time I felt alone. The chorus would loop in my mind as I walked the crowded hallways, a soundtrack to my isolation, because deep down I knew I didn't have any real friends. It stung, but my pride was dense and my head hard, so I wouldn't allow myself to make up with my friends. If they wanted to be friends again, they would have to talk to me first. They never did . . .

What would I do? I had no idea. I was so concerned about what people thought of me standing around alone, I had to do something and fast. I started tagging along with another acquaintance from grade school. We didn't talk much, but he was cool and allowed me to hang around him and his friends. Perfect, I thought. Anything was better than standing around alone. Even when I did find myself hanging out with these so-called friends, I knew deep down it wasn't real. I was just doing it to feel like I mattered, to have some sense of significance in a world where I felt invisible. This is when things really began to shift, as I felt I was an outsider on the bottom, just feeding off whatever scraps were laid out before me. I needed more, even if "more" meant going in the wrong direction. I knew my life would never be the same.

And so I began to morph everything about myself. I started to slick my hair back with enough hair gel to protect a football player from a tackle. I wore giant baggy pants and ugly green Reeboks. I literally became someone I wasn't overnight, all for the sake of "likes." Not Facebook likes. Facebook was still about twenty years away. I'm talking about real likes. Did it work? Not really. Nothing was working. And playing on the tackle football team didn't make me significant either, because I was definitely not your *Friday Night Lights*' superstar. I hated getting hit, and being one of the smaller players, I became an easy target for others eager to showcase their tackling skills. It was painful as I would lay on the ground after most tackling drills, trying to recover. I figured I had to do something different. Maybe I'd become an outlaw. Maybe that would earn me some respect.

High school was worse. Still hanging on to my gangster look I tried hanging out with some of the guys I played youth football with, the jocks. I looked out of place so I'd just stand out on the edge of their group, far enough away so they wouldn't bother me and close enough to where I didn't look like a loner. I was basically perfecting the art of social camouflage. Turns out I had all the stealth capabilities of a neon sign in a dark alley and I turned into someone they could bully when they got bored.

One day, one of them walked up to me and said, "Why do you even hang out over here with us? Nobody likes you," and rammed me with his shoulder. The impact sent a jolt through my collarbone and my backpack slipped awkwardly off my shoulder, but the physical pain was nothing compared to the words that seemed to hang in the air around me, visible to everyone passing by. That one stung, and I'm not talking about the shoulder—I felt it for days after. My chest tightened like someone had wrapped a belt around it and pulled. At night, I'd replay those words in my head, each repetition like a knife twisting deeper. I'd walk the halls with my eyes down, stomach in knots, dreading the lunch bell. Why didn't I stand up for myself? Why didn't I just knock that prick on his ass? I hated school with a passion.

I heard one of the Physical Education teachers was opening up the weight room during lunch breaks. So instead of hanging out with people who didn't like me, I began lifting weights at lunch. The problem was he didn't always open the gym, so again I'd have to make a decision to stand around alone or stumble back to the jocks for some lunch time abuse. The thought of facing them again filled everyday with dread.

One day as I was walking up to the group and out of nowhere I got shit on by a seagull in the middle of the courtyard, and everyone started laughing. Their laughter echoed in my ears like they were all standing inside my head. My face burned with shame, and I wanted to disappear, to melt into the concrete beneath my feet. I didn't think my freshman year could have gone any worse. Problem is, things can always get worse.

> "Why didn't I stand up for myself? Why didn't I just knock that prick on his ass? I hated school with a passion."

My neighbor, a so-called friend who sometimes came over to play basketball, decided to target me in class to build himself up. Being significantly larger than me, he knew he could get away with it and began unleashing a barrage of big nose jokes while shoving me around. Then he grabbed my head and proceeded to rub my hair until it was a dried-up mess sticking out in all directions. With that much hair gel, the damage was catastrophic—I looked like I'd stuck my finger in an electrical socket or auditioned for the role of a shocked cartoon character. The humiliation burned through me like acid as laughter erupted around us. I fought back tears but failed miserably, breaking down right there in front of everyone. In that moment, I wasn't just embarrassed—I was defeated, emotionally spent by this betrayal from someone

I'd considered a friend. Each laugh felt like another nail hammered into the coffin of my dignity. I was at a breaking point.

And so I stayed away from the jocks and my friendly neighbor and started hanging out with some less popular guys who seemed to like me for who I was, gangster look and all. We talked and laughed, played basketball in the back of the school at lunch. It was a much better existence. These guys were real friends, but something inside me still wasn't satisfied. I desperately wanted to feel significant, to be somebody who mattered. And in my teenage mind, I was willing to do almost anything to achieve that feeling. The respect I craved wasn't coming from my grades or my athletic abilities. I needed to find it somewhere else, even if that somewhere wasn't the best place to look.

A chance to break free from "loser" finally came for me in the form of a driver's license. I took the classes, got my permit, and passed my driving test the first time I took it. I drove to school the very next day. I know you remember the incredible feeling you got when you first took the wheel and drove down the street. Alone! No mom, no dad, alone, free. It's one of the greatest feelings a young kid could ever have. Suddenly, you feel like you can go anywhere, your world expands. The radio plays your favorite tracks, bass thumping through the speakers at a volume that would make your ears ring later. A sea of endless possibilities calls to you. It truly is a rewarding day. While everyone else was still walking, riding their bikes, or getting dropped off by their mommies, I pulled up in my mom's Isuzu Trooper, an ugly, boxy, top-heavy SUV. I didn't care what the car looked like; it just felt so good to be rolling.

When you have wheels, you are no longer confined to the school grounds for lunch. You can now leave and get lunch almost anywhere you like, as long as you get back in time for your next class. So on my first day of driving to school, I took my average, slightly nerdy friends to Blondie's Pizza right up the road. The next day, we went to the mall and ate at the food court. It was glorious. It was freedom! However, much like the man who wins millions in the lotto, friends began popping up with smiles on their faces, and I was beginning to feel a little touch of significance.

It wasn't long until a different crowd started to notice me. Not your average nerdy guys, but the bad guys, the hardened ones, the guys who were already having sex and drinking beer. The ones who cut school and smoked a ton of weed. The ones who grew up early . . . yeah, those guys. Those guys made an impression on me. Why? I don't know why. Probably because they fit the description of what all the rappers like NWA, 2 Pac and many others rapped about. These rappers glorified criminality. My role models. It was the lifestyle that grabbed me and would not let go. The baggy jeans, the I don't give a fuck attitude, the rebelling against all adults and all authority, including the law. It was the power we thought we had. It was everything a shy boy needed to feel alive, to feel like he mattered. It was the significance I was looking for. I was trying to fill a gap in my existence. I looked up to the outlaw way of life, and with my car, I finally got an in.

I was already getting to know these guys a little before I got my wheels, but when I finally showed up rolling, suddenly they wanted to go to lunch. Suddenly, with a big smile on their faces, they came up and said, "What's up, Jono? Let's all go to lunch." To be seen rolling with the outlaws? I couldn't say no. They jumped in and told my average, nerdy friends to hop in the back. They complied. I remember glancing at them through the rear-view mirror. They looked clearly unhappy and saddened, maybe disgusted at what I had just done. They sat in the trunk like lost puppies, tails tucked between their legs, quiet and shamed. I didn't care because I was now rolling with the bad guys. And so once again, I lost a set of friends. It would be the last day I'd talk to those nerdy guys. Apparently, they didn't like taking a back seat to all my "cool" friends.

This incident represented a life-changing moment for me, and not for the better. While it would still be a year or so before I really went off the rails, that was the day I sold out my friends and, most of all, sold out myself. From there on, I'd be stuck walking on a deeply rutted road.

I began cutting classes and showing up late to school. I started using drugs and alcohol. Sometimes, I'd show up in class with a nice buzz on. I loved this because suddenly I had confidence. I could laugh and crack jokes in class. Insecurities fell by the wayside. I no longer gave two shits about anyone's opinion. Even when I wasn't buzzed, I began to just not give a damn. I was riding a wave I knew nothing about, and didn't appear to notice that sharks were circling my surfboard. Falling off would have dire consequences, as I'd soon find out, but that wave felt astonishing to me, so I kept riding it.

I became someone I wasn't in hopes others would like me. I became a criminal, an outlaw, a convict, and I sold myself out for such a low existence. I basically spit in the faces of the friends who actually liked hanging out with me for who I was, and for that, I will always be sorry.

I will never forget one of the last things one of my old friends said to me that day before I officially moved on. "Jono, listen. Those guys . . . those guys aren't your friends. They don't give a damn about you." It was the truth, and I knew it then, but I still ignored it. I let it go because being cool meant more to me, whether it was real or not. There were girls on this side, wild parties, and a feeling of belonging and significance, even if it was fake.

Don't Sell Yourself Out

Here's the truth that nearly destroyed me: never sell yourself out. Not once. Not ever. I know how tempting it is—trust me, I've been there. That moment when the cool kids finally notice you, when fitting in seems worth any price. Those moments when who you are gets tested against who others want you to be.

But when you sell yourself out, your whole life unravels. You toss aside real friends for fake ones who wouldn't piss on you if you were on fire. You put

> "You'll never find one second of real happiness until you learn to love the person you actually are."

yourself in situations that make your gut scream "wrong," but you ignore it because you're desperate to be liked. It's the kid who torments others just to hear his "friends" laugh much like my neighbor did to me. It's the married person who throws away twenty years for a quick hit of validation from a stranger. It's abandoning your deepest dreams for a cheap thrill that fades by morning. My Uncle Bill, drops this truth bomb whenever I see him: "Short-term gain, long-term pain." That's selling yourself out in five words.

I started selling out young, and it bulldozed me into years of ruin that took twice as long to climb out from. I had to rebuild everything: relationships, self-respect, my entire identity. Because here's what nobody tells you: you'll never find one second of real happiness until you learn to love the person you actually are. Not the person you think others want. Being fake might get you temporary attention, but being authentic earns you genuine connection. And nothing, not drugs, not status, not any amount of "cool points," feels better than that.

Living as someone you're not is like wearing shoes three sizes too small. At first, you just notice the discomfort. Then comes the pain. Then the wounds. Your body and mind start breaking down under the weight of your own bullshit. The emptiness grows, the stress builds, and eventually, something gives. For me, that "something" was everything, as you'll see in the chapters ahead.

If you're already struggling with self-esteem like I was, faking it doesn't just fail to build confidence, it incinerates whatever fragments you were clinging to. Every fake smile, every forced laugh, every compromised moment burns another piece of who you really are. Rebuilding takes work. Hard, painful, worth-every-second work. Because without a solid sense of who you are, you'll never master anything else in life. You'll fold at every obstacle, always searching for the approval that never quite satisfies.

We're born with certain truths in our DNA. When we betray those truths to please others, we lose our center. It's buying status symbols to impress people you don't even like. It's treating others like garbage to hear your "friends" laugh. It's risking your freedom and your future for a fake version of significance. And goddamn, do I know that road by heart.

Oscar Wilde nailed it: "Be yourself; everyone else is already taken." Trying to be someone else is the biggest lie you'll ever tell, and you're telling it to the one person who matters most—you. Those who shape-shift to fit every room are drowning inside. Real peace only comes when you can stand in your own skin anywhere, anytime, without apology.

Maybe you're in that dark place right now. Maybe you're watching someone you love disappear into it. I see you. I was you. But trust this hard-earned wisdom: the path gets ten times harder when you abandon yourself along the way. The real you is worth fighting for. Always.

2

Dreams Die

"Picking up the pieces of a shattered dream is better than having no pieces to pick up at all."
—Matshona Dhliwayo

On a cold, dark February evening, I sat brooding in my old, gray, sun-faded 1986 Honda Accord. I paid $600 for that car. It was my first. It was one of those cars that never dies, even after 300,000 miles. I beat that car to hell. Bounced over curbs, took it off road for no reason at all, crashed it into parking poles because I didn't know how to park. I worked that engine hard and it just kept going. It reminded me of the Energizer Bunny. It just kept going and going and going. Most of us have had a car like this. Usually it's our first.

That evening, as I sat in the warmth of that old faded bucket, I watched the class resume without me. Outside, as the darkness enveloped me and my old ride, I watched as the light inside the dojo shined bright on all the students at William Kim's tae kwon do studio. I saw Master Powell instructing the class that I had faithfully attended for two plus years.

Now, I no longer wanted to be a part of it. At least, I thought this was what I wanted. It was what I kept telling myself.

I watched as they performed kick after kick, punch after punch, and put on their gear and sparred with each other. What used to bring me joy and happiness was now fading. I was losing interest, and I couldn't muster the energy needed to get my ass out of the car and into the studio.

I stared down at the class until the sweat steamed and the humidity fogged up the glass and I was no longer able to see in. In a way I felt a bit of resentment towards my taekwondo training. It never helped, it never worked. My brother and I joined to learn self-defense but the bullies kept coming and later I'd still get my ass kicked a dozen times over. Even though I loved it, I still rotated the key in the ignition, I heard the old four-cylinder sputter to life. I shifted down to reverse. Yeah, buddy, it was a stick shift. Who drives those anymore? I backed out of my spot and disappeared into the night. Only a puff of exhaust remained, fading away in the thick, cold air. I would never return.

The medals I won in my tae kwon do career, before I threw it away.

Though I made a ton of bad decisions in my life, this one stands out. It might seem unimportant, but it had a huge impact on my life. It was the night I once again changed for the worse, not for the better. The night I let one of my childhood dreams die.

The new me would make all of his decisions based on instant gratification. I'd go on to make choices based solely on how it made me feel in the moment and how it made me look to my friends and peers. I wanted to be someone, and to be that someone now, not tomorrow.

When I was younger, I'd walk around telling everyone I wanted to be an actress, not knowing the difference between actor and actress. I always had big dreams, dreams of becoming an action star like my heroes, Bruce Lee and Jean-Claude Van Damme. My tae kwon do training gave these dreams substance. I could feel the power in my body during practice, my muscles remembering every move, every stance, each motion bringing me closer to the hero I imagined I could be. My best friend Adam and I—yes, I had a couple good friends outside of school—even started making cheap VHS movies of fight scenes and stunts all around my house, the camera shaking with our laughter as we attempted to mimic our heroes. We'd spend hours rewinding and watching our clumsy roundhouse kicks, imagining ourselves as the next big thing in action films.

The night I drove away from the dojo, I buried those dreams beneath the weight of my own self-doubt. I can still feel the decision sitting heavy in my chest. It hurts. I chose a road of ruin and despair, of drug use, money, guns, and jail cells. With each step down that darker path, I could feel those childhood dreams fading, struggling to survive as I smothered them with each bad choice. I chose these things over my dreams, over my long-term gain, trying to ignore the voice of that hopeful kid still whispering somewhere inside me.

> "I got so wasted one night I woke to find myself behind a dumpster. The worst part? It didn't even seem all that bad at the time."

High school became something I only went to when I felt like it. I soon found myself using drugs. All kinds of drugs. I got on meth pretty bad, but I didn't like who I became on that stuff: skinny, with sunken-in eyes and cheeks, looking like a zombie from *The Walking Dead*. I'd stay up all night tweaking out, stealing stupid shit for a buck. It was a low existence. I got so wasted one night I woke to find myself behind a dumpster. The worst part? It didn't even seem all that bad at the time. I just simply woke from my slumber and began walking home in a daze like the zombie I'd become. I was living the life of a true loser. Even in my low state, this was a jarring reality for me. I had never wanted to be on the bottom. I had always strived to be on the top. I just happened to find the wrong place and the wrong "top."

I was demolishing my future with the precision of a wrecking ball, like so many young adults do, in search of something bigger, something we think is better. The grass is greener on the other side, we think. For some, that "something better" means going the conventional route of staying in school, going to college, and following the path of least resistance. The path that society tells us to follow. School, more school, career, a good job, family, a five-bedroom house with a pool, seventy-inch TV, etc. I always heard the same damn line over and over again: "Go to school, get a job." Let me guess, you've heard that shit too? Cogs in a wheel. I hated the idea of our dreams being slowly beaten out of us. The conventional route wasn't for me.

Few people tried to steer me straight, and those who did couldn't break through my walls. If anyone could have, it would have been my grandpa, Justice John E. Benson. He was a high-profile judge in San Francisco and a high-grade example of the benefits of becoming a cog in the wheel. Behind the stern courtroom demeanor, he was the grandfather who planted slobbery wet kisses on our cheeks that made us squirm and giggle. He went to school, graduated from college, and became a lawyer and then a judge. He was a perfect example of what hard work meant. He showed everyone in the family that if you do the work and stay persistent and never give up, you will be rewarded. His work must have been his dream because he sure did spend a lot of time in his office.

What my grandfather never understood was how much I struggled with school from the beginning. I was always placed in the "special" classes, what the other kids called the "retard class." Learning disabilities made every assignment feel like climbing a mountain with weights strapped to my back. While other kids breezed through their homework, I'd sit for hours, the words swimming before my eyes, my frustration building until I began walking out of class. Teachers would sigh when calling on me, their patience wearing thin as I stumbled through reading assignments. School wasn't just challenging, it was humiliating. So when I heard people say, "go to school," all I could think about was signing up for more years of feeling stupid and worthless.

Grandpa ultimately died of lung cancer. As his health was fading, sucking on bottles of oxygen to breathe, he placed his hands on my shoulders and, taking a few ragged breaths, spoke his last words to me, "Go to school." His grip tightened as if he wanted to shake some sense into me. Of course I smiled and said, "Okay, Grandpa." We never spoke again.

Grandpa saw all of my mistakes unfold. He witnessed the revolving door of jail cells, the hollow look in my eyes from drug use, the rebellious attitude that pushed away anyone trying to help. The disappointment in his eyes cut deeper than any judge's sentence ever could. Sometimes, in moments of clarity or achievement now, I wonder if he's looking down, finally seeing what I've become, the transformations I have made despite the challenges I face daily—and nodding with a smile.

School isn't the only way. It was definitely not the route I was going to be taking, no matter what Grandpa or anyone else said. Quitting tae kwon do class was a critical decision in my life, a pivotal moment, and I blew it. I was going to make my own decisions. No one else would have any influence over me. As the old knight said in *Indiana Jones and the Last Crusade*, "He chose poorly." I had made one of the many bad decisions I would continue to make in my life for a long time to come.

We all have these "What could have been?" moments. We can't regret them because they are what shape us into who we are today, but it still stings when we think of how much better off we might have been had we chosen differently and stayed on the path toward our goals and ultimately our dreams.

Smoothing Out Our Rough Edges

We are like clay. In the beginning, we have guides to shape and mold us: our parents, grandparents, mentors. Eventually, we have to start trying to figure it out on our own, and for me, that meant going down all the wrong paths. The older I got, the more stuck I got.

The clay begins to harden, and the older we get, the harder it is to grind out the rough edges of past mistakes. That's when we have to bust out the power tools, grinders, and Dremels. We have to grind away at ourselves until our hands bleed. In time, we *can* change, if we put in the effort. In time, we *can* learn to smooth out all those jagged rough spots and straighten out those knobby curves. In time, with more precision hand tools, we can chip, whittle, and resculpt ourselves into somebody new. With patience and bravery, we can become something alluring and magnificent.

It's hard to tell this to a seventeen-year-old who has already been struggling with who he is and where he is going in life. I had a destination picked out, a dream to be an actor, but failed to make that happen, or even try. How was I to see my fault in this choice I made? How was I supposed to see past the adolescent stage and look at the bigger picture? How was I supposed to look at what really matters? I couldn't. Many of us struggle with this. We think we know so much at this age, but our pride gets us into trouble.

We can get advice from well-meaning family members who say things like, "Go to school!" I received such advice, but I always just laughed it off. I didn't give a shit about school. And it was extremely hard for me. I had no direction, but I wasn't too worried. Sometimes we just have to learn things the hard way. We have to get smacked in the face, dragged across the concrete, thrown in the slammer, wake up hungry and bloodied behind dumpsters, boiled hard. Only then might we come out on the other side with a new perspective on life. Only then can we learn. Only then, after the mistakes are made and the adversities are dealt with, will we realize what we must do. It's unfortunate it has to be this way, how much pain has to be involved—and some don't even make it out on the other side alive, free, or healthy. But for people like me, that is our path. It has to be done. We were too stubborn. We were surfing that wave again, riding high even with sharks still right there with us, and then we slipped, we began to fall, and right before we hit the water our life, our past, flashed before us. Fuck! This is going to be a wild ride.

The Greek philosopher Heraclitus said long ago, "The content of your character is your choice. Day by day, what you choose, what you think, and what you do is who you become." So remember that from here on out. Maybe you squandered a lot of time; you still have some left. There is always time to become better than you are right now. Decide who you want to become, find that dream again, and let that be the reason for your choices. We can choose to see our past disasters with the hardheaded perspective we used to have on everything, or we can choose to see it with fresh eyes.

Be kind to yourself. Learn to be patient in the suffering that it takes to get to the life you desire. Don't settle for who you used to be. You're better than that. You say you've been through hell? You've reached your breaking point? Good! That means you've learned a lot—a whole lot. All the obstacles, struggles, pains, and hardships you have been through have taught you valuable things. They taught you important life lessons like strength, resilience, perseverance, and persistence. You learned fortitude and willpower. Where most people would look at your life and see it as a tragedy or calamity, you can choose to see it as an opportunity for growth, because it's those of us who have been through deep struggle who are now more equipped than ever to travel down the hard path. Not the destructive path, but rather the challenging yet satisfying path that leads to the life you have always dreamed of. I know, because if you had an inner rebellious attitude like me, you also felt you were meant for so much more. We made all those past mistakes because we just didn't know any better at the time.

> "You say you've been through hell? Reached your breaking point? Good! That means you've learned a lot—a whole lot."

Now, it's time to travel the road you always felt you were meant to travel. Those scars you carry? They're not just reminders of pain. They're proof you survived. Use them. Every single one. You will find they are invaluable to your life as you move forward and back into your dreams.

3

The Ghosted Advisor

> *"The teacher who is indeed wise does not bid you to enter the house of his wisdom but rather leads you to the threshold of your mind."*
> *—Khalil Gibran*

My sophomore year in high school, 1995, was a tough year for me. I was in a rapid downward skid, headed for all the problems that would eventually arise in my life. I was no longer hanging on either side of the fence, but rather falling off the wrong side. The environment I chose was providing me with a false sense of significance, every bad decision reinforced by the people I surrounded myself with. I had quit tae kwon do, abandoning the discipline and structure that had once kept me grounded. School no longer had an appeal to me unless I was getting drunk or high, and hanging out with so-called friends and ditching class. Breaking the rules felt good, especially when everyone around me celebrated each act of defiance. I was, however, still going to some classes here and there, so I hadn't fully quit school yet. I was in the "I don't give a shit" state of mind and nothing anyone said mattered. I was smarter than everyone and had no need for school or guidance from anyone.

I was in my old, dusty, high school woodshop class. A place I had always found enjoyable no longer could hold my attention. The positive environment that once inspired me now felt foreign, like I no longer belonged among people who took pride in creating something worthwhile. I was lucky to even be in the classroom that day, as Mr. Hair, our woodshop teacher, began to explain the off-campus project we would be working on. We were going to be framing some sort of shed foundation and pouring the concrete. Most of the students knew what this class was all about and were excited to head off to work on something bigger than all the little projects in the shop. This was big for anyone who dreamed of building things with their hands. As for me, this was disastrous. Once I heard we were leaving campus for the day, which meant I would not be able to ruin my life just a little more than yesterday. I had to figure out how I was going to get out of this, one way or the other. I needed a plan.

"Alright everyone, time to go. Please go get in your assigned car and we will head to the project. I will meet you guys over there in twenty minutes," Mr. Hair yelled. Each of us was to hitch a ride with one of the students who volunteered to drive a couple of others to the site. This was perfect. My opportunity seemed to just fall right in my lap. The student vehicles were parked out back, but Mr. Hair just so happened to have parked his truck in the teacher parking lot, which was out front. I would just walk away from the car and smoothly walk to where all the other losers ditching class hung out. It would be a sly escape.

I slowly made my way to the back door with all the other students. Just as I was about to go through the door that led out back I turned my head and to my surprise, Mr. Hair was right on my tail with a big smile on his face. I tried to act normal and smile back as I turned back forward, however that smile quickly became a nervous look of *Oh shit! This guy is going to jump in the back seat with me and put on my seatbelt.* Now, Mr. Hair knew I was already headed for disaster, so he was trying his best to get me back on track. What the fuck was I going to do now?

Sure enough, he watched me right into the back seat of the car I was assigned to. "See you guys in a few," he said, and slammed the door behind me. *Ha! So he thinks he has the upper hand. No way I'm going. I'll show him*, I thought. We sputtered away, bent around a corner, and the second I saw we were no longer in Mr Hair's crosshairs, I said, "Pull over. I'm getting out." The driver turned to look at me. "What! No way, Jono. I'm not letting you out. I will get in trouble." My face quickly distorted in anger. "Pull the fuck over and let me the fuck out of this piece of shit you call a car." With no more words, the driver pulled over and let me out of the car. I hurried off before Mr. Hair came driving down the street.

Like I said, *Not this time, Mr. Hair. I win.* I imagined his face when all the students arrived on site. He would do his count and realize I wasn't there. I laughed at the thought of the surprise on his face. Did he really think he could beat me? I was such a tough guy. I didn't give a shit what anyone said, and when people told me I had to do something, I always did the opposite. Always. Back then, I thought this attitude made me strong. I didn't realize how the crowd I ran with was shaping me into someone I was never meant to be. Even today I do this, but I've weaponized my defiance for good. When someone tells me I can't follow my dreams, can't write my book, start my business, be a public speaker, or beat cancer, I don't just ignore them, I use their doubt as fuel. Their "you can't" becomes my "watch me." That resistance that once made me a troublemaker? Now it's my superpower.

The next day in class, Mr. Hair walked up to me and said, "What happened yesterday? You were in the car. You were almost there." And with no shame in my voice, I simply said, "Well, I didn't want to go, so I didn't go." He shook his head and walked back to his desk, reached in a drawer, pulled out a book, and handed it to me. "Read this book. It just might change everything for you." Without even glancing at the book, I took it, all the while thinking, *Really? A fucking book? What is this guy trying to pull?!* To be nice, I shoved it in my backpack. "Thank you."

> "That resistance that once made me a troublemaker? Now it's my superpower. Their *you can't* becomes my *watch me.*"

That night, I pulled the book out and looked at it for a moment. I hadn't read a book since maybe the fourth grade. I thought books were stupid, a waste of time. Why the hell was this book so special? Flipping it around, I read the title: *The Way of the Peaceful Warrior*. Stupid, I thought, as I began to read.

So this is the part of my life where I tell you I read that book my high school woodshop teacher gave me and everything changed for me. Suddenly, I saw everything clearly. I knew what I was supposed to do, and in my case, not do. From reading that one book, I knew the exact path I was supposed to take to live a life of happiness and success. Isn't that the case in most success stories we hear or read about? How does something so simple change everything?

I wish I could tell you this is what happened. I wish I could tell you I went on to follow my dreams and desires and never looked back, and that all the problems and adversities I have been through and created for myself... well, they never happened. However, my story isn't that simple. This isn't a Hallmark Christmas movie. In fact, for most of us, this is usually not how it works out. When you're in a death spiral, spinning out of control, but for some reason you think you have total control, then you are delusional, and the only way to regain control is to simply crash.

A couple of weeks later, I walked into the class, fashionably late as usual. Woodchips and dust fill the air. The sharp, sweet scent of fresh-cut pine filled my nostrils as the students moved about, working on their artistic joys. A kind of calm and pleasure shone in most of their eyes, as they were content in their craft, something I had lost and at the time had no idea how to get back. That time for me had passed, for now.

I didn't want to be the guy who never gives things back, so I pulled the book from my pack and handed it to Mr. Hair. He said, wearing a smile, "Well, what did you think?" With a smile, I said, "Oh, it was a really good book." He said, "Oh, really? What was your favorite part?" Ouch! He got me there. I had only read a couple of pages of that mysterious book. With the sounds of wood being chopped behind me, I came up with something I read in the very beginning. He took the book and said, "Jono, you're going down the wrong path and hanging out with the wrong crowd. Thank you for returning the book." And he walked away. With the saws still tearing through wood in the background, I knew that he knew. I felt deep shame in my heart. A total letdown, to say the least. I ghosted him without a word, letting his wisdom fade into silence as I walked away from both his guidance and my education, as I'd drop out shortly after.

Mr. Hair saw right through my bullshit. This bullshit detector is something a lot of us master as we get older and gain experience in the real world, and we become well-versed in it while on the streets. I know this stuff all too well now. He knew I had not read one single chapter of that book, and I felt his disappointment as he walked away. He could see the people I decided to surround myself with would only be leading me down the wrong road. Every person I chose to spend time with, every place I chose to hang out, was another nail in my coffin. He had given up. I was a lost cause who wouldn't accept the obvious. I was at the point of no return. I could see all this, yet still I was unable to change my trajectory.

Mr. Hair was a great teacher. He was the last person to try to save me from my demise. Looking back at it now, all he wanted to do was help. He saw the potential in me and tried to stop me from hitting the ground on the wrong side of the fence. Of course, all his attempts failed. He threw me a rope, and I failed to reach up and grab ahold.

Mentors: The Shortcut I Should Have Taken

The late and great Hall of Fame coach Bill Walsh said this: "Find a great mentor who believes in you; your life will change forever." Was my woodshop teacher the mentor who would change my life forever? Maybe, maybe not. But he could have been the light I needed to find my way out of that dark path. But I refused to see it. A mentor was something I needed in my life at that time. As a positive influence, Mr. Hair was just a few years too late. My state of mind had already reached a point where the only things that could penetrate it were negative consequences. I just wasn't in a place where I could be reached. Sure, Mr. Hair could have tried harder. If movies and sitcoms tell us anything about reality, he would have followed me home, demanded I read the book, and taken me under his wing. Unfortunately, this isn't Hollywood.

> "I chose to reject the creative, supportive environment of that woodshop class for the destructive influence of the streets."

The people you choose, the things you choose, and the places you choose to spend your time have the power to impact your life positively or negatively. Some aspects of our environment we can control and others, like family, not so much. But every day we make choices about the company we keep, the places we go, the attitudes we embrace. I chose to reject the creative, supportive environment of that woodshop class for the destructive influence of the streets.

Les Brown, one of the world's foremost motivational speakers and thought leaders on self-improvement and goal-setting, started off life in a rough way. He was born on the floor of an abandoned building and things never got better from there. He struggled in school and he was labeled "educable mentally handicapped." He also had a twin brother who was pretty smart, so students began calling Les "DT," for the "Dumb Twin." Ouch.

One day in class, a teacher asked Les to come up and solve a problem on the chalkboard, but Les refused and said he couldn't. "Of course you can," the teacher responded encouragingly. "Young man, please come up here and solve this problem for me." "But I can't," said Les. "I'm mentally handicapped." That's when the rest of the class began to laugh hysterically. So the teacher walked over to Les, looked him straight in the eyes, and said, "Don't ever say that again! Someone else's opinion of you does not have to become your reality."

Les never forgot those words, and he spent the rest of his life overcoming adversity and charging forward toward his goals with passion and intensity. Thanks to that one teacher, Les made it to the top of his field and has lived by the words he is most famous for all over the world: "You have greatness within you."

If someone ever gives you as much effort as Mr. Hair gave me, give them a moment. Hear them out and listen. Because someone believing in you when you don't believe in yourself? That's rare. That's sacred. Don't throw it away like I did.

What if you could spend time with your heroes, with someone you look up to, with the person who is doing the things you would love to be doing? Who would that be to you? Think about how much you could learn from their years of knowledge, their wisdom and their insights. Think about how much they could share with you. This stuff would be invaluable. Think about how fast you could get to your desired destination, as they could help you develop a road map for success, while saving you from pitfalls and other unforeseen adversities that only they can see. Because they've already been there. When someone comes into your life and they are trying to help you, accept it gratefully. Learn what you can from them. Devour their teachings and insights. Observe them with hunger and excitement, and you will begin to see how far you can go.

Now, I know my path wasn't exactly in woodworking or carpentry, as you have read, or I would have taken it up by now, but the expertise I would have gained from such a relationship would have been highly impactful. The knowledge and physical practice of woodworking transfers over to many other industries: creativity, the arts, reading and writing, business, hands-on trade professions, etc. Writing a book is like crafting a fine piece of furniture. Rough out all the pieces, design the look, put it all together with precision and passion. Sand it down and polish the final piece to be shared with the world. Everything is connected, and therefore we will evolve into the exact person we were meant to be.

Marcus Aurelius wrote over 2,000 years ago: "Take a good, hard look at people's ruling principles, especially of the wise, what they run away from and what they seek out." The environment you choose today is who you become tomorrow. I learned this in jail cells and behind dumpsters. You don't have to. That's why I'm telling you now.

4

"Right Between the Eyes"

> *"One's dignity may be assaulted, vandalized, and cruelly mocked, but it can never be taken away unless it is surrendered."*
> —Michael J. Fox

In the middle of winter 1996, I was driving down the road in my beat-up, gray Honda to pick up a couple of friends. The sun was quickly on its way out. At this point, I was no longer welcome at my parents' house. "Get your shit together or get out," my father had said a few months prior. I wanted nothing to do with getting my life in order, I was having too much fun breaking rules to let it end.

I pulled up to my friend's house, its paint worn, the grass a patchy mix of brown and green. They were waiting outside. "Let's go!" I called out. "Hold on. We have to get our things," one of them replied. They headed back inside. I pulled over, shut off the engine, and waited. For the next fifteen minutes, they moved in and out of the house repeatedly, whispering with a girl inside and casting sly glances my way. Something felt off. When people are up to no good, they seem to have a terrible way of hiding it. Even in the darkness of the night I could tell they were up to something.

"What's taking so long?" I finally shouted through the window. They said goodbye to their friend and climbed into my car. As I shifted into first gear and began pulling away, a burgundy Oldsmobile appeared. "That's Zach," I said. "Yeah, let's see what he's doing," my buddy replied. "Nope," I responded, continuing to drive. I thought I'd dodged a bullet. You see, Zach was after me. He had been accusing me of spreading serious rumors about him, telling all our friends I was a backstabbing piece of shit they shouldn't associate with. I knew he wanted to confront me physically. So I quietly retreated, pretending it was no big deal as we headed to my place.

Years later, I would discover the full extent of the betrayal: my supposed friends had orchestrated the entire confrontation. Their repeated trips in and out of the house, the whispered conversations, the meaningful glances, it was all a calculated delay, giving Zach enough time to arrive. They had called him the moment I pulled up, trying to ensure I wouldn't escape what was coming. Looking back, I realize they knew exactly why I had tried to avoid the confrontation.

Secretly, Zach terrified me. He was older and bigger, and his reputation even larger than that. He excelled at intimidating others with words alone and frequently played psychological games. Once, he drove us to Oakland for what he claimed were the best tacos around. Only after I'd finished eating did he reveal I'd consumed tongue, watching with amusement as I nearly vomited in the street.

Back at the house I was staying at, we were smoking and engaging in meaningless conversation when someone knocked on the door. My heart raced, nobody knew this location. My buddy answered the door and sure enough, it was Zach, with four more of my supposed friends, demanding I come outside. Again, how the hell did he get this location? My old friend's voice rings in my head, "*Those guys . . . those guys aren't your friends. They don't give a damn about you.*" I hesitated, knowing there was no escape. This was the reality of trying to be a tough guy: if you wanted to hang with that crowd and break rules, eventually there would be consequences. Though I hadn't actually spoken ill of Zach, he had an agenda. As an alpha personality, he seemed threatened when I stopped hanging out with him. His solution was to start trouble, paint me as a piece of shit, and simultaneously demonstrate my weakness so others would abandon me. Brilliant tactic as it worked well.

I made my way to the large, brown front door. As I stepped into the cold darkness, Zach's round, chubby face twisted with anger. He grabbed my shirt at the collar and yanked me outside. I stumbled down the three front steps, barely maintaining my footing on the grass.

"Why did you call me a wetback?" he demanded.

"I never called you that, Zach!" I protested repeatedly, eventually realizing this wasn't about alleged slurs, it was about humiliating me in front of everyone.

For twenty minutes, Zach pushed me around the street, pretending to investigate while demonstrating his dominance over someone clearly smaller and weaker. This was classic bully behavior, targeting only those they knew they could defeat. I had never felt such profound embarrassment, unable to muster even a bit of resistance. I felt pathetic as everyone watched me stumble around in the quiet suburban darkness.

Finally, under the orange glow of a street lamp, he stopped. His smile confirmed his victory, but he wasn't finished. As I looked around at the spectators, knowing they wanted me to respond somehow, Zach reared back his head. In an instant, he launched the largest, wettest glob of saliva imaginable directly between my eyes.

"What the fuck? You spit on me?" I sputtered, wiping the stinky fluid from my face. I had reached my lowest point, as he laughed and everyone stared in disbelief. Spitting in someone's face is the ultimate disrespect, and I didn't think there was anything worse that could happen to me at the time. To my relief, someone shouted "Cops!", and Zach fled with surprising speed, along with his four companions. I have no idea why he ran, as the cops never came and what he did was hardly breaking any laws. I made the long walk of shame back inside, where I remained motionless and quiet on the couch for the rest of the night, marinating in misery and wishing again that I could sink into its depths and vanish from existence. Maybe part of me was upset he ran off. Maybe if it had kept going I would have grown the balls to put my fist in his mouth. But it went far enough and I did nothing.

> "I had never felt such profound embarrassment, unable to muster even a bit of resistance."

This incident haunted me for years. I hated myself for not defending my dignity. I resented my tae kwon do training for failing to prepare me for real confrontation. That's why every kid signs up for karate, at least that's what the movies show. I mean, I did watch *The Karate Kid*. The shame persisted far too long, my hatred for Zach matching my self-disgust. Those "friends" disappeared from my life that very night, except for rare, awkward street encounters. My buddy's voice as he hopped out of the trunk of my ride, "Those guys aren't your friends." He was right. And this surely was not the significance I was looking for.

This incident crystallized two realizations: I was far from being any kind of gangster, and if I wanted to become one, I needed to experience more fights—both winning and losing, so this would never happen again. I vowed to confront Zach if our paths ever crossed, believing redemption would heal this wound.

I began initiating fights regularly, regardless of my opponent's size. Sometimes I won, sometimes I lost. I started doing cycles of steroids and a one hitter quitter in front of a bar provided the significance I still craved. Between jail stints and beatings, I grew stronger and larger, until I resembled an aggressive pitbull. I even unconsciously became a bully myself.

Years later, while fueling my motorcycle at a Shell station, my muscles straining against my too-tight T-shirt, a beaten-up truck pulled up. "Hey, what's up, Jono? Nice bike," called a familiar voice in a friendly tone. To my disbelief, there sat Zach with his friend, wearing that same grin from eight years prior. My heart raced, my blood boiled, and my cheek twitched. My moment had arrived.

"Fuck you! I have no respect for you," I shouted, dropping my helmet and drug-filled backpack to the gasoline-stained ground. It was time for my revenge and he knew it. However, he wasn't expecting that response. He still saw me as that frightened boy from years ago, that privileged weakling who couldn't hurt anyone. He hadn't witnessed my transformation in the intervening years. Without another word, he accelerated away, wanting no part of the confrontation, as I threw up my hands, wishing he'd come back. It never happened.

The Transformation That Mattered

Did this moment provide closure? Hell no. I wanted blood. I wanted him humiliated in front of everyone, just like he'd done to me. Eventually, after years of eating myself alive from the inside, I learned to forgive him. More importantly, I learned to forgive myself. Because carrying that shame around? It was killing me. Slowly. Every single day. I had to face the truth. I chose those people. I surrounded myself with fake friends who didn't give a shit if I lived or died. That spit running down my face? That was the price of my choices.

Witnessing my brother's lifelong struggle with bullying, combined with my own painful experiences throughout middle school and early high school, eventually transformed me. These formative experiences as a bullying victim taught me compassion for others in similar situations, particularly for young people targeted by those seeking significance through others' degradation.

The truth about bullies, young or old, is that they are all cowards. My own experience, and watching others get bullied, revealed that bullies exclusively target those they perceive as weaker or smaller, rarely challenging equals or superiors. Nine times out of ten they retreat when confronted with resistance or powerful self-advocacy, just as Zach drove away that day at the gas station. The lesson wasn't in the violence I initially sought, but in the strength I finally found in letting go.

The journey from that humiliating night to genuine peace wasn't about physical confrontation or revenge, it was about understanding that holding onto past shame only helps to maintain our pain. For years, I carried that moment like a weight, letting it drive me toward increasingly destructive behaviors in search of redemption, in search of that elusive significance.

> "The lesson wasn't in the violence I initially sought, but in the strength I finally found in letting go."

True strength didn't come from the fights I won or the punches I landed. It came from finally understanding that forgiveness was the only way out. Forgiving him. Forgiving myself. That was the real fight. This realization didn't come easily. It required acknowledging that my choices had placed me in that situation and accepting that no amount of retaliation would erase what happened. By releasing the grip of that memory and the shame attached to it, I found a more authentic form of power: the ability to define myself not by past humiliations but by how I chose to move forward. Here's what I learned: Sometimes the most courageous thing you can do isn't throwing a punch. It's refusing to let shame turn you into someone you're not. It's standing up to your own demons and choosing to walk away from the darkness. That's real strength. That's what actually matters.

5

So You Wanna Be a Gangster

> *"We all do things we desperately wish we could undo. Those regrets just become part of who we are, along with everything else. To spend time trying to change that, well, it's like chasing clouds."*
> —*Libba Bray*

I'd moved on from the past and graduated in the streets. In my eyes, I was no longer a nobody, I was royalty. My rise to the top happened quickly. I turned heads at every corner in my Chevy Tahoe with twenty-inch rims, which nobody had in the nineties. The problem was I attracted attention from people I should have avoided.

My inventory was extensive: weed, cocaine, ecstasy, and anything else that would generate profit. I had a girlfriend who probably only stayed with me because of my status, but that didn't concern me. Ever since abandoning my high school friends, I'd stopped caring about authentic connections. This shallow arrangement suited me fine.

One sunny afternoon, while driving with my girlfriend, I had a duffel bag containing four pounds of weed and a

THE BREAKING POINT

kilo of cocaine. Suddenly, an unmarked police car appeared behind me. "Oh fuck," I said, attempting to maintain composure. When you've operated in the streets long enough, you develop a sixth sense about these things. Perspiration formed instantly as terror washed over me. Interesting how fear only surfaces when consequences become imminent. The officer activated his hidden lights and pulled me over.

I steered into a Safeway parking lot, convinced this was the end. He approached my door. "License and registration, please." After handing them over, I asked why he'd stopped me. Without answering, he returned to his vehicle. The entire time, my duffel bag of drugs sat openly behind my seat, completely visible and undoubtedly reeking of marijuana. All he needed was one glance. The officer returned promptly, handed back my documents, and said, "You can go." As he walked away, relief flooded my system. My shaking hands steadied and my sweat-soaked shirt began to dry as I drove off. *Sign number one I should have quit.*

"What the fuck was that?" I said to my girlfriend in the passenger seat. "They're on to you, Jono," she replied.

By this point, I had my own apartment and money literally spilling from my pockets. Despite the warning, I wasn't prepared to surrender this lifestyle and return to being an average nobody. I despised mediocrity too much. Young and foolish, I couldn't see the disaster waiting ahead. The path I'd chosen offered only one exit, but I was too blinded by false success to recognize it.

On a crisp, cool October morning, I said a quick goodbye to my girlfriend and her son as she drove away to take him to school. It is 7:30 a.m. as I walk back up the spiral metal staircase leading to my second-floor apartment. Those stairs, which have a striking antique appearance, are the only way up to my place. As I reach the top of the stairs, I grab the door handle and take a look over my shoulder. Suddenly, the hairs on the back of my neck stick up. Am I being watched? It is a strangely quiet morning on a fairly busy street, and I feel a sense of eeriness as I stand there, poised to enter my apartment.

I'm still just waking up as I head to the bathroom. Despite having my own place, I carried no real responsibilities. Throughout my life, I had consistently attempted to project an identity that wasn't authentic. I sought external validation, constantly trying to make others love me while searching for a sense of power that eluded me. At this moment, I believed I had finally reached a position that rendered all past struggles irrelevant, the bullies, the isolation, the feeling of insignificance—because now I stood at the top. Selling drugs and driving an SUV with 20-inch rims gave me status. People admired me, and I relished the respect. As Ray Liotta says in the film *Goodfellas*, "Everybody wanted to be a gangster." In my social circle, this sentiment certainly rang true. Of course, such artificial power only persists until shit gets real.

As I walk out of the bathroom in my pajama bottoms and old moccasin slippers, I hear a strange *thump* sound come from below. Below me is the parking garage, so I think, no big deal, must just be the neighbor coming home. The place that I lived in was a duplex. I had the upstairs unit. I crack the curtain and look around. Not a soul is stirring. As I start to walk back to my room to get dressed and start my day, I hear another strange sound. That's odd. Is that somebody coming up the stairs? Those rickety old metal stairs . . . It was near impossible to come up those stairs without making noise. I creep slowly and quietly to the window.

Something is definitely not right. My sixth sense kicks in and I feel it in my gut. I know you know what I'm talking about. We definitely forgot to add the gut sense to the other five senses. The gut sense is real and we have all felt it before. I slightly pinch the curtain with my thumb and index finger, because if anyone is out there, I don't want them to see I'm looking out. So I do this as discreetly as I can and crack the window open just enough to peek out. Heat surges through my body, my heart sinks in my chest, and my stomach turns over about a dozen times. I'm stunned by fear and sadness at the same time. All these feelings and emotions rush in me

My apartment and the spiral stairs that led to the front door. One agent stood about midway up with his AR pointed right at me.

in a matter of seconds because, apparently, I don't have much time. I say to myself, "So this is it. This is how it's going down." What I feared all along is winding its way up my rickety metal staircase. I suppose it's time to face the music.

> "This is beyond ugly. A scene you'd think you'd only ever see in the movies is actually unfolding right in front of my face."

I walk to the door, composed, but not ready to face my reality. I'm not willing to let this situation get out of hand, so I grab the knob and swing the door open wide so all of me is displayed. The sun is shining low through the trees, creating a beautiful cascade of sunshine across my doorstep. I squint my eyes as I look out at such a wonderful morning. It's a shame it has to go away. I take my gaze off the nature and blue sky to look down at my new reality. Ugh!! This is beyond ugly. A scene you'd think you'd only ever see in the movies is actually unfolding right in front of my face.

As I gaze out, I see the county's hit squad, special agents strategically placed behind cars and trees with their eyes and fully automatic ARs pointed directly at yours truly. They came, bulletproof. Shit, they probably even had a couple grenades and flash bangs ready to blow me and my pad to smithereens. But like I said, I wasn't dumb. I knew what this was and out of common sense I knew how to act and compose myself. If you want them to respect you, then respect them back. There will be no problems except the one huge problem I created in the first place, and it's a little late to deal with that one at the moment.

There is one agent on the spiral stairs pointing his assault rifle dead at my chest. Guess he picked the short stick. Or maybe it's just that he was the bravest man, willing to take point. All these men have to be brave, just like soldiers in war. Someone has to go in and deal with idiots like me. The rest of the scene was like a blur, but this is the gist.

"Hands up! On your knees! Now, hands behind your back!"

I comply. I do not question. I do what I'm told. I'd rather not be shot today. At this very point in time, their guns are off-safety. They are on go-mode and they are taking no chances. It's kill or be killed, and I was the odd man out, the bad guy, "the gangster" I so desperately wanted to be. They didn't know me. They had no idea if I was going to get violent and try to shoot it out with them. They knew of my prior gun-related charges, and that automatically marked me as a threat they must approach with caution. We never think we will end up the bad guy in the story, but here I was. Well, here you go, son, this is what gangsters get. After they get me up and handcuffed, I watch as they clear the rest of the house, which takes them about five seconds. These guys aren't messing around.

After this, the regular street cops come in to take me to the back seat of the police car. A walk of shame. As the officer guides me down that metal staircase, the neighbors are out, all wearing the look of disgust on their faces as I make my way across the parking lot, head down, trying not to look at the guy I just had a well-meaning conversation with a couple days ago. The cop opens the door. I duck in and he slams the door shut. I keep my head down with shame and embarrassment. It truly is a shitty feeling.

What's more, I was wearing slippers. I remember asking the officer if I could get some shoes so I didn't have to wear my slippers into the jail. He asks the agents, but they say no. Maybe I'm trying to pull some kind of escape attempt? Or maybe I have a gun in my shoe? Yeah, right. So much for respect. Now I have to go into that hellhole with slippers on. Can you believe that!? You have to be tough to survive in jail, and starting off in my slippers didn't feel tough to me.

Looking back on that day, years later, the whole thing seemed like a waking nightmare. I've been in the back of a cop car many times, but that time was different. I felt sick to my stomach. This situation was really bad and I knew it. The officer drove me to the police department for some kind of processing. I looked at him and asked, "I'm pretty screwed, aren't I?"

"Yes, you are not in a good spot."

"How much time do you think I will get?"

"It's hard to say, but with all your charges, I'd say three to five years."

He was just assuming, because of course you never really know what to expect until you get in front of that judge and he tells you how your life will go, but I put my head down, sullen. I knew it was bad, but to hear it from someone else made it real. The officer pulled me out of the car, brought me inside, and put me in a small holding cell. This thing was maybe four feet by four feet, all concrete, with a nice, cold concrete seat to relax on. I was holding it together as best as I could right up until he shut the heavy steel door on me. Once that door closed, I felt my future closed with it and I broke. I sat down and cried, emotions pouring out of me. In a blink of an eye, my reality had changed from living high to dark and dire. The consequences were bleak, and all I could do was imagine what was going to happen to me, and in a situation as negative as this, only the worst outcomes come to mind. There was no way to be positive. At least, not in the beginning. They don't put up motivational posters in jail cells.

I knew I didn't have long before the officer would come to take me over to the county jail two blocks away. I let myself pour out the pain for about thirty seconds before I told myself to man up and move forward with the situation I had put myself in. I took a few deep breaths and did my best to wipe the tears from my face. I'd be damned if I was going to let myself move to the next stage of this process with tears in my eyes. Slippers are one thing, but tears are a sign of weakness. "Don't show those tears, boy, or you're gonna look like a bitch, so man the fuck up, right now!" I muttered to myself.

You see, I wasn't born tough or hardened. To some, I could have even been considered a momma's boy early on. Shy, timid, weak, I would cry about anything as a kid. As you already know, I had sold my true self out to join the outlaws. While I was still soft and had feelings, I was no longer a wimp. I stood up for myself and no longer tolerated disrespect, which may have been a form of growth for me at the time, but which I now know is also a sign of weakness. It's funny, but in life, when you put effort into something you want badly enough, sure as shit you will get what you sow.

Sitting in that small cell, the adrenaline finally wore off. My heart drained and refilled with regret. I'd go on to spend months behind bars, caged like the animal I'd become. There was no way out and I was left with nothing but wasted time to think about my life and the road I had chosen. The life I had been carving out for myself to this point had been reckless, fake, and in the end would only get me the knowledge I'd pull from the pain of becoming a convicted felon and having my freedom stripped away.

Bit by bit, from selling myself out to making the choice of quitting my dreams, my trajectory had been a path of destruction and pain. A young innocent boy with dreams and ambitions had slowly become something I didn't even recognize. I had gone so far off into the wrong direction that finding my way back was going to be no easy task. I'd first have to go down, and go down hard.

Use Regret as Fuel

For years I felt intense regret for this era of my life, a regret that at times was almost paralyzing. But eventually I figured out how to move beyond regret. Now, instead, I look back on this time and use it as fuel to propel myself forward. I don't want to be the man I once was. I am so much better off now, but I know we are always one wrong decision away from "choosing poorly" and turning our lives into dust. Thinking back helps me see where I've fallen. It helps me to choose the right actions every moment, based on what I want my future to look like, not what is going to make me feel good right now.

Lucius Annaeus Seneca, the ancient Roman philosopher, once said, "The issue isn't the limited duration of our lives, rather, it is our tendency to fritter away a significant amount of it." When we spend years wasting time on things that move us to the bottom, it's hard to get back up. You also never get that time back. I was on the top, at least I thought I was. Instead, I found myself on the bottom, broke, with only a couple outfits to wear, no more SUV, no more house of my own, no cash, no girls, nothing, not even at the level of your average Joe. I was at the bottom, but was it really my bottom?

Bruce Lee once said, "If you love life, don't waste time, for time is what life is made up of." Bruce died in his thirties and never reached his full potential, but he did extraordinary work with the little time he had. You could say he didn't waste a moment.

I wasted a ton of time, but there is absolutely nothing I can do about it now. It's how I had to learn. Back then, I was concerned about what people thought of me and focused entirely on instant gratification and what made me feel the best I could as quickly as possible. Selling drugs and rolling around in the hottest ride with a pocket full of cash and a pretty lady on my arm made me feel significant. It made all the years of being a nobody in school irrelevant. Why? Because I was the man now. While everyone else drove around in buckets and lived with their parents, I had my own place, my own life. I was respected by my peers. It felt good, until it didn't.

> "It's in your darkest moments, in pain, struggles, and adversities, where you will find the most growth and ultimately the true depth of your resilience."

And so, all of my crazy life experiences shaped and molded me into the man I am today. It was a hard path to travel, but it's something I will never regret. Drew Barrymore once said, "I never regret anything. Because every little detail of your life is what made you into who you are in the end." Wise words from Drew, as she had her own setbacks and struggles. She's someone who knows the cost.

Acknowledge your mistakes, own them, be grateful for them. You are you because of them. Hiding them causes more pain and stress. When you do make your mistakes, let that be the end of it. Don't repeat them, and don't wallow in regret. Move forward. Grab the lesson and go. It's in your darkest moments, in pain, struggles, and adversities, where you will find the most growth and ultimately the true depth of your resilience. You will have so much more to offer by extracting these lessons. You will become a force for good with the ability to help others. You will become a bank of original wisdom that nobody holds except you, and you can use that wisdom for good. Learn to see your past setbacks as fuel to thrive on today, and always ask, "Yes, that sucked, but what good came from such a shitty situation?" When you extract meaning from difficulty, you gradually unlock the person you were meant to become.

Don't let past regrets eat you alive. Transform them. Turn that pain into power. Turn those scars into wisdom. Because the only thing worse than carrying regret is wasting more time dwelling on it. Be aware of where you are now and decide to move forward, despite what's in the rearview mirror, because every breaking point offers a new beginning.

6

Pay Your Dues

"Being held accountable is an act of generosity and compassion. It is a gift that someone gives us to correct our wrongs, unlearn, and do better for the sake of our own growth. It might be uncomfortable, but it is worth the discomfort."
—*Minaa B.*

I sat in the Bullpen[1] waiting for my turn to see the judge and my lawyer. I was nervous, but not scared. My lawyer had been giving me the run around since this whole thing started. It seemed every time we talked my expected sentencing would change, and not for the better. I'd always give him the benefit of the doubt. I'd already been in for two weeks and had done many little stints like this before due to previous bad choices, so I thought, "I can make it. I can do this." So I was feeling half-okay as I waited for my turn.

There were about fifty of us in a room that could probably seat twenty. The Bullpen was packed with a bunch of knucklehead convicts trying to find a spot to sit. The day was going

---

[1] The Bullpen is basically a large holding cell for all the convicts who are waiting to see the judge and get sentenced, hear their charges, or even be released.

pretty well. No fights. That's pretty good when you think about it. We are all being held against our will, waiting to be sentenced. Understandably, this is a very stressful situation for convicts. It certainly was for me. I wasn't a badass, hardcore convict like some of the men around me were. However, in this environment, you had to learn to be tough or you would be taken advantage of quickly. So even though I didn't start out as a tough kid growing up, living this lifestyle I had chosen for myself had forced hardness into my soul. In jail in my late teens and twenties, I had caught a couple beatdowns because I'd look at someone the wrong way. I even fought in a cell over orange juice. What a joke! Of course, orange juice is big business in jail. Orange juice is one of the main ingredients we used to make pruno, alcohol fermented from sugars. Anything with sugar can be used, Kool-Aid packets, chunks of pear from our lunch trays, and anything else we could find that had sugar in it, so fighting over it was inevitable. Of course, you remember from earlier in the book, "You become who and what you surround yourself with." I became this.

The waiting was the hardest part. It was wall-to-wall orange jumpsuits, and it smelled like a mixture of body odor and shit. Men were on edge. Everyone was stressed out to the max, waiting for their turn to see the man in the black robe who would decide their fate. They called name after name as the day dragged on, but it really didn't matter who went first since we all arrived on the same bus and we would all leave on the same bus. After you learned your fate and were finished, you returned to the Bullpen, sat down, and continued to wait until everyone else was done.

PAY YOUR DUES

There were about six stainless steel toilets that just hung off the wall. No privacy. We were far from such luxuries as privacy. The toilets were right there in the wide open, so if you got to go, guess what? You got to do it in front of everyone. Thank God I was still young and didn't have an overactive bladder, nor did I have to take a dump. I'm not a fan of using the bathroom in front of others. Even today, I hate it. Taking a piss is one thing, but a number two in front of all those convicts would have been uncomfortable. With all those men, some were bound to do it, and they did. Some guys just don't give a damn. When you gotta go, you gotta go.

At last I heard my name. "Gilardi!" "That will be my turn to see the judge," I thought. They led me to a small room with a desk and two chairs and a dim light, like an interrogation room but much smaller. The guard told me to have a seat as he

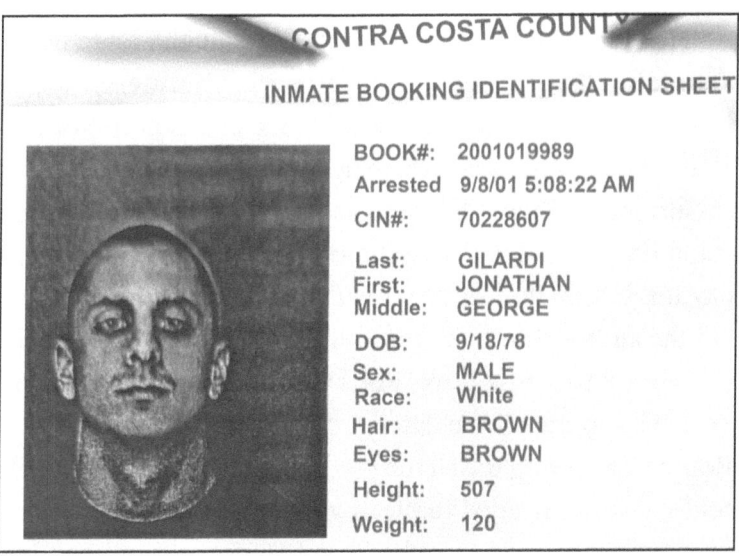

My inmate booking and identification card. I made sure to look the part. *photo courtesy Ali Gilardi and Karen Ng*

closed the door, leaving me all alone to ponder my fate. About one minute later, I heard keys rattle and the lock clanked free. In walked my wonderful lawyer, Ronnie. The hardest guy on the planet to get hold of. Everything he had told me so far had been a lie. Did he even know what he was doing?

"What the hell is going on, Ronnie?" I blurted out aggressively from pent-up nervousness. "You told me I would never get locked up. First you said I would get house arrest for two months. Then it escalated to three months jail time. What's the fucking deal?"

"Well, John, I didn't know all your charges and all the details when I talked to you. This is bad, so you should be happy with the deal I've worked out for you."

"It's John-Oh," I said. "Just like you'd say Bono. How can I trust a lawyer who can't even get my name right? I must've told you a thousand times."

He didn't even respond. "Figures," I thought. I had heard Ronnie the lawyer was a dirtbag of a lawyer. I even found out he was into cocaine and would take payment in powder. That's the definition of a dirtbag lawyer. You probably won't be surprised when I tell you he was the cheapest lawyer I could find. I need not say anymore, except you get what you pay for. Normally I don't go with the cheapest of anything, but the authorities took everything from me. I was broke.

With an intense look, Ronnie read off my charges and explained to me all the details of my case. I almost felt as if Ronnie was trying to sell me the deal he had worked out. He told me why I needed to plead guilty and that there was no way to fight these charges because I was caught red-handed. "This isn't good," I thought, "not good at all."

So here came the moment of truth where I would find out my sentence. The judge would make it official when I stood in front of him. I was led by a guard down a long corridor, red doors on both sides. There were about five of us convicts in a row, shackled from wrists to ankles. We reached the end of the dimly lit hall and the guard opened the door in front of us. We were ushered right into a small glass box off to the side of the courtroom. It separated us from them, the chained from the free, the caged from the ones who could just get up out of their seats, walk to their cars, and go home. A crushing wave of despair washed over me as I realized how such a simple act of freedom, once taken for granted—now existed in a world beyond my reach. I was brought down to such a low level in life I couldn't help but feel inferior.

> "A crushing wave of despair washed over me as I realized how such a simple act of freedom now existed in a world beyond my reach."

On the other side of the glass, seated in rows of wooden benches, I could see family and friends waiting to hear the fate of their loved ones. I looked around. No family, no friends. My girlfriend said she would be here, but I couldn't find her in the crowd. Our relationship was doomed from the start, anyway. However, the pain I felt and the stories I heard about from the streets of her doings made my time much harder than it needed to be. Relationships in this context are usually a struggle, and even though I was hurt, years later I'd learn what a blessing in disguise it was for us to go our separate ways.

Saddened, I slowly moved my gaze to the front of the room. There he was, up on his high chair, humorless and completely focused on the task at hand. A man who took his job seriously, a man consumed by his work and who, I imagined, had mostly neglected all other things in his life, like family and fun. A memory exploded in my head and for a brief moment I saw my grandpa staring back at me in his black robe, serious as always. He spoke with intensity: "I told you to go to school." I looked down, and in that moment I said to myself, "I'm sorry, Grandpa." I so desperately wanted to walk out of this glass shell and through that back door that led to the untying of the ropes around my heart, but life doesn't work that way. You pay the price for your mistakes.

I swallowed the sorrow. This was no place for tears. Deep breaths calmed my nerves and prepared me for my upcoming judgment.

"Mr. Gilardi, you may step to the front. Mr. Gilardi, you are here by . . ." The judge read me his lines and rapped off my charges. My head stayed down, stomach in knots. I listened intently. "Mr. Gilardi, how do you plead?" Ronnie, standing close on the other side of the glass, whispered my response. "No contest," I said weakly. "Mr. Gilardi, speak up, I cannot hear you." The judge spoke in a tone that insinuated, "You're a worthless sack of shit." I felt disrespected. "No contest!" I said, much louder this time.

"Mr. Gilardi, I hereby sentence you to 365 days of imprisonment. Oh, and before you go, I'm not sure how you got away with this deal, but if I see you in here again, I will not go lightly. Do you understand?" I just nodded and shuffled to the bench behind me.

I had known this was coming. Earlier, back in the interrogation room, as I liked to call it, Ronnie broke it all down for me. "Three hundred and sixty-five days, as long as you plead no contest to all charges, and please sign here." Ronnie had a smile on his face, looking like he did me a damn favor. My heart sank again, my stomach turned, and I got that knot in my throat, you know, the one that tells you you're about to cry. Yeah, that one. I told myself not to cry, not in front of another man. I swallowed it down and spoke as clearly as I could.

"A whole year!? You said three months tops! What happened to that?" I asked, with a rising anger and sadness in my voice.

"This is the best they are willing to do for you, Jono, and considering the circumstances, you are very lucky. You get to do this time in the county jail, so you will not be going to San Quentin or any other prison in the state. You need to look at this as a good thing! You have a lot of charges here and one year in the county jail is cake. Not to mention, this is the second time you have been busted for sales. And this is your second firearms case, as well."

His words upset me, and I raised my voice in reply. "Ha! That's easy for you to say. You don't have to do the time!"

"I get it, Jono, but you are the one who committed these crimes. I'm just here to try and make things easier for you. Which I feel I have done," Ronnie stated with an air of finitude. I can tell he was more than a little frustrated with my ungrateful attitude, but at the time it was hard for me to see 365 days in jail as a good deal.

"You know, maybe this wouldn't be so hard to take if you hadn't misled me the whole time," I said. My voice was crackling, but I still successfully held back tears. He could tell I wanted to cry, and he got a little sympathetic.

"I'm sorry, Jono, I did my best. You know, with good behavior, you can get an early release." What he said about early release was true, if I were to take school courses and have good behavior, but then he went and fed me another bullshit line. "If you take the drug program course, I will have you out of here in three months."

Three months came and went. I passed the drug program and I never heard from old Ronnie the lawyer. So much for the class and his false promises. A whole year locked in a miserable place was a tough pill for me to swallow. It literally made me sick to my stomach. It took some time to get over it, and I held it together for the most part. You can't be seen crying around a bunch of hard-ass criminals. There were a couple of times I broke down, but I made sure to do it in private.

This wasn't the first time I had been in jail, but it was the longest stretch. When I think about it now, Ronnie the lawyer did a pretty darn good job for a dirtbag lawyer. I was sentenced to a year in county jail, but with good behavior and school I was out in eight months, not bad for all the charges I had, especially considering the firearms enhancements. Everyone I talked to thought I was going to do multiple years, but Ronnie's strategy was to say the ecstasy and cocaine I had in my possession were for personal use only, not for sale. And his ploy worked! By designating those charges as being caused by "drug use," we were able to say that my actions were committed because I was an addict and that I just needed rehab, not years in prison. And because of Proposition 36,[2] they actually had to comply. So what if I looked like a total dope head and belonged in the drug rehab program? That was far better than spending multiple years in the state prison system.

I had reached my breaking point, or so I thought. Nonetheless, at the time of sentencing I was heartbroken and had no idea how I'd get through the next year. My former life, gone. All that clout and significance I was chasing, gone. The power I had as the man on the block that could get you anything, gone. Now I was reduced to a miserable convict in orange clothes wearing the same shit-stained boxers as everyone else.

Stop Acting Like a Child

Accountability is a funny thing. There I was, staring at this heavily armed task force with their guns pointed right at me, and I knew I was wrong, so I didn't try to fight it. And then, only a couple weeks later, I'm busy blaming everything on my lawyer! So much for accountability. How could I have sat there and blamed this on him? Because he promised me this wouldn't happen? Because I paid him and felt it was his job to keep me free? My expectations were too great, and I got let down. Sometimes shit happens and we have to be prepared for it. I assumed everything would work out and that I would be let off easy. I still had something in the back of my head telling me I'd be allowed to go back to my apartment, back to my girlfriend, and back to my former life as kingpin.

---

[2] Proposition 36 is a California law allowing nonviolent drug offenders to serve their time in a drug treatment program rather than jail.

THE BREAKING POINT

I was shocked how differently things turned out, so, unwilling to be held accountable, I blamed my lawyer. But *I* was the one who assumed wrong. That was all me, not Ronnie. Looking at it now, it was for the better. Things could have been worse.

In the moment, it can be hard to see your own fault. It's easier to blame someone else. Have you been there? Have you done what I did and shirked accountability? There was no one else to blame but me, but I wasn't prepared to accept that blame. The simple truth is, whether I had the highest-paid lawyer or someone like Ronnie, I put myself there. It was my doing, and not the shitty, cocaine-addicted lawyer's fault.

The crazy thing about my story is that it happened right after 9/11, literally within a couple weeks. I remember watching the two towers crumble on the TV with a bunch of other smelly-ass convicts. I was hoping I'd be let out of jail and allowed to go fight those bastards who attacked us. Unfortunately for me, there was no escaping accountability for this one. Just like Al-Qaeda and Osama Bin Laden, who had to take full accountability for the actions they took when they flew the planes into the twin towers, I was going to have to do the time the district attorney and my lawyer agreed upon.

If we can't learn to be accountable for our actions, then we are but children, not men. James Matthew Barrie once said, "I'm not young enough to know everything." Only a child is allowed to get away with blaming others for their faults. Only a child knows everything, including right from wrong. I know lots of men and women who can't take responsibility for their condition in life. Grown adults, adults older than I am, adults in their sixties and seventies, who still blame others for their issues. It's quite pathetic to watch grown-ass men blaming others for their depressing lives. They blame the government, the president, the economy, millionaires, their parents, their bosses . . . anyone who is better off than them is a target for their blame. But never themselves. Blaming others is a coward's way out. It's the excuse we use to make our miserable lives seem okay. I've got plenty of excuses I could use right now to permit myself to take the easy way out of working hard and taking accountability for my life, but I choose the higher path for my future self, for my kids, and for you reading this.

> *"Anybody* can turn things around for the better and start working toward a much better future."

If you learn to take full responsibility for all areas of your life, you will learn that all things are in your hands and in your control. Wealth, health, financial freedom, happiness, and all-around success come from taking accountability for all your mistakes and victories. If you are like me and have a tattered past full of mistakes, you must own up to the consequences and demonstrate a full commitment to make things right and better for yourself, and for the people around you. Here's the truth: You will never create the life you want until you stop pointing fingers and look in the mirror. That's where accountability starts. That's where everything changes. Believe me when I tell you that I know it can be difficult. But if you glean any lesson from my mistake-filled life, let it be that anybody can turn things around for the better and start working toward a much better future.

7

There's Good in All Adversity

"The most successful people see adversity not as a stumbling block, but as a stepping stone to greatness."
—Shawn Anchor

One month went by in jail, and I was trying my best to keep to myself and serve out my time without any major problems. I was starting to get used to my surroundings, the other convicts, the routine (breakfast, lunch, and dinner), and, of course, the stupid politics of life behind bars. It's funny how we humans, no matter what the situation is, will find a way to adjust to our surroundings. Even people in some of the most horrendous situations are able to adapt, to a certain extent. Viktor Frankl, who was a prisoner in 1942-1945 of four different Nazi death camps, who also wrote the book *Man's Search for Meaning*, believed that even in the most dehumanizing and brutal conditions, individuals could find meaning and purpose in their lives. He said that those who could find meaning, whether it was through maintaining their inner values, helping fellow prisoners, or focusing on a future goal, were more likely to endure the suffering and survive. He wrote that: "Everything can be taken from a man but one thing: the last of the human freedoms, to choose one's attitude in any given set of circumstances, to choose one's own way."[3]

It's how we choose to perceive our situation. We can adapt. No matter how grimy the situation, we humans can find a way to make things work.[4] Don't get me wrong, I'm not comparing my situation to that of someone who went through the Nazi death camps. My time behind bars is like a few trips to Disneyland compared to something like that. However, our situation is exactly that: *our* situation.

> "Time locked behind bars is some of the slowest time you will ever know."

I eventually got to the point where I was laughing and making friends in jail. It didn't take long. Hugo, my then-cellmate, was a twenty-two-year-old Russian with a deep accent. The many teeth already missing from his mouth suggested he started using drugs at an early age. As we sat in our bunks clad in our orange jumpsuits, Hugo told me he was learning to use mind control to move things about the room. I thought, He's watched a lot of *Star Wars* movies, huh? I was glad he couldn't see my facial expression down on the lower bunk. As he was just about to

---

[3] Frankl, Viktor E., *Man's Search for Meaning* (Simon and Schuster, 1985)
[4] Side note: this is one of the main reasons men and women stay in the jail system. They become used to life behind bars. The longer their stay, the more they become dependent on the system to take care of them. After years of prison time, the ex-con has no idea how to live a normal life. Without the right support, he will never survive in the world as a free man. Inevitably, they go back to what they know.

show me how it works, a voice came up on the loudspeaker and said, "Lockdown! All inmates back to your cells."

We were already there, so we simply closed the heavy door. Upon closure, you hear the loud *clunk* of the locks being thrown. Can't get out now. It had been free time before the announcement, when us convicts are allowed to move freely inside the block, as well as outside in the yard. We tried to guess what had happened.

"I bet someone got a beat down," I said.

"Maybe someone tried to escape," added Hugo. "Not likely, unless they beat you to the task of figuring out the whole mind control thing." I laughed.

We stopped talking and waited. Time locked behind bars is some of the slowest time you will ever know. It crawls like a snail across the concrete before the sun is about to rise. You want so desperately to reach the shade but can't seem to get there fast enough. Patience becomes the ultimate virtue inside places like this. As we waited, I was startled to see a deputy suddenly standing at our door peering through the small rectangular window. No expression on his face. Psychopath? Maybe. Very rarely would you find a guard with a sense of humor. His keys rattled, the lock clanked free, and he opened the door.

"Mr. Gilardi, let's go."

"This can't be good," I said to Hugo as I got up to follow the deputy. I was not really worried because I hadn't done anything. Not this time! I'd been in my cell the whole time learning about the Force from a Jedi knight. For all I knew, my lawyer could have been there with the good news that I was about to be released. You can hope and pray all you want, but things often don't go your way in there. The deputy led me down to a row of other inmates. Obviously some kind of lineup. I kept my cool.

Well, it seemed as if my guess earlier was the correct one. An inmate got his bell rung because more than likely he did something that went against the politics of life behind bars. These are inmate rules imposed by the inmates. The two sternest rules are: snitches end up in ditches, and any kind of child molestation or rape is the ultimate offense and isn't tolerated by inmates. These rules are serious—you just don't break them. There are a bunch of other rules, including race-related stuff; however, these two have grave consequences if you break them. There are no warnings for offenders who commit these acts. The inmates will find out about it and they will come after you when you're least expecting it.

As the deputy started telling inmate after inmate to head back to their cell, there were only a few of us left, and I was beginning to feel a knot forming in my gut. That damn gut sense again. Let me guess the description of the inmate: white, with a shaved head. Awesome. I fit the bill perfectly.

Finally, there were only two of us left. I've got a knot the size of a tennis ball in my stomach. After a quick talk through his radio, the deputy walked forward and told the man next to me to head back to his cell. I was dumbfounded, still not believing what was happening here. He pulled me to the backroom and told me that the "Rat" had positively identified me as the one who beat the crap out of him. "Are you fucking kidding me?" I yelled. He asked if I did it and I said no. I was in a rage.

Apparently, a pair of inmates had entered the Rat's room (I'm calling him the Rat because I don't remember his name) and given him a beatdown he would never forget. He *was* a rat, and he got what inmates call "rolled up," which means they beat the crap out of him and sent him on his way to protective custody, where he would stay if he wanted to remain safe.

I couldn't believe this guy was actually accusing me of this, and it seemed as if the deputy in charge couldn't care less if I did or didn't do it. They just needed someone to take the blame. That someone? Yours truly. At the moment, I had no idea all this was even taking place, but it didn't matter. I didn't think I'd ever seen this guy's face before this scenario took place. How does this happen? It's that paranoid feeling you get when bad shit keeps happening to you, and you think everyone is out to get you. It's where the victim resides. Did I really think something good was ever going to come of all this?

They put me in a holding cell and asked me again if I did it or knew who did. They wanted me to rat. These bastards probably knew I was innocent, but they were punishing me in hopes of getting to the real culprit. And I *did* know exactly who did it because I had a series of conversations with other inmates who were trying to ensure I wouldn't rat. I knew one thing was for sure: I wasn't about to become a rat myself. I had way too much time left to have to deal with beatdowns and protective custody. Life here sucked enough. I already felt broken and mentally defeated. Add all of that nonsense about ratting people out and you're really gonna feel it.

THE BREAKING POINT

My reward for doing absolutely nothing was a twenty-one-day, forty-seven-hour lockdown. Much like solitary confinement. I'd get one hour out of lockdown every other day to make a phone call or take a shower. It was one or the other, because the showers fill up fast, and so do the phones. So, your only chance was to get to either one quickly the second those cell doors opened.

And so I was shipped off across the jail. My new home was a dark, cold cell, complemented with dirty floors, walls, and a bed. Everything was dirty. Imagine that you are trying to sleep. You roll on your side facing the wall, and staring back at you are a dozen or so greenish-brown, dried-up boogers smiling back at you. *Fuck my life!* While you still have a bunk, blankets, a cellmate (due to overcrowding), and a place to relieve yourself, this place is misery at its finest. I was allowed to bring my books, nothing more.

My celly was a man fresh off the streets. He laid under his covers for five days straight, shivering, and repeating over and over, "Kicking this heroin, kicking this heroin, kicking this heroin." Sharing a cell with a man who is going through major withdrawal is disgusting. The next five days I listened to him constantly barfing and relieving his bowels in the toilet bowl. It was pure agony, and just when I thought this couldn't get any worse, the smell hit me. You haven't lived until you've smelled something so horrible. Eventually, my friend moved on and wasn't replaced. I had the place to myself for the remainder of my time.

Patience was key . . . I *knew* that. But now I thought I was losing it. Randomly, I'd hear screams from other inmates that gave me the feeling of being in some sort of mental institute.

Eventually though, I found joy in a howl of tension release. I'd try to work out, but the food was inadequate to provide the energy to do so, so we screamed like loonies in the night instead.

When you are bored and confined to a six-foot by ten-foot cell for days on end, you'll do anything to occupy your time. I had three things. Yelling was one, wetting wads of toilet paper and throwing them on the air vent to try to stop the cold air from coming in was another, and, lastly, I did my schoolwork.

I had made a crucial decision when I first entered jail a month earlier: I had started taking my high school courses again, mostly because you can shave days off your sentence by doing so. I never really thought I'd finish. I just wanted to get out of there as quickly as possible, and shit gets done when you have time and ample determination. During my time in lockdown, I spent twenty-one days studying and doing work in history, science, and math. These books were thick, but I was able to complete my high school credits. Sure, the tests were open book, but who's judging? I got it done.

Adversity Is the Way

Have you ever been in a predicament so grim there was no upside? Has something ever gone so poorly you couldn't imagine there ever arriving a brighter moment in time? We've all had junctures in time like these.

Zig Ziglar once said, "Sometimes adversity is what you need to face in order to become successful." Soon after they released me from jail on a warm sunny day in the middle of June, I got a package in the mail. It was a high school diploma from the Board of Education. It brought back all the memories of being stuffed inside a cold cell, fighting my way through adversity, grinding away to get it done. I was prouder of myself at that moment than I had ever been before. My diploma was a tangible piece of success that showed me I was capable of doing so much more, no matter what life threw at me.

The main message I'm trying to convey in this book is this: no matter how bad things get, no matter how stuck you feel, and no matter what you're currently going through, you can, and you *will*, get to where you want to go. All you need is the will to put in the effort to get it done. I was able to summon that will while stuck in a smelly jail cell. You, too, can summon that will, regardless of your circumstances. I love this quote that is often attributed to John Keats, "Impossible is for the unwilling." You can accomplish anything in this life if you are willing to sacrifice. It's just that simple.

> "No matter how bleak the situation you are in, there's always something good that may be plucked from the pain. There is purpose in dark times."

By earning that diploma, I accomplished something I had never thought I would. It's not the diploma itself that matters, it's achieving it while behind bars that feels so victorious.

My situation sucked, but I was able to extract a very useful lesson from it: no matter how bleak the situation you are in, there's always something good buried in the pain. You just have to be willing to dig for it. Even when your hands are bloody and your body is broken, you dig. There is purpose in dark times. We don't go through the hard times just because that's how life is. We go through the hard times so that we come out the other side stronger, more resilient, and ready to face adversity. Sometimes, these lessons come right away, and other times it doesn't register until years later, when suddenly you come to appreciate the nightmare you went through. That's when you realize the thread of purpose that had been hidden amongst the terror, and finally understand the reason for your suffering.

My high school diploma was earned in West County Detention Facility during my 21 days of lockdown.

8

One Bad Decision from Disaster

> *"Once you make a decision the universe will conspire to make it happen."*
> —Ralph Waldo Emerson

I hadn't learned my lesson after jail, even after the judge warned me never to appear in his courtroom again, his voice edged with disappointment. I was still up to no good, even though I knew if I got busted again, I'd go down for a long time. Old habits die hard, especially when they've been your only companions for so long. By this point, I'd been breaking rules for some fifteen years, each promise to change fading faster than the last. I remained firmly on the road to nowhere.

It was a freezing night in the middle of February. I had just told a close friend of mine, Jay, that I knew about someone who was selling weed that they had ripped off from somebody in Jay's hometown. As it happens, someone had recently robbed weed from Jay's house, so I put two and two together and figured maybe these guys were also the ones who had robbed Jay's. So I set up a meeting and told these guys that my buddy wanted to buy a pound of weed. The meetup was set for 7:00 p.m. that night.

As I pulled up to the house where we were going to meet, I was struck by a fear of what might come. Jay didn't come alone. He had his brother and a couple other hard-headed outlaws in the car. If you're not used to these types of guys, as I was early on, they will make you feel uncomfortable. Real gangsters, unlike me, are unpredictable. They just don't give a fuck. It was at this point that I knew this was serious business for them. They let Jay out of the car and pulled over a couple houses down to sit in the dark of the night. If anything went wrong, they would be going down in a blaze of glory. Unfortunately, my name isn't Billy the Kid, and this isn't a movie.

I didn't think about where this might lead. I didn't consider all the possible outcomes and potential consequences of my decision to arrange this meeting. All I wanted to do was help out a friend. Yeah, that's me, pure innocence at work. Right? My buddy Jay holstered his 9mm pistol and we entered the half-lit garage.

In the murky shadows of that musty smelling garage, they handed Jay the weed, and as he turned the bag over and then opened it up to squeeze a few buds to get the true aroma out, my mind was consumed with panicked thoughts of what I have gotten myself into and the possible life-altering outcome. But there was no turning back now.

This scene could turn into a real catastrophe in the blink of an eye, or, in keeping with the theme of this book, turn into one of my worst adversities ever. Jay could find that the weed wasn't the same weed that was stolen from his home and we could all part ways with no problems. Or, a much more terrifying situation could occur: Jay could find that this, in fact, was the weed that was stolen from his home, draw his firearm, and things could go very wrong very quickly. The owner of the pound of weed could resist or pull his own firearm, which would necessitate the squeeze of the trigger from either side. This would more than likely end in murder or attempted murder. Either way, I'd find misfortune as I was right smack in the middle of the action.

As I was the only one known by both parties, more than likely, I'd be the first person picked up by the investigation team and be asked to either snitch and give up my friend or take the fall. At this point in my life, my pride would have gotten the best of me and I wouldn't have become a rat, sending me to my demise. I would have received a sentence of life in prison. Or, at the very least, I would have spent a long time behind bars, making my last stay of eight months seem like a blessing.

I told my mind to shut up. The decision had been made, *my* decision, and there was no stopping the ball in motion. To my great relief, things turned out okay and I was able to dodge this ball. Jay eventually came to the conclusion that it was not his weed and we all parted ways on good terms. Oh, how easily that ball could have crashed right into my nut sack, like it did for a friend.

A few years before my situation with Jay in the garage, a friend was not able to dodge the ball of fate when he found himself in a predicament remarkably similar to mine. However, things didn't go as planned. Guns were drawn and a man was killed. While my friend wasn't the one who pulled the trigger, he was there and, of course, he was the only one they caught. His pride kept him from ratting, and they sentenced him to life in prison. Like me, he had made his decision, and like mine, it was a bad one. However, I lucked out. That ball was set in motion the moment they decided to rob another man. The universe conspired to work things out in the exact way it was supposed to. Cause and effect. One man was dead and another man's freedoms were completely stripped away from him.

Yet Another Bad Decision

One late afternoon, on a beautiful warm spring day. I was cruising down the highway on my motorcycle with a backpack full of weed and cocaine, making my rounds, not a care in the world, a couple grand stuffed in my pockets from a couple hours of some easy-money work. One hand on the bars, the other on my hip, tinted face shield so nobody could see my face. Yeah, I thought I was pretty cool. I felt pretty significant. I was enjoying this shit too much.

Cruising along to my next stop, I took a look in my rear-view mirror and saw Mr. Policeman right behind me. My heart skipped a beat, but thankfully he pulled off the freeway. Relief! Everything was all good. As I moved to my exit, a big, sweeping right turn off the freeway to a stop sign, I checked my rear-view mirror, and who did I see sweeping around the exit? That's right. My friend, Mr. Policeman. It was the same car, I was sure of it. Since he got off and then got back on the freeway and followed me to this exit, I could tell he wanted me. I had a plate on the back, so if he got close enough, he would run it. Whether or not to have plates is always a tough

ONE BAD DECISION FROM DISASTER

decision to make when you're a bad guy on a motorcycle. On the one hand, if you don't have plates, a suspicious cop can't run the number, which probably means you're getting pulled over. On the other hand, having plates means you can't allow them to get too close because then they can run the number and get you later. Decision time, Jono.

Mind made up! I slapped it in first and rolled the throttle, banked a hard left, straightened out, and kicked up to second, already doing about sixty. I smack third and hit about eighty, then ninety on a two-lane road. I glanced in my mirror and saw lights flashing behind me. My engine noise was tacked to the max and the wind was blowing hard. I was crouched as tight as I could get to the gas tank of the rocket I was sitting on. I warped into tunnel vision. I was probably two hundred yards ahead of Mr. Policeman when I saw my next obstacle: a car in front of me and another coming down the other side of the road. Of course, all three of us were going to come together at the same time. Why on Earth would it happen any other way? Why on Earth would this be easy for me? We are on a thirty-five mile per hour, two-lane-road and I'm now doing over one hundred.

> "I chose the latter, put my head down, and squeezed down the middle of both cars at high speed."

Another decision had to be made, and quickly. Do I hit the brakes hard and slow down so I can pass these cars safely and risk letting Mr. Policeman catch up? Or do I roll the throttle back and bomb right down the center of the two lanes on top of the double yellow line right in between the two cars? I chose the latter, put my head down, and squeezed

THE BREAKING POINT

Spinning at a high rate, doing burnouts in the middle of an intersection in San Francisco. Being reckless made me feel good back then. *photo courtesy of an unknown bystander (thanks!)*

down the middle of both cars at high speed. Holy shit! What a rush! As I moved back to my lane, I spotted a man working in his yard. He was frozen, eyes wide as the size of two silver dollars, probably saying to himself, "That guy is a fucking idiot and will be dead soon." I was utterly reckless.

At that point, the police were way back there, lights still flashing. I slowed down to bank a right turn and accelerate out and up the hill with power and speed no car can match. Most cops would give up the chase at this point because trying to catch me was only risking the lives of everyone involved, including me! I assume he gave up chasing me, because I never saw him again, at least not that I know of. We may have crossed paths again, but he never got close enough to make out my plate or get a clear identification. Thank God, because they would have been at my house that evening dragging me back to my favorite vacation spot, the county jail.

I took the long way back around through town, watching not only my back but my front left and right. Who knew how many cops were now on the lookout for me? I made my last stop and called it a night. I'm not sure my heart ever stopped pounding that evening, and I don't think I slept either. It was a total adrenaline spike that wouldn't let up.

The Consequences of Dumb Decisions

Life is one big series of decisions. Every minute of every day, we are faced with the unending need to make decisions (sometimes upwards of 35,000 decisions per day![5]). We can choose to make good ones or bad ones. Our decisions move us either forward or backward in life, health, work, business, relationships, and any other area of importance. Some decisions keep us stuck in the same place forever. We must learn to make our decisions wisely and think about them profoundly, at least the important ones—because once you have made a decision, either for good or bad, the ball is set in motion and you must take ownership of whatever results.

> "Sometimes, the worst decisions we make are the ones we don't suffer obvious consequences from, because we don't learn the lessons we need to learn."

---

[5] Marples, Megan, "Decision Fatigue Drains You of Your Energy to Make Thoughtful Choices. Here's How to Get It Back." CNN, 21 Apr. 2022, www.cnn.com/2022/04/21/health/decision-fatigue-solutions-wellness/index.html

Evading the law on my motorcycle was one of the worst decisions I ever made, even though nothing bad actually happened. Sometimes, the worst decisions we make are the ones we don't suffer obvious consequences from, because we don't learn the lessons we need to learn. We fall into the trap of believing our decision must not have been that bad since everything seemed to turn out okay, but this is a lie we tell ourselves so we can continue our dumbassery. The truth? Getting away with it is worse than getting caught. Because every time you dodge the bullet, you start believing you're bulletproof. And that delusion? That's what kills you. Trust me, I spent many long years rationalizing things this way. I risked a lot that night, not just my life but the lives of the people in the cars and nearby on their lawns. Sure, they probably would have been alright, but what if I had crashed and sent my bike flying down the street, taking out the guy working in his yard? I could have killed him in an instant. I probably bragged about this to my friends like it was a great accomplishment.

Your Future Is in Your Hands

In the movie *Back to the Future Part II*, Marty McFly, one of the main characters, learns of his precarious future by using a time machine to jump forward several years. He learns that a series of bad life decisions led to crippling debt, physical ailments, and an otherwise pathetic life. He discovers the one particular moment in time when things took a turn for the worst: the moment he decided to drag race with someone at a stoplight. Needles, the antagonist, revved his engine, bucked like a chicken, and goaded Marty into racing with him. Marty took the bait, got into a major accident, and ruined his life.

When present-day Marty comes to this life-altering moment in time, he chooses wisely by backing up his car in true Hollywood fashion instead of racing forward. He changes his future by making the smart decision in the moment. Yes, he had the knowledge of his future helping him, but he still had to get over his irrational fear of someone else thinking he was "chicken." He still had to make the right decision in the moment, and this is never easy. But you must do it! Remember, short-term gain, long-term pain. Choose wisely, my friends.

The power of decision making is huge. It's the closest you will ever get to being able to write your own life's story. And it's the closest you'll get to time traveling like Marty, because what you choose to do right now wildly affects your future self. How many men and women didn't dodge the ball in the garage like I did and are locked in prison for life because of the poor decisions they made? How many humans are confined to the streets because their decision to use drugs outweighed their desire to put in the work to enjoy an actual good life? A really good friend of mine, someone I rode motorcycles with, made the poor decision to roll on that throttle, much like I did, except he rode right into a car that had suddenly turned out in front of him, ending his life much too early. A friend of my father's is paralyzed from the neck down because of his awful decision to jump off a bridge into the unforgiving waters below. How about the man or woman who sacrificed their family because of a sexual desire they couldn't control? But just like all the bad decisions and the dismal roads they open up for us, we can also make good decisions that unlock brilliant opportunities.

What happens when you make the decision to wake up early every day and exercise? In time, you get stronger, leaner, and healthier, you lose weight, and you feel better about yourself. Your confidence begins to soar. What about when you follow through on the carefully constructed decision to start the business of your dreams? You find joy and happiness and become wildly successful in whatever manner that means to you, even if you fail at first.

Every decision has a path attached to it. It doesn't matter the size of the decisions you make, good or bad, because they all converge and compound into whatever path that decision leads you down. What matters is that you must try to see the path that each given decision will lead down before you begin taking action. Once you have determined it is the path and direction you'd like your life to go down, then, and only then, may you step forward and begin to carve out that life.

I'm extremely grateful I'm alive today to be able to share these stories on the power of our decisions. I hope my stories serve as examples for you to see what the consequences of our decisions can be, good or bad, great or small.

One of the greatest motivational speakers of all time, Jim Rohn, said, "It does not matter which side of the fence you get off on sometimes, what matters most is getting off. You cannot make progress without making decisions." Get off the fence and start making decisions that propel you in the direction you want your life to take. Each day, make the proper decisions that have the path attached to them that lead you toward your finest life.

Ask yourself right now, Where do I want to go in life? Am I making the right decisions to lead me there? Do I like who I am? Are my choices creating who I'd like to become?

If you answer no to either of these, adjust and realign yourself toward the desired outcome you want. I've fucked up plenty, and you'll read about more of my mistakes in coming chapters. But here's the thing: nobody's perfect. We all screw up sometimes. It's inevitable. What matters is how we handle it when we do. If you can see a mistake for what it is, just a mistake, you can pick yourself up to keep moving in the right direction. Even with the setback, even with the mess you made, that's when you know you're on the right track in life. And this is where the real work begins, because it's an ongoing process. It's how you grow as a person. It's not about never falling. It's about getting back up every damn time and pushing forward. That's when transformation happens. That's when you become who you're meant to be.

9

Change Hurts

*"A dog is the only thing on Earth that loves you
more than she loves herself."*
—*Josh Billings*

The most genuine soul I had in the early part of my life was my pup, Blue. She was a pitbull, on the small side, white fur with gray patches (which for some reason people refer to as blue in dogs). Blue was mostly well behaved. She was also very protective of me, which made me feel really good. Being with her was exactly what someone like me needed, and of course, what's a drug dealer without a pitbull?

Blue and I went everywhere together. From the day I got her as a pup, I put her in the front seat of my truck, and that is where she stayed. Everywhere we went, her head was out the window, tongue flapping in the wind, dried up slobber across the whole side of my black truck. It was nasty, but I wouldn't have had it any other way. She was my road dog, and even once protected me from the police when she kept them from using their K-9 to sniff out my truck. Bullet dodged! We went to the park every day, and she chased rabbits until she finally tired. One time, she chased a rabbit so far off into the hills I lost sight of her. When I did finally catch up, she was laid out in a patch of tall, dried weeds, breathing hard in exhaustion. That rabbit almost ran her dead.

She also loved chasing squirrels up trees. Literally, I would tap the tree and tell her, "Get him! Up!" If the tree had any angle on it at all, she would cruise up and balance herself on different limbs, searching for that squirrel. It was one of those things you see from a distance and say, "Is that a dog in a tree?" It was remarkable. Blue and I were inseparable, two peas in a pod.

My dog Blue, roughly 15 feet up in a tree searching for squirrels. The picture does not do it justice. Actually watching her navigate through the tree was amazing.

My brother, Brian, was down on his luck. He was at a loss and had nowhere to go, so I offered him to stay with me. I had plenty of room, so why not? The problem was, he brought his pit bull along with him. Another female dog. I should have smelled trouble right from the start.

One day, I returned from taking both dogs to the park and letting them have a good run. They were tired, and I felt they would be fine if I left them alone in the house while I went to do a couple errands. Looking back on it,

Blue and I were inseparable, right to very the end.

I remember seeing my brother's dog having blood on its mouth after the park. I didn't know what she got into or why it was there, but I thought nothing of it.

I had a few calls to make and had to go make some drops. I figured I'd just leave both dogs in the house. What could possibly go wrong? I wouldn't be long because I was taking my motorcycle. As I'm walking out the garage door, I noticed Blue standing at the back slider, wanting to get in the yard. She seemed pretty adamant about it. I recall how in that moment I had a glimmer of insight that maybe she didn't want to be left alone in the house with my brother's beast of

THE BREAKING POINT

an animal, but I ignored the thought and left her. It was one of those decisions in life that I truly should have spent more time considering.

I arrived home about forty-five minutes later, and as I walked back into my house, with my motorcycle helmet still in hand, I wondered why Blue wasn't there to greet me. I look around and to my horror, all I see is red blood everywhere. I mean *everywhere*. The carpet was soaked in it. It was splattered on the walls. I've never seen so much blood. Starting from the living room, the swipes and splatters on the walls moved back down the long hallway that makes a left turn, and that's when I saw what I will never forget. My brother's dog had Blue by the neck.

> "I couldn't bring myself to stab a living thing to death, no matter how bad I wanted to. I'm no killer."

I lost it completely. With rage I began to beat my brother's dog with my motorcycle helmet yelling, "Let go of my dog, you fucking piece of shit!" and cursing to no end. It didn't matter where I hit the dog, how loud I yelled, or how hard I swung; his dog wouldn't budge. It didn't even flinch from the massive, full-swing motorcycle helmet slams. If you've ever held a motorcycle helmet, you know they're pretty solid and robust. I must have hit her over the head at least fifty times but the dog wouldn't let go. She just kept trying to drag my dog away from me, absorbing the blows like they were pats on the head. Still in a rage, I ran and got a big kitchen knife, intending to stab the dog to death. I ran at the dog and raised the knife over my head, my face distorted in madness and tears as I thrust it downward. Right before I plunged the knife through this vicious, blood-thirsty dog, I held myself back. I stopped. I couldn't bring myself to stab a living thing to death, no matter how bad I wanted to. I'm no killer.

I looked at Blue and could see that my pup was already gone. Probably for at least ten minutes already, maybe longer. I'm no expert, but her tongue was hanging limp out of her mouth and her body was already quite stiff. This wild dog had been dragging Blue around my house like a savage beast. I commenced kicking and stomping the dog as hard as I could. Finally, she broke her hold on Blue and I ran her out the back door.

I returned to Blue, fell to my knees, and cried my eyes out. In those first few moments of being alone with her, I hoped maybe she would come back to me, but she was gone. I put my head on hers and held her and kept on crying. I told her over and over how sorry I was for leaving her there with that beast.

It was one of the most emotional days of my life. I was hurt badly and continued to hurt for a long time afterward. It took several months to get past the pain and move on. It's one thing to lose your loved ones to natural causes, but one in a manner like this, taken totally by surprise, is absolutely cataclysmic.

I've had people say things like, "Who cares? It's just a dog." Those people just don't get it. Unless you're a dog lover and have had a relationship with a dog like I had with my friend, you may never understand the depth of one's true bond with their dog. For three years, it had been just me and Blue. There had been nobody else, other than a few girlfriends here and there. It was just me and Blue every day together, everywhere together, and she was truly my best friend. I'll never forget her. The emotions, the pain, and the horrible scene I came home to were terrifying, crazy, and just heartbreaking. It was near the end of an era for me and yet another stone I had to step onto and move forward from. It was another piece of my journey in adversity I had to endure.

In a way, it made the change I was about to make a lot easier. In all things bad, there is always something good we can mine from it. The loss of Blue more easily allowed me to move on from all the bad things I had accumulated in my life. Her death allowed me to say goodbye to a life I no longer desired. In that pain, I was able to see my life from a different perspective and finally say, "I'm fucking done with this shit." Why this happened, I don't know. Maybe in the deepness of the pain I just felt I couldn't bear anymore catastrophes. Running from the police on my motorcycles. Constantly watching my back for not only the cops but for thugs who will put a bullet in your head for a couple grand. A few months earlier someone, probably someone I knew—had broken into my home and swiped five grand from my room. Shit was starting to get ugly. Also, the thought of getting busted one more time would lead me to a disastrous, life-altering outcome. Like the judge said in the courtroom, "Mr. Gilardi, do not let me see you back in here." I didn't listen to him. However, Blue's shocking death made me realize I'd better stop now. Somehow, something inside told me it was time.

And so I said goodbye to my friend and to my reckless lifestyle. With a heaviness in my heart, I sold all my material possessions, my boat, all of my motorcycles, and walked away from my house and let it go into foreclosure. It was in the middle of the 2007-2010 financial crisis anyways so who cared, everyone was doing it. That final day, I stepped through my front door, closed it firmly behind me, and made a silent vow to rebuild my life from scratch. Some journeys require us to lose everything before we can see clearly again. Sometimes we need to return to solid ground before we can move forward with purpose. Blue's absence created the space for me to finally face the truth I'd been running from, it was time to become someone new.

> "Some of the deepest lessons in life can only be learned in our darkest of times."

Seek Out Your Change before It's Thrust upon You

Sometimes, we need to reach our breaking point in order to change our ways. In my case, this breaking point came with devastating force. For me, Blue's death was like being hit head-on by a speeding truck. But apparently I needed something harsh like that to finally light the fire up under my ass and force me to make the changes I needed. The fire came as a sacrifice, but a meaningful sacrifice, as hard as it is to say. Sometimes in life, we get the opportunity to change before it's too late. And for some of us, that hint comes with a stiff cost. But when it does come, take that hint:

- The abused wife takes one last blow . . . Change
- Another jail term to realize how much you've screwed up your life . . . Change
- Can't afford to feed the family . . . Change
- Stricken by disease . . . Change.

Change is good. To see that you need to change is even better. Jim Rohn once said, "You cannot change your decision overnight, but you can change your direction overnight." Take the hint and make the change you desire for yourself. Better yet, make the change before you get hit with a life curveball, because let me tell you, they will come. It's often thrown so fast it hits you in the head, and it's only from that hit that the light bulb goes off and you begin to think.

It's much better to make the change without a major painful episode beforehand. Listen to that little voice inside, nagging you to change. To do better. Don't wait, like I did. It would have been much better if I were to have thrust off my old life before Blue was gone, because then I could have taken her with me! The problem is, we don't often get the motivation we need until after something very painful happens. I don't know for sure why this is. But I guess it's because some of the deepest lessons in life can only be learned in our darkest of times. Here's what I do know: Change is coming whether you're ready or not. Life will break you open eventually. The only question is whether you'll choose to crack yourself open first, on your own terms, or wait for life to do it for you. One way, you're in control. The other way, you're just bleeding. The best way I've found to stay ahead of this change is through awareness, watching for the signs before the universe forces your hand. Pay attention to the voice inside telling you something's wrong. Notice when you're making excuses instead of progress. See the patterns before they become disasters. Don't wait for the grim reaper to swing his ax. Get busy living your preferred future right now!

10

A Message from Hell

"An arrow can only be shot by pulling it backward. So when life is dragging you back with difficulties, it means it's going to launch you into something great."
—Paulo Coelho

I stared up at the ceiling in my hospital bed, the harsh fluorescent light burning into my retinas. The mechanical rhythm of heart rate monitors echoed through the room, a cold reminder I was still alive. The IV dripped . . . dripped . . . dripped into my veins, each drop a ticking clock marking time I hadn't planned on having. The papery hospital gown scratched against the raw stitches crisscrossing my arms as my consciousness fully returned. "Well, I guess I'm still fucking here," I thought, the realization both a disappointment and strange relief.

After leaving my home I had bought in Antioch, California, I moved to a dark apartment in Lafayette about twenty miles away. When I say dark, I mean the place didn't get any sun, ever. The days were dark, the nights black as ancient obsidian, and the cold seemed to bite more, as if it was blown in from the frozen glaciers of the Arctic. My little one-bedroom apartment on the second floor was a cave, which was not quite ideal for me. I've found over the years that I do better in the spring and summer, whenever that big ball of fire is burning bright and I can absorb its healing powers and vitamin D. I could never live in a city or state that's always overcast and cold. No sun equals depression for me.

Despite the gloomy aura of this place, I did appreciate its location, cradled in the embrace of majestic, towering redwoods, with a creek flowing alongside the complex. Yes, those beautiful trees blotted out the sun and cast shadows into my Arctic cave, but it's hard to complain about redwoods surrounding your home. Still, as I mentioned, I'm a bright and sunny type of guy. As time passed, the dark and gloom of the place had a negative effect on me. And so, my fall began.

Each day, I fell deeper and deeper into a pit of despair and hopelessness. I missed Blue, and I had just broken up with my girlfriend. I was stuck in my new existence, which felt foreign to me. I felt like I had it all back in Antioch. Nice home, boat, motorcycles, and other toys. It was all gone. Now the money stopped flowing and I was struggling to pay the rent. A rent payment that used to literally take me one minute to make had now turned into a month's worth of hard work.

I started seeing a therapist, but I never really connected with her. I should have searched for another, but I guess I felt I'd do the easy thing and just stick it out. I thought it would just get better in time. Unfortunately, things got even darker the further down I went. The way I saw it, life was not looking promising. I felt I was taking all the right actions, but still nothing was working.

I realized that my first step out of the darkness had to be to get out of that shadowy, depressing apartment complex, so I began my search for a new place and totally lucked out. My brother and his young family were moving out of their two-bedroom home in Martinez, about ten miles up the highway, and I was able to slide right in. My new home was brighter. I had more room for my truck and all my supplies for the swimming pool business I had started. Unfortunately, it wasn't in the greatest part of town. You could literally see the Shell gas station refinery and its towers pumping out their toxic smoke above. My lungs weren't loving my new location, but at least I had vitamin D now, so yay for me!

Feeling a little better, I began hanging out with friends again. However, we partied a lot, which turned out to be the slippery slope that led to my last descent into the abyss below, before I smacked hard into rock bottom and bruised my soul. Alcohol, girls, boats, MDMA, cocaine, and more alcohol. Oh, and don't forget steroids and dumbells so we could look good doing it. The darkness began to squeeze down on me until I felt trapped. I'd feel okay for a bit while drunk and high, but when I came down, I would just squirm into that dark crevasse a little bit more, a little bit deeper. Over and over. It clenched down on me tight and I could feel no escape, except for the ultimate way out.

Imagine you are one of those cave divers who scrambles and squirms their body through those dark caves to search and explore the innards of those forlorn places, for God knows what. Maybe they're looking for buried treasure or monsters that will rip their bodies in half? I felt like one of them, except I got stuck and couldn't get out. Panic sets in. It becomes hard to breathe. You can't think clearly, and calming yourself is out of the question. You scream in fear. You scream for help, but no help arrives because you've slipped too deep into the cave and no one can hear you. Reminds me of a favorite horror movie of mine, *The Descent*.[6]

I would sit in my living room alone in the dark, trapped in feelings of despair and worthlessness, contemplating whether it was worth going on with my miserable existence. The transition I was attempting to make in my life seemed impossible, too big of a challenge. For fifteen years I had made easy money and had everything I needed or desired. Now I was dropping it all and starting over from the bottom. I was broke and missing all the joy in my life. Not to mention I still had friends who were living the lifestyle I had just left and watching them make money did not help.

In my depression, seeing no way out of that deep, dark cave I was stuck in, I exploded into a decision that will forever be my nightmare. That day, I popped oxy pills one by one to numb the pain. The constriction of the python snake wrapping itself around my body lessened. I drank straight from a bottle of Captain Morgan spiced rum. The Captain stared back at me with his blue cape flowing behind him and one brown leather boot up on a barrel, as if to say, "Drink up, life is a bitch." I enjoyed glorious relief, but it was ultimately short-lived. Captain Morgan smiled at me upside down as I polished off the bottle and laughed back at him. "Who cares anyway, right?"

---

6 Watch the movie *The Descent*. It's about a group of adventurous girls who venture into an unknown cave. It brings up all the feelings of being trapped in a cave, stuck in tiny crevasses, and getting attacked by strange creatures.

Sitting there realizing what was going to happen, I stumbled my way out to my work truck. If I was going to go I wanted to make sure to finish the deed. Fumbling around in the dark, I found my tool box and pulled out a rusty old razor. Staggering back up the stairs and into my home, I crashed into my couch head first, flipped myself up into a slouched seated position, and carved at my arms. My left arm was a complete bloody mess when I finished with it. I couldn't even see a good spot to cut anymore, so I began on my other arm.

> "Death spoke to me that night. He sat right beside me and told me, 'Let's go, Jono, there's nothing here for you.'"

I was not blacked out yet because I could still see myself there in that room, slouched over like a drunk bum on the streets. A broken man. A sad, totally incoherent piece of shit. Death spoke to me that night. He sat right beside me and told me, "Let's go, Jono, there's nothing here for you. Let me put you out of your pathetic misery." I gashed at my wrist hard with no concern for the blood running down my arms and soaking into the couch and the carpet and everything else nearby.

I began to cry, mixing the tears with my blood. I thought that I was truly doomed. I sat and cried for twenty minutes, feeling more and more drowsy. But suddenly, in a flash of desperation, some part of my soul rallied and fought back. I texted my brother, "I need help." I don't know exactly what went through my head at that time, maybe I didn't want to really die. Maybe I got scared. Maybe it was the rational side of me coming out and commanding, "Stop! Don't do this anymore."

My brother, who lived about two blocks away, arrived in a flash. He walked in the front door, his face distorted in horror as he yelled "What the fuck are you doing?!" I could barely hear him. The room was spinning. Then in a blur I saw him run out. Coincidentally, I lived right next door to the local fire department, so everyone showed up in record time, including the sheriff and my ride, the ambulance.

Once I started seeing the flashing lights, something in me panicked. Maybe it was the ex-convict instinct, or maybe just the drugs and alcohol clouding my judgment. Now, I'm a small athletic guy, and hopping a fence is usually easy for me, but not that night. I stumbled out the back door, barely able to keep my footing. I managed to climb over the fence, but instead of my usual nimble vault, I found myself awkwardly sprawled across the top before dropping like a sack of potatoes into the neighbor's yard. I lay there in the dirt for what felt like forever, my cuts still bleeding, my mind drifting in and out.

After a few minutes, I somehow found the strength to get up. I staggered to the front where the whole crew was gathered and just collapsed on the ground. They immediately started working on me, putting pressure on all of my cuts to stop the bleeding. I tried to resist again, like I was in trouble for something. I struggled like a fish out of water to break free of the EMTs' grasp. But finally I went limp and they dragged my sorry butt into the back of the ambulance.

Suddenly, I heard a voice saying, "Hey, Jono, do you remember me? It's Mike, from high school." Mike, an old acquaintance from high school, was one of the EMTs. Ouch! What an embarrassing moment. It didn't really matter, though. I couldn't see anything, let alone get a good look at Mike's face and remember who he was from fifteen years ago.

They rolled me into the emergency room and Mike said before parting, "I hope you get better, Jono. Good luck." I mumbled something unintelligible back to him, something like, "Thankith yoooo." The whole episode came to a close as they stitched me up and detoxed my sorry ass.

As I lay in that hospital bed, bandaged and sedated, I was forced to confront a truth I'd been running from: I had hit rock bottom. The ultimate **Breaking Point**. The only direction left was up, if I was brave enough to make the climb.

Bear Your Scars with Pride

When I chose death over life, when I cowered away because shit got tough and things weren't going my way, it was a bitter pill to swallow. Actually, it was a lot worse than a bitter pill. It forced me to confront just how badly I had fucked up my life. It showed me how weak I was, made me come face to face with the stark fact of my lack of resilience in the face of such adversity. I ran from the challenges life had thrown at me, hoping to find a permanent escape from that short-term pain. In that moment of desperation, I chose the easy way out, to be the coward, the chicken shit, the yellow belly, the craven, and the candy ass. That exit out of life would have left a wake of devastation for those who cared about me, who loved me. My attempt to flee from life's struggles actually highlighted how ill-equipped I was at the time to face the harsh realities of existence.

Looking back, I realize I was lucky in a way most people wouldn't understand, lucky that I was a felon, I couldn't

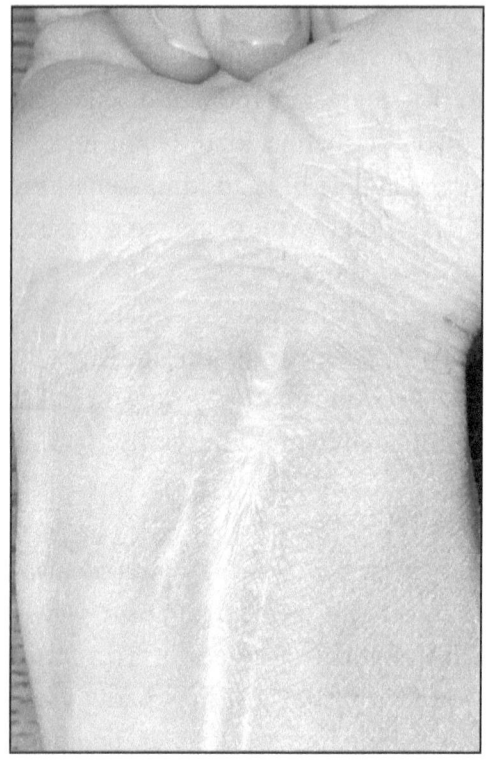

The prominent scar on my right wrist is a constant reminder of how far I've come.

legally own a gun. A gun would have been much quicker, and there would have been no second chances, no opportunity to text my brother, no possibility of changing my mind. Sometimes the restrictions we resent the most end up being the ones that save our damn lives.

Let's face it, life isn't always sunshine and rainbows, and problems pile up daily. But it's how we perceive and deal with these problems that makes all the difference. We've got to toughen up and accept that sometimes life just sucks. It's going to drag us through the mud, and we'll suffer because suffering is a part of the deal. But as Jordan Peterson said, "Life can be meaningful enough to justify its suffering." A season of pain can be followed by a season of joy. But those wonderful "golden ages" won't ever come around if we fail to learn and grow from the bad times. If we get stuck and fail to keep moving forward.

I fell into the trap of playing the victim, blaming the circumstances themselves instead of blaming me, the person who created them. I blamed the people around me for my problems. I pointed the finger at the psychiatrists for handing out high-dose depression meds like candy. But at the end of the day, *I* made the choice to pop those oxy pills, knowing damn well that mixing them with booze and other drugs was a recipe for disaster. I had walked my ass to the liquor store and invited Captain Morgan to join me in my pity party. Sure, the antidepressants as well as the labeling the therapist and psychiatrists placed on me, probably dug the hole a little deeper and screwed with my decision-making that day. But I'm the one who must own up to my choices, past, present, and future. The truth is, some of us don't need those fancy pills. We just need to suck it up and push through the tough times. There are plenty of natural ways to cope with the darkness.

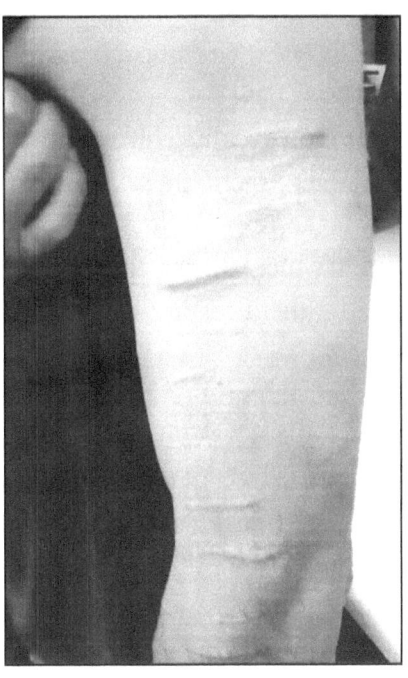

In the moment of cutting or self-mutilation, the pain dulls the battle with a troubled mind. *photo courtesy Ali Gilardi*

THE BREAKING POINT

After this episode, I finally decided to stop playing the victim, and doing so opened the door to integrity, honesty, and a sense of authentic pride I'd never before experienced. No longer was I letting life's curveballs extinguish my fire to strive for something extraordinary. I got out of my own way and focused on being a better person to myself and others. The moment you stop telling yourself that life is crushing you and start believing it's crafting you into something stronger, your entire reality shifts from a prison of pain to anything is possible. Practicing self-love and self-kindness every single day is the key to unlocking an extraordinary version of yourself. It's the path to self-mastery. Wear your scars with pride and let them inspire wisdom in your life and in the lives of others.

Lao Tzu said, "A journey of a thousand miles begins with a single step." We'll never stop being the pity of the party until we decide to take that first step away from victimhood.

Rock bottom is a dark, deep hole, and it's a real bitch to climb out of. The darkness feels like it's swallowing you whole, just like my gloomy apartment in Lafayette. You can't see a damn thing to grab onto to start your climb out. But as someone who's been to one of the darkest places a person can go, I'm telling you, those steps, those handholds, *are there*. You'll find your way out if you choose to look for them. So never stop looking. Never give up.

Therapists and psychiatrists? I know they work for many people, I know that talking it out is priceless, but they were not my saving grace. Maybe I should've kept looking until I found one that I really connected with. But honestly, a lot of them are just robots, asking the same predictable questions, slapping you with a diagnosis and sending you on your way with a prescription that may or may not work. You'll have to play Russian roulette to find out. But some of them are alright and will put in the effort to help you sort through your shit. Although that wasn't my experience, it has been for some of my friends. Since then I've found that working with someone who has actually been through it rather than just studied it has been more beneficial to me. As I understand and they understand better.

So, I had to go it alone. I knew I needed to make some drastic changes if I was ever going to see the light again. Step one: cut ties with almost everyone from my old life. I distanced myself from anyone still caught up in the partying and drug scene. If you've ever tried to do this, you know how hard it is, because they never stop trying to lure you back in, and when you're at your lowest, the escape they're offering sounds like heaven.

So, how did I resist? I found something else, a substitute, something that gave my life meaning and purpose: my swimming pool service and repair business. I poured my heart and soul into making it a success. I became a sponge, soaking up everything I could learn, attending every pool maintenance convention, hitting the books, and getting my contractor's license. I set big goals. I fell in love with what I was doing, and it gave me a reason to keep going.

Because my life was becoming so much fuller, my past wasn't haunting me as much, begging me to come out and play. Sure, it still tried to pull me back sometimes, but the momentum in my life had shifted. My mindset had changed, and slowly but surely, things started falling into place.

Happiness became a more regular visitor, and you could see it, feel it radiating from me. And when you start putting out that positive energy, you attract even more good things into your life. That's the turning point, the moment when angels start to appear.

When you find your purpose, whether it's a passion, a business endeavor, a cause, or a challenge that lights a fire under your ass, pour everything you've got into it. Let it consume you in the best way possible. When you find a reason to rise each morning, to push through adversity, that's when healing begins and strength takes root. That's when you start to see the beauty in life again, even with its many flaws and hardships.

Surround yourself with positivity, with inspiration, with love. Take care of yourself physically, mentally, and emotionally. Exercise, eat right, get enough sleep, and find healthy ways to cope with stress and pain. Meditate, journal, read, create art, pour your heart out to a trusted friend. Do more of what makes you feel alive and less of what numbs you or makes you feel like shit. This may seem like a daunting list of stuff, but believe me, once your life is headed in the right direction, it all starts coming together synergistically.

> "Your scars? Wear them like badges of honor, reminders of the battles you've fought and won, reminders of your grit and toughness."

Then of course you need to find people who support your journey, who lift you up instead of dragging you down. For me, I'll be forever grateful to the successful guys in the swimming pool industry; their positivity and uplifting encouragement fuelled me past the down slumps I'd still sometimes find myself in. Their healthy desire to grow and improve their businesses invigorated my drive to do the same, and helped place me in a happier state.

Then of course, there were one or two good friends who helped me along, jumping in to support me when I needed them. One day I was slumped over feeling miserable, not wanting to do shit. My buddy Jeremiah knew the state I was in and recognized I wasn't doing well. Suddenly I heard a honk outside. I swung open the door and there he was. "Get some clothes on. Let's go!" he yelled. "I'm not going anywhere!" I yelled back. "Get some damn clothes and let's go!" he repeated.

I yielded and clumsily hopped in his truck. "Where are we going?" I asked, my head down. Jeremiah took me to a Warriors basketball game that night. It was the perfect medicine. I smiled, I cheered, and I laughed. I didn't think about my problems because I was enjoying life. Sometimes it just takes a good soul to lift you out of a funk. It's the friend who can make you laugh no matter how down and crushed you feel at the time. It's my old buddy Nick, who sat with me in the dark and just listened because maybe he didn't know what to say, but it was his listening that mattered most.

Changing your life for the better is a beautiful process that never ends, because if you want to stay away from the dark side of life, then you must apply consistent attention to working on yourself, to bettering yourself through personal development. There's no other way, no secrets to uncover. Like most everything good in life, it simply takes work.

Remember, healing isn't a straight line. You'll have setbacks, moments when you feel like you're slipping back into the darkness. But that's okay. Be kind to yourself, forgive yourself, and keep putting one foot in front of the other. Celebrate every victory, no matter how small. And never, ever give up on yourself.

So, when life keeps yanking you back, whether it's your own demons or some outside force you can't control, remember that eventually you've got to propel yourself forward. Let go of what's holding you back and set your sights on the right target. Reach out for help if you need it, but ultimately it's up to you to release that arrow. Aim high, straight out of that dark cave you've been trapped in, and shoot for something extraordinary. Your scars? Wear them like badges of honor, reminders of the battles you've fought and won, reminders of your grit and toughness. They're proof that you're a fucking warrior. So go out there and conquer your world, one purposeful step at a time.

I owe my brother everything. That text I sent him, those three words—"I need help"—gave me a second chance at life. He didn't hesitate, didn't judge. He just showed up. We all need someone like that. And if you're in that dark place right now, reach out to whoever that person is for you. If you feel you don't have this person, then call or text the National Suicide Prevention Lifeline at 988, or contact the Crisis Text Line at 741741. These are lifelines staffed by people who genuinely give a damn and understand what you're going through. Making that call or sending that text could be the most important thing you ever do. There's always another way forward, even when the darkness tells you there isn't.

11

Bottomed Out

> "The best thing about rock bottom is the rock part. You discover the solid bit of you. The bit that can't be broken down further. The thing that you might sentimentally call a soul. At our lowest we find the solid ground of our foundation. And we can build ourselves anew."
> —Matt Haig

I was sober now, lying in another hospital bed. This, however, wasn't the typical hospital, this was the mental hospital, the looney bin, the cuckoo's nest, where they keep the wackos, the crazies, the unpredictables, and the unstables, like I had become. I never felt more alone or more lost. Well, the night before was bad, but I had been drugged up and there was a lot of alcohol swishing around in my belly. I've been in some messed up places and seen some fucked up people, but this place took the cake.

I looked at my surroundings. I was in a small bed with a gray wool blanket, you know, the type that makes your skin itch if you let it touch you. The sheets and pillowcase reeked of bleach. At least they were clean . . . right? There was a wooden desk and a chair to my right. Nothing screams insane asylum more than the buzzing fluorescent lights overhead. I looked to my right! "Fuck," I whispered to myself. There was another bed in the room with the same exact gray, scratchy blanket. And there was someone in it. I couldn't see them because they were completely covered, head to toe. Not moving, not snoring, nothing. Must be asleep. I hoped they weren't dead.

I got up to better inspect this luxury hotel. As I looked to the floor, hoping to find some kind of shoes or slippers, I was delighted by the sight of my own shoes. Well, I wasn't in jail, so that was good! But I quickly realized the laces had been removed. They did this because nutters like me can use them as something to hurt themselves with. "Good luck hanging yourself with shoelaces," I thought. I slipped the shoes on and clunked over to the door. Peeking through it, I looked left, then right: long hallways both ways, with white walls and a floor littered with ugly light blue linoleum tiles. Fluorescent lights all the way down, doors on each side. A man turned the corner in a hospital gown, brown hair looking like he just stuck his finger in a light socket. He was getting closer. "How's it going?" I asked him. He didn't even look at me, just kept walking, muttering something that sounded a little like a mix of *abracadabra* and *yabba dabba doo* in a low growl. He was clearly in no mood to have a convo, but neither was I, for that matter.

I made my way down the hall, clenching my toes to keep my shoes from falling off. I was definitely looking the part of the wackadoo, even if I didn't want to admit it. Thinking about it now years later, I must have looked like a rejected extra from *One Flew Over the Cuckoo's Nest*, that classic movie about a mental institution. Not even Jack Nicholson would have wanted to share a card game with me. As I got to the end of the hall, I came to what looked like the command center for this shit show. There were two women working their computers behind a large desk that separated their space from ours, safely tucked behind clear plastic all the way up to the ceiling.

Nearby me was a guy yelling into a wall-mounted phone. As I was staring at him, I was tapped on the shoulder by a little woman with a lazy eye. She explained to me, "Don't mind him. He does this every day at the same exact time for ten minutes. He's not even talking to anyone." She left and dragged her feet through a set of double doors.

I heard a loud scream from down the hall and two orderlies dressed in white, keys swaying to and fro on their sides, burst out of a door and ran down toward the scream. My eyes went wide with curiosity. However, as I looked around, I saw that nobody else seemed to mind much, not even the two gals behind their plastic bunker. This must just be another daily routine.

I heard laughter coming from behind the double door, so I slid my feet over to take a peek. There was a TV with about six or so people glued to the screen. Three of those people were sitting on an old brown couch. The others were seated in some chairs they had pulled over from nearby tables. At the tables, there were a couple guys playing a board game of some sort. The laughter I had heard came from a ping-pong table in the far corner. Some of the faces in this room seemed happy and content, others lost and confused. "Wonderful. One big happy family," I said under my breath.

I turned and began walking back toward the front desk, but not before I was cut off by another raving loony walking close in front of me yelling, "Ba, ba, ba ba, ba, ba." He startled me so much that I prepared myself for a fight, but like most of the others in here, he was in his own little world, and nobody else even seemed to notice.

I arrived at the plastic command center and said to one of the ladies behind the desk, "Okay, I'm good now. All sobered up. My mind is right. I'm ready to go home."

She took a good look at me and smiled. She glanced down at her computer, clicked a couple times with her mouse, and looked back up. "Mr. Gilardi, I'm sorry, but you are on a forty-eight hour hold where at the end of that forty-eight hours you will be assessed by our in-house psychologist."

"What?! You can't hold me here against my will. I've done nothing wrong except to myself."

"Exactly," she replied.

"This is bullshit," I said, clearly upset. "I do not belong here. Look at these people. They are fucking crazy."

She looked at me with the slightest hint of sympathy and calmly said, "I'm sorry, Mr. Gilardi. There's nothing I can do. You must go through the process. I will have the doctor come speak with you as soon as he's available." Through a tiny slot, she slid over a small cup with one pill in it. "Please take this, it will help you relax. There's water right there behind you." With no hesitation and no care in the world, I swallowed that sucker and chased it with water. I didn't give a shit at that point. The night before I had tried to off myself, so why would a little pill bother me? I threw the cup in the garbage, turned around, and once again assessed my situation.

I looked around at all the wackos and then looked down at myself. Stitches ran up and down my arms, with one weaving its way up my right wrist. It began to sink in. I was surrounded by zombies and other head cases, but who was I, shuffling about the place with wide eyes and a railroad track of stitches on my arm? I was clearly no better off than any one of these people. I was just as fucked up as them, but in my own way. If they let me out of here, what do I do? Go on another binge and take another crack at it?

I dragged myself back to my room and took a look at my roommate, still unmoved beneath his blanket. I laid down and threw my blanket over my head as well. It seemed like the best thing to do at the time. Hide from it. I was surrounded by people, but I had never felt so alone in my life. I began to weep quietly. How did I get here? What kind of future did I have?

> "I looked around at all the wackos and then looked down at myself. Stitches ran up and down my arms, with one weaving its way up my right wrist."

As I lay there, the reality of my situation crystallized with painful clarity. This wasn't just a bad day or a rough patch, this was rock bottom. My body bore the physical evidence with its stitches, and my mind was just as scarred. That phrase "rock bottom" suddenly wasn't just some expression anymore, it was my address, my current residence, the cold hard surface I'd finally crashed against after years of free-falling.

THE BREAKING POINT

Rock Bottom

Rock bottom. We've all heard the phrase, all known people who have been there. Nobody wants to go down there, but many of us find ourselves slapping hard against that unyielding bottom. For some of us, it comes out of nowhere. A tragic mistake, a terrible incident, maybe even something that wasn't your fault, and boom, there you are, at rock bottom.

For many others, including me, the descent is a long time coming, the slow, almost inevitable end-product of years of bad choices. Even so, to my self-deluding mind it seemed quick and sudden. Yes, I knew I was living a life that consisted of making all the wrong decisions, but hitting rock bottom still seemed to happen in an instant. Smack! Suddenly this vicious blow hit me hard. I saw stars and had a ringing in my ears like I had just been hit by Mike Tyson's right hook. And I'm not talking about the fifty-year-old Mike Tyson, I'm talking about the twenty-something Tyson who was knocking people out in seconds. It was a devastating feeling. Mentally, I was checked out of the game, and physically, I had nothing left. Death seemed like the only answer.

If you've hit rock bottom yourself, or been in the neighborhood, you quickly realize that nobody close to you understands unless they themselves have been to the bottom. Family and friends can surround you with their love and good intentions, but still you feel so far removed from them. You may smile and laugh back, but it's fake. You may act happy for their benefit, but deep down you are greatly hurt and troubled. Troubled by the choices you've made in your life. Troubled by the type of people you choose to surround yourself with.

The troubles we face are ours alone, and can make us feel extremely isolated. We find escape in a bottle or a drug. When we are down at that stony bottom and feeling this alone, we tell ourselves that nobody will understand. That nobody will get it. People try to help and say things like, "It's going to be okay" or "This too shall pass." The problem is, when you are in the moment, you feel like it will never pass, like things will never get better. Suffocation. You can't see a way out and you dig a deeper hole for yourself, making things even worse.

> "I came to understand that rock bottom isn't just a place of despair and defeat, but also a foundation upon which to rebuild."

At the loony bin, I found my rock bottom, and it was miserable and frightening. I had no idea how I was going to escape this hellhole I had dug for myself. The impact of being trapped in a place like that on your mind and emotions, even if for only forty-eight hours—is profound. Nightmarish. Finding yourself in a mental hospital and having that 5150[7] file on your record will tell you real quick where you are in life, how bad it's gotten, and that you have one of two choices remaining. Nobody describes those two choices better than the wise words of Morgan Freeman as Red in the movie The Shawshank Redemption: "Get busy living or get busy dying." That's deep. I'd prefer to get busy living, and once I did start thinking hard about my life and my circumstances, my whole attitude began to shift and became more positive.

---

7 A 5150 is the California code for an involuntary 72-hour psychiatric hold that can be initiated when someone is deemed a danger to themselves or others due to a mental disorder. It allows for temporary detention for evaluation and treatment.

I came to understand that rock bottom isn't just a place of despair and defeat, but also a foundation upon which to rebuild. Remember that Matt Haig quote? "The best thing about rock bottom is the rock part." That shit hit differently when I was staring at my stitches in that hospital. The solid ground beneath me wasn't just the bottom of a pit, it was the starting point of my climb.

> "Today, I look at the scars on my arms like a map of where I've been. The mental hospital, the 5150 on my record, the scratchy gray blanket I hid under, they're part of my story now, not shameful secrets but markers of a journey I survived."

I'm not gonna bullshit you with some fairy tale about how I magically transformed overnight. Those pills didn't work for me. My climb was messy, with plenty of slips and falls. But I began to move, first with small, desperate grabs at anything solid I could hold onto. A day of sobriety. A real conversation where I actually told the truth about how fucked up I was. A phone call to someone who hadn't given up on me yet.

Each of these micro moves, as I call them now, was like finding a tiny ledge on that rock face. Nothing monumental, just enough to keep from sliding back down. But these small victories became evidence that I wasn't completely broken. That maybe, just fucking maybe—I could claw my way back to something resembling a life.

Today, I look at the scars on my arms like a map of where I've been. The mental hospital, the 5150 on my record, the scratchy gray blanket I hid under, they're part of my story now, not shameful secrets but markers of a journey I survived. That miserable rock bottom became the foundation I built myself back up from, one painful inch at a time.

If you're down there now, wrapped in your own version of that scratchy blanket, feeling like the world would be better off without you, I need you to know that the solid ground beneath you isn't just the end. It's also a beginning. The first handhold is waiting for you, even if your fingers are shaking too badly to see it clearly. Grab it anyway. The climb is brutal, but I promise you there's air up here. Real, breathable air. And enough space for all of us who've been to the bottom and found our way back. Your journey to greatness starts with a single step of courage.

12

An Angel Emerges

> *"So, I love you because the entire universe conspired to help me find you."*
> —Paulo Coelho

I walked out of the mental hospital and she walked into my life. Well, I'm making it sound easy, but it wasn't that easy. I was so far from perfect and so far from being in a good place in my life. She didn't care. She had seen me in my worst possible form. She had seen the police and firefighters rush into my house. She had watched as the ambulance drove away with my tattered soul inside, and with a smile, she waved hello when I came home after my stay in the cuckoo's nest. I was still so lost then, still not in a good place. She didn't judge or shame. She felt my pain and offered a helping hand. They have a name for people like this; they call them angels. I just call her Ali.

A few weeks before the incident, we were just starting to cross paths more often. Everyone has that neighbor they try to avoid, but in this case, she didn't avoid me, nor did I avoid her. There was just something special about the connection. I felt it and she did as well.

We talked a lot from porch to porch about life, past relationships, and our values and thoughts. I shared that I was working on building a life I could be proud of by building an ethical business I didn't have to hide. She seemed impressed that I was deliberately moving from a childish life to a more responsible way of living. Good women like this sort of thing, and that was different for me. Responsibility is sexy.

Every day I stepped forth from my porch, our paths crossed. She'd smile at me as her eyes caught my gaze. I'd smile back. She would knock on the door and say, "I'm walking to the corner store, would you like something?" She brought me back Red Bulls. I eventually started to bring her Go Girl energy drinks in return. It felt good. Our friendship was blossoming, but neither of us knew where it was headed, if anywhere at all. She was still in a dysfunctional relationship herself and not happy, and I wasn't sure what that meant for us.

Then, the hellacious night happened. In its aftermath, to my surprise, we became closer on an emotional level. She saw me at my worst, my very most vulnerable point of existence. But miraculously, instead of this event shutting down the friendship due to fear, it gave us the freedom we needed to open up to each other about deeper things in life. I had obviously hit rock bottom and was just starting my climb up, but to my credit, I was beginning to learn how to communicate on a deeper level.

She had a Halloween party and invited me over. I had a little fun, but I soon disappeared. Still feeling down for what

I had done to myself, finding joy was a difficult task. When Ali realized I was gone, she came looking for me. It wasn't hard to find next door. There was a knock at the door. It was Ali, dressed in a sexy Eve from the Garden of Eden costume. I took one look at her beautiful face and pulled her through the door. We stumbled to the ground and in a passionate entanglement we began vigorously kissing. Just kidding. That didn't happen. What did happen was I got that feeling in my gut. You know, those corny butterflies. I was feeling those, and so was she, at least I think she was. A feeling that had been dimmed for so long, it felt foreign but so natural.

> "Instead of this event shutting down the friendship due to fear, it gave us the freedom we needed to open up to each other about deeper things in life."

"Why did you leave?" she asked.

"I'm just not feeling it at the party, and the beer I had didn't make me feel any better." Before she could respond, we heard the loud rumbling of her slightly drunk friends making their way over. They stayed for a little while chit-chatting about nothing special, while Ali shot me a few eye rolls and encouraging smiles. They eventually left. Thank God, because I just wanted to be alone. Later that evening, Ali would begin to spill the beans through text messages.

She wasn't happy in her one-sided relationship and she had never felt more alone, unworthy, and unloved. She shared with me that it was finally time to throw in the towel and move on to start a new life, a happy life. And so, after seven years, she did just that. She moved away and got a place of her own. It was hard for her at first, but she made it through. I was sad she was no longer my neighbor, but, again, everything happens for a reason. Although I felt a door was closing on me, I somehow had the wisdom to know I just had to be patient and wait for it to open once more. Looking back, I guess that, maybe, that little bit of insight was a sign of my growth as a person.

A bit of time passed, and then I did slightly crack the door open again: I found the courage to ask her out for dinner. The door swung open wide as she enthusiastically accepted and we went on our first real date. I remember she was super shy, as she had not been dating in quite some time. Luckily, I was well-versed at the art of dating, so there were no weird moments or awkward silences, at least not for me. We just really hit it off and enjoyed each other's company. We then began regularly hanging out as more than just friends. It was a rough start because her ex caught on and made things harder as he thought we had conspired this the whole time. We told him there was never any cheating, and that she had left and broke off the relationship as soon as she started to have feelings for me, but she would have left anyway, and that the universe brought us together, sorry. I felt sort of bad for the guy because it was never my intention to steal his girl. However, I began plans to make Ali mine forever, so you can tell I didn't care too much about his feelings.

Eventually I moved out of that old house in Martinez. Mostly because every time I walked in the door I saw a man sitting on the couch, bloodied and slumped over in a drunken daze, a nightmare I didn't want to have to confront every day. So I got a nice townhouse that overlooked the ghetto in Bay Point, California. Ali eventually moved in with me and we began our life together. We did everything together: ran marathons together, went backpacking together, went to the movies together, cooked together, made every holiday special together, and just spent as much time together as we could, being our true selves, laughing and enjoying the simple things in life. I was falling deeply in love and I knew she was too. Boy, how life had taken a turn for the better! If I had died that gloomy night back in my Martinez home, I would have never gotten to experience true love, something I wish everyone can experience in their lifetime.

On a beautifully clear New Year's Eve night, I took her on a dinner cruise out on the San Francisco Bay. The water lay still while my breath clouded in front of me. I couldn't ask for a more perfect setting. We ate and danced and as the clock struck midnight, fireworks boomed overhead. With the lighted San Francisco Bay Bridge in the distance, I softly asked her to marry me. She looked at me with tears in her eyes and said, "No! Sorry, Jono. I can't. I would never marry such an ugly duck."

Just kidding! Of course she said yes, and I wasn't kidding about the tears in her eyes. It was perfect. We were two peas in a pod and totally in love.

A few years later, we welcomed our first child Gio into the world, a handsome little boy with Ali's smile and my stubborn streak. He's smart and funny, maybe the next great comedian. Then came our daughter Olivia, who is the most kind, loving soul we have ever met. She's creative and loves all the arts. Watching these two tiny humans grow has been the greatest adventure of my life. Nothing puts your own journey into perspective quite like seeing your kids discover the world with fresh eyes.

Every time I look at them, I'm reminded of how close I came to missing all of this, the midnight feedings (where I learned I could actually fall asleep standing up while holding a bottle, a talent no one tells you about in parenting books), the first steps, even the tantrums that somehow make me laugh even when I'm exhausted. And just when I thought I understood what love was, having kids showed me a whole new dimension, a love so fierce and protective.

Having children is a challenge but extremely rewarding in so many ways. If I could go back and tell that broken guy in the mental hospital that one day he'd be teaching Gio how to ride a bike or braiding Olivia's hair for school, he'd never have believed it.

Love, the Greatest Gift

Ali is absolutely beautiful and the love of my life. She makes my heart skip beats. She is funny and weird, just like me. Still to this day, we make stupid jokes other people wouldn't find humorous at all, but we find them funny, and that's all that matters. Our values match up like an easy puzzle that takes no time to complete. We have similar goals for the future and for life.

Was it the totally unorthodox way it all began, or did the universe truly conspire to bring us together? Looking back, I can't help but think about that quote at the beginning of this chapter, about the universe conspiring to help people find love. Did some cosmic plan know that my one-year rental

AN ANGEL EMERGES

agreement was up at my apartment and to free up the house next door to her so we could find each other? I don't know. However, it sure does feel that way. All I know is that your next good thing might be just around the corner. Everything won't continue to go poorly forever, so long as you keep your head up and keep moving forward. Because when you make the choice to follow the positive path, life begins to unfold its treasures before you.

Life with Ali is still challenging because that's just life. There's always suffering, but having her by my side makes it all more bearable. Lao Tzu once said, "Being deeply loved by someone gives you strength, while loving someone deeply

My beautiful wife Ali, the woman who didn't run when she saw my scars, but instead helped me heal them. She is my heart, my home, my reason to keep fighting. *photo courtesy Kim Salvato*

gives you courage." I love my wife and kids so much it provides me with the strength to sacrifice and take care of my mind and body, and to continue to strive for my goals every day.

Finding love can seem like such a daunting life adventure. Think about all your greatest successes and wins in life. Did they come easy? Championships are not won without long hours in the gym. What you don't see is all the other relationships I've had, the pain and heartbreak, the lying and stealing, the cheating and the leaving, the lonely nights and the tears. Every bit of adversity I went through in those relationships accumulated into lessons that prepared me for Ali. I grew and learned to communicate, so when she did come, I could be equipped to have and keep such a wonderful person in my life.

> "Love gives my life meaning. When I think of the pain and struggles I'm forced to go through, I think of my wife and two kids and that pushes me through."

Once you find that person with whom everything aligns, it feels amazing. But soon the smoke settles and the work continues. Life throws you double the challenges, yours and theirs. Then add kids to the mix. However, now you have a steadfast partner standing by you no matter what. As a pair, you're together so much stronger. That's why love is still one of life's greatest rewards.

Love gives my life meaning. When I think of the pain and struggles I'm forced to go through, I think of my wife and two kids and that pushes me through. One of my favorite things is the shared experiences we have together, even the simplest things, like surprising Ali with flowers at work and hearing the joy in her voice when she calls to say thank you.

The best part about a great relationship is when you can talk about your goals and dreams with someone who believes in you and supports you. It's this inspiring of each other that's so joyful. If you don't have this, work to achieve it, because communication, saying the "I'm sorry's" and the "I love you's," is what makes it worthwhile.

My advice for finding love? Stop searching and start working on yourself. Begin to live a positive life and focus on your happiness. Learn to love yourself first, because we cannot extend to another what we don't have for ourselves. This was my precise stumbling block for so long. I used to tell friends I was going to be the guy who never found love, the one who always showed up alone. I didn't believe it would happen, so it never did. But when I finally let that shit go and steered myself in a positive direction, I found myself in the loving relationship I have today.

13

Hello, Grim Reaper, My Name Is Jono

"Challenging the meaning of life is the truest expression of the state of being human."
—*Viktor E. Frankl*

In April 2019, I fell ill. At first I thought, "It's just a common cold, no biggie, it will be over in a couple days." However, I wasn't getting any better. Each night I'd go to sleep, I swore I'd wake up the next day feeling better. Instead, each day I woke up feeling slightly worse. It was still nothing too concerning, but the fatigue was driving me nuts. I was used to having a ton of energy to run around and do whatever needed to get done. Now, I was slogging around the house like a three-toed sloth playing hide and seek.

Lying around the house too tired to move got really old after a couple days. A week had passed and I watched just about every show on Netflix, a cloud of restlessness fell over me. I wanted so badly to have my energy back, to get back to working and exercising again, to enjoying my family and doing fun things. But it wasn't happening.

A couple weeks went by, and Ali and I finally decided it would be best for me to see a doctor, just in case. They did some tests, gave me some antibiotics, and sent me home. After a few days, I was still not getting any better. I actually felt worse. So we headed back to the doctors and they did a series of blood work tests to see what they could find. Each time those results came back, the doctor would come in and say, "We still don't know what's going on with you, Mr. Gilardi. We need to run some more tests." So back to the lab I went to get more blood drawn. Thankfully, needles don't bother me too much, so this was no big deal. Two months passed like this. I was still not 100 percent, but I was feeling a lot better. Not because of any medication, but because I was just naturally beginning to fight the invader inside.

But then, things changed. On what I assumed would be another routine visit with no meaningful results, I finally got something different from the usual "We don't know." What I got was still not a concrete answer, but this time my doctor told me they had finally found something. Uh oh! I wasn't ready for this . . . She told me my blood was creating too many proteins, which could mean a number of things, so she referred me to a hematology specialist at UC Davis Medical Center in Sacramento, California.

My wife and I drove down to see the specialist two weeks later. It's a two-and-a-half-hour drive, so we made a day of it. We hung out, ate at a nice restaurant in the city, and enjoyed ourselves on the little trip. There are lots of great restaurants in Sacramento. I mean, it's the capital of California, so it must be good, right? The restaurants are terrible where we live in northern California, so it was a delight to have a great meal out.

We arrived at my appointment and went in to see the doctor. She was an older woman with a warm demeanor and intelligent eyes. Instead of the typical lab coat, she wore professional clothing with just a simple name tag. This small detail immediately put me at ease, well, as much as possible considering I was there to discuss why my blood was creating abnormal proteins.

She sat us down and rapidly explained what my labs and blood were pointing toward. Suddenly, I heard the word, the word nobody ever wants to hear. The word that has been said way too many times to way too many people. The word that has taken life after life with no remorse. The word that represents the reaper himself. *Cancer.*

My heart shifted in my sternum as if it wanted to launch itself to the moon. My stomach turned over about a dozen times, just like it did back in my apartment when I first realized the task force was about to drop in and take me away. Two very similar feelings. Two totally opposite scenarios. I felt as if I was going to barf up my lunch all over this smart doctor's desk. Was she serious? I mean, really, did she just say I may have cancer? I looked over at my wife, who already had tears in her eyes, her heart breaking. I held back my own tears for the moment because nothing was for certain yet, and asked, "How do we know for sure?"

"We need to do a bone marrow biopsy," the doctor said.

"A bone marrow biopsy? What is that?" I asked, already fearing the worst. Nothing good will ever follow a question like that one.

"It's where we go inside your bone, usually the back side of the pelvic bone, and remove a blood sample so we can see if there are any cancerous cells inside," she explained.

"So it sounds like it might be painful and you will have to put me under, right?" I responded, hoping for the best but expecting the worst.

"Actually, no, we won't put you under. What we do is numb the top layer of the skin so you won't feel a thing as we tap a hole in the bone. However, I must warn you that when we go in to pull the sample, the pain is usually quite excruciating. You will be okay, but it's not going to be pleasant."

"Wow, it sounds intense," I said. I tried to smile at my wife, but probably actually looked more like fear itself had taken over my face.

"Some people can tolerate it better than others, and we don't have to do it today. We can reschedule this procedure for another day, but since you guys drove over two hours to get here, I will squeeze this in now, if you'd like." It was super nice of her to offer that, because I imagined her schedule was most likely extremely busy.

I sat and pondered. This process sounded miserable. All I really wanted to do was schedule it for another time. I wanted to just leave with my wife, go eat some good food, and then head home and hang out with her and the kids. I was already scared enough, since she said I may have cancer. Deciding about the bone marrow biopsy on top of that seemed like too much. I tried to stay positive about the whole thing, but it was taking every ounce of my self-control.

I quickly realized I didn't want to wait. Why put it off for a couple more months and put myself through all that anxiety of wondering whether I have cancer or not? Sometimes in life, it's just best to get matters like this done and over with so you can just move on with your life, whichever direction that may be. I hated procrastinating, but the fear was intense. Taking a deep breath, I made my decision.

"Let's just get this done now. I don't want to wait," I told the doctor. My wife looked at me like I'm crazy, but my mind was set. I can be a stubborn bastard, but let no one say I'm a coward.

"Are you sure?" the doctor asked.

"Absolutely. Let's go!"

"Okay, let me get things together and I will return so we can begin."

With that, she walked out. My wife gave me a big hug and teared up again. "You are so brave, Jono. I would have never done it right away. I would be too scared!"

"You know my mantra of pushing through fear, right? We can't hesitate about this. I'm ready to get better and this is the next step, even though it's going to be horrible." Ali leaned her head against mine and I felt her warmth and tender love in that moment. On the brink of mortality, it was comforting to know I had her total support.

The doctor came back in, wheeling a cart with several different tools and supplies on it. She was accompanied by an assistant. I thought, "Great, the needle is so big she needs someone to help carry it and then insert it. Well, whose bright idea was this fucked-up plan after all? Oh yeah, it was mine."

"Are you ready, Mr. Gilardi?" she asked, bringing me out of my latest bout of internal morbid sarcasm.

"Yes. Let's do this."

She had me lie face down on the bed and pull my pants down, not too far, but far enough so I could feel the cold air slap my ass. I was a little embarrassed, but what could I do? I noticed two handles down by my head.

The doctor said, "When we begin to pull samples, you will want to grab on tight to those handles."

Awesome! My anticipation grew as I firmly gripped the "oh shit" handles.

She started by numbing the area, which gave me a sensation like bees were swarming my ass and stinging me repeatedly. We let that sit for about five minutes, ass still exposed while I stared at the floor. I couldn't help but think, "Is everyone staring at my butt right now?" while also trying to remember if I'd bothered to shower that morning, not exactly how I planned to introduce my backside to medical professionals. And then the hammering began. How crazy is this? The doctor was literally hammering into my pelvic bone, the same way you would see someone using a hammer and chisel. I looked over at my wife, and her eyes were as big as saucers. Ali had front-row tickets to a torture chamber event. At that moment I thought, "Oops. I'm glad she is here, but is this too much for her? I must be strong for her sake."

I couldn't see anything that was going on, so a lot of this was relayed to me later on our drive home from Ali.

"Okay, it's time to begin the hard part," said the doctor, with a passing look at Ali. "Are you ready?"

"Yes."

She pulled out one of the biggest needles ever. I never saw it, but Ali said it looked something like one of those marinating meat injectors with the giant needle heads. The doctor inserted this into my bone and began to slowly pull the plunger upward and, *Oh . . . my . . . God!* The pain was intense. Easily one of the worst physical pains I've ever felt in my life, and you know I've been through a lot. It made me grunt and curse loudly enough so they could hear me at the front desk. "Sorry," I gasped. They said don't worry about it. They totally understood. This wasn't the first time they'd heard it, and it wouldn't be the last.

This first pull lasted for about five seconds, but she still had to do it three more times. I tried my best not to scream, as I gripped the handholds as tight as possible. My whole body constricted, just like she said it would, and the pain reverberated right down through my legs. It was a hellish experience, but I was glad I was getting it over with. After the last pull, the doc patched me up and told me she would call in a couple of days with the results.

I thanked her for all she was doing for me. My wife, completely stunned by what she had just seen, managed to squeak out her thanks as well. Ali appeared to be more traumatized than I was. She told me on the ride home that it was the most intense thing she had ever seen, with blood everywhere. Some doctors are able to do this cleanly, making very little mess, this time, however, apparently it was a bloody mess. For her, the size of the needle was the scariest part. For the next couple days, I tried to act as normal as possible. I tried to be positive and tell myself it would be okay and that the results would be clean.

A week later, I was sitting outside on a beautiful, warm fall day, watching my kids play on the front grass, when my phone rang. I grabbed it and noticed it was from UC Davis. I answered. It was my doctor. More suspense.

"Hello."

"Hi, Mr. Gilardi, how are you? I wanted to call you personally to tell you I'm sorry, but you definitely have multiple myeloma cancer, and we are going to need to begin treatment soon." My heart broke, and I felt like throwing up at this devastating news. I talked to the doctor for a moment longer and then we hung up. Thankfully, my mother-in-law was at our house just then, able to watch the kids. I needed to be alone.

I hid by doing some work outside, staying away from my children because I felt interacting with them might trigger my emotions, and I didn't want to go there right now. The last thing my family needed at that moment was for me to lose it and scare the kids. Ali was still at work, so I would have to wait for her wise counsel and warm support. I was in shock, even though I secretly expected this, ever since receiving my first negative result.

It was not until Ali got home later that night that I told her the news. As I shared it with her, my emotions broke free and I, Mr. Tough Guy, began pouring out the tears. We cried in each other's arms for a long while, unsure of what the future held.

Crying in my wife's arms was one of the hardest moments in my life. What once was almost perfect was now sliced into a million pieces. We were so young. My kids were two and four. It hurt so bad. I could hear that Kansas song playing in my head: "All we are is dust in the wind." My future, my dreams, everything my wife and I had built, it all seemed so fragile and temporary now.

A Life Shattered? No! I Refuse to Answer Death's Call!

When doctors first diagnosed me with cancer, my whole world crumbled right out from under my feet. In something of a daze, I commenced the long, arduous process of cancer treatment. During the first part of chemo, I just let myself go. The pain of thinking about what my death would do to my family was too much to bear. I ate garbage food, didn't exercise. I let negative thoughts overtake my mental state. I let my fears overcome my mind and I grabbed hold of whatever would give me immediate comfort, which too often included copious amounts of ice cream and other horrible lifestyle choices.

This whole thing was bullshit! Why me!? Why, after everything else I had been through, did I need to face this down as well? I became a victim to my circumstance, and I wallowed in self-pity. This is easy to do when you're faced with the realities of cancer and what chemotherapy does to your body. The barfing, diarrhea, constipation, itchy rashes, fevers, lack of energy, and night sweats that leave you drenched from head to toe. "This just isn't fair," I'd say to myself.

But then, somehow, a spark was lit within me. Was this really how I was going to live out my days? Sad and weak? Was I going to let my kids see their father act like a coward and bow down to this disease while it ravaged my body, or would I get up and fight this thing with all I had in me?

Facing cancer is much like when I stood in front of the judge so many years ago, waiting to be sentenced. Both situations stripped me of control. With the judge, I had to accept the consequences of my actions. With cancer, I was trapped with a threat I didn't create but still couldn't escape. Either way, I had to stay the course. I must endure. I must embrace it and find a way forward and accept the things I cannot control.

One morning as I sat at my desk, grappling with feelings of hopelessness and defeat, I squeezed close my eyes and pushed out two tears, one for sadness and one for fear. I raised my head and wiped my eyes dry so I could see. Right there in front of me was my answer. Right there was everything I needed. It was my why, my passion, and all the fuel I would ever need to keep going.

> "Was I going to let my kids see their father act like a coward and bow down to this disease while it ravaged my body, or would I get up and fight this thing with all I had in me?"

I was looking at two pictures, mounted in one of those desktop picture holders with a nice shiny pen and a numberless clock. One of the pictures, from 2015, was of my wife lying in a hospital bed, me standing over her with one of those light blue, stupid-looking hospital hair caps on, a big smile on our faces. I'll never be certain how she pulled off her smile because on the other side of the curtain her stomach is being put back together from her emergency C-section. In the picture, we are holding our slimy newborn son, Gio, for the first time. The other picture is identical; same scenario, same stupid-ass hat, different year, 2017. This time, it's our newborn baby girl, Olivia. These pictures weren't just memories, they were my battle cry. In their innocent faces I saw my purpose: to fight with every cell in my body, to show them what true strength looks like in the darkest hour, to be the father who refused to surrender when death came knocking. What terrified me most wasn't dying, it was leaving them behind. I couldn't stand the thought of my children growing up without me there to guide them, to protect them, to love them. Cancer was trying to take me away from them, but I wasn't going to make it easy. Long after I'm gone, whether that's years or decades from now, they'll carry not just my name, but the legacy of a man who stared down death and said, "Not today."

I began doing everything to optimize my health and well-being; strengthening my mind and body was the key to getting better and living longer. I changed everything about my lifestyle and my diet. I held my every thought captive and made sure I was thinking positively. Day in and day out, I began doing things that were difficult. Like an addict saying no to a bottle of booze, I am now able to walk past Cold Stone Creamery without hyperventilating and say, "Nope! Not today."

We will talk more about discipline and self-control in part two of this book. These lessons don't just apply to fighting cancer, they're the foundation for conquering any challenge life throws at you. The same mental toughness that helped me walk away from drugs and crime became the weapon I used against cancer. Discipline isn't just about restriction; it's about freedom, the freedom to choose your future rather than surrendering to your circumstances.

I knew that if I could turn my body and mind into a sacred place, I could improve my chances of beating cancer. I've heard fellow cancer patients say, "If I'm going to die, I'm at least going to enjoy myself." I used to think like that too. But for me, those perspectives no longer fit. I needed to become a conqueror, not for mere survival but to thrive, to be there for my family. My kids deserved a father who fought with everything he had. There aren't many things in this world more relentless than cancer, but I intended to be one of them.

With this change, my mentality shifted completely. I learned not to waste another minute forgetting to tell my wife I loved her. I learned to tell my kids they could realize their wildest dreams. I found joy in the simplest things, watching my son catch his first fish or my daughter at her dance recital. I took bigger risks so that when my time comes, I won't look back and regret yesterday. I learned to live deep in life and be fully present.

I believe so strongly that the road to greatness and survival comes down to your why and your meaning and purpose. Remember this: The ability to do the work most are unwilling to do is what separates mediocre from extraordinary and life from death. I don't just know it, I expect it!

Staring Death in the Face to Find Meaning

So many questions pop into your head when this kind of shit happens, starting with the obvious: How long do I have? Why me? What's going to happen to my wife and kids?

Dealing with this kind of major adversity is one of the biggest challenges and lessons you will ever experience. It reveals the raw power of confronting your own mortality. What do I mean by this? When you're face to face with death, you gain a heightened awareness and appreciation for your precious time here on Earth. Yes, this awareness brings chaos initially, but ultimately it guides you forward. The person who claims to have never faced life-altering challenges isn't displaying a badge of good fortune, they're confessing to a life half-lived. A major part of life is suffering, and those challenges that completely upend your world aren't just possible, they're inevitable. You can be as positive as you want, but you better be ready for the left hook to come out of nowhere and smack you in the jaw.

Nobody can tell you what the meaning of life is. It's not their job. That is a deep personal question only you can

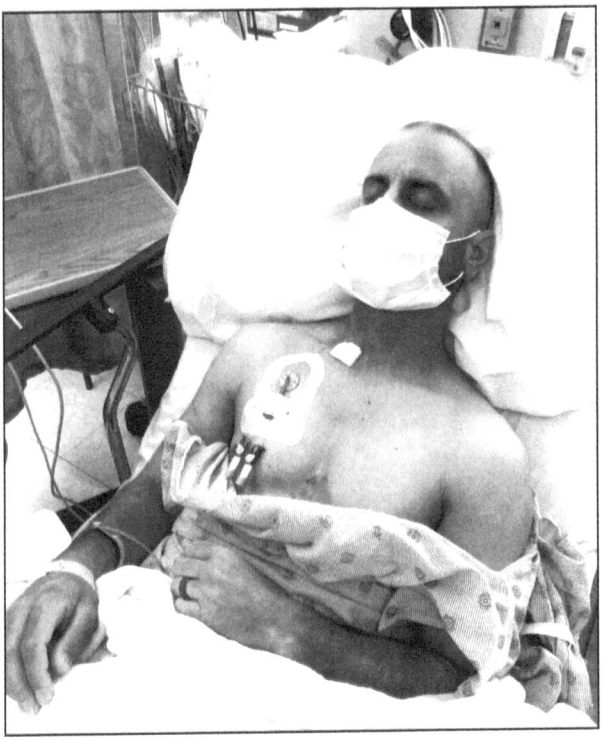

I had to wear this port for over a month. It had to be covered for showers and somehow kept clean. Just a small inconvenience. *photo courtesy Ali Gilardi*

answer. Your meaning of life is how you define your life's path and how you choose to live on this planet here and now, today. It's what makes you feel the most alive. It's how you define happiness and joy. It's about what gets you out of bed in the morning and gets you excited for the day. It's your purpose and your passion. It's your dreams and desires. It's your relationships and loves, your kids, your spouse, your extended family, and all the little moments in time that make extraordinary memories. It's the stories you will tell about those memories, memories that will never be forgotten.

Your meaning of life is what pulls you beyond the difficult, horrible calamities.

When you truly face your mortality, your perspective transforms. As I go through life now, taking medications, getting blood work done constantly in hopes the beast will not rage up, I am forced at each of those visits to confront the possibility of my end days. Most people avoid thinking about death,

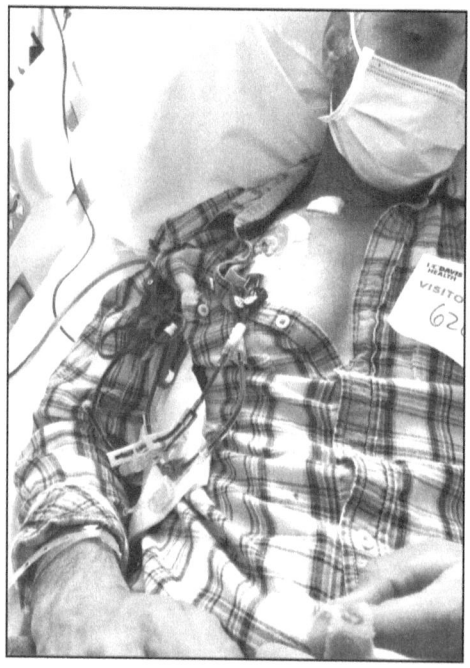

Having my stem cells removed in preparation for a stem cell transplant. I eventually opted out of this major treatment and to this day have not done it. I'm doing great! *photo courtesy Ali Gilardi*

not talking about it because they consider it depressing. It's not. It's actually the most powerful subject you could ever consider.

This awareness of your finite existence forces you to deeply consider where you are and what you truly want from life. You realize that what's important is not how much time you have, but rather the quality of life you have and what you live for. As you have read in this book, I have not always lived purely and virtuously. None of us really have. And if you have, you're either super boring or have led a sheltered life free of experiences. I was the bad guy in the first half of my story, but I have learned so much through my many ups and downs. Things are much different here in the second half; I am now the good guy. I live my life with purpose and compassion. I love myself and then love others. I show my kids, and whoever else needs it, what strength in adversity really means so they can be inspired to live a life of extraordinary proportions.

> "Your meaning of life is what pulls you beyond the difficult, horrible calamities."

Thinking about your mortality forces you to zoom in on your life and figure out what matters to you. You focus on those around you with a new urgency, and your goals begin to align with greatness and goodness. You learn that nothing can be taken for granted.

Odds are you are not faced with your mortality today in the way I am, but you can still connect with it now by imagining the following scenario: You're on your deathbed. All your family and close friends are around you, but you're clearly in a state of regret and unhappiness. You realize you didn't live your life to its potential. You never found true meaning. You could have done more, been more, loved more. You gave into comfort and a life of ease. You never developed into your full self, and truthfully, you never even got close.

Imagine this scenario so fiercely your heart starts beating faster in your chest. A bead of sweat drips down your temple. If you really dig into this exercise, you might even want to run away, dropping this book to the ground in fear. Don't run. Stay with the pain. Stay in this moment. Consider these questions and even ponder some of your own:

- Did I pursue the visions that set my soul on fire, or did I leave them to smolder and die?
- Did I step into the arena of life's greatest challenges, or did I watch safely from the sidelines?
- Did I find joy even in life's darkest moments, or did I let circumstances dictate my happiness?
- Did I create something that will outlive me, or will all traces of my existence fade within a generation?
- Did I create moments so powerful they're etched into the hearts of those I love?
- Did I lift others toward their greatness, or was I too consumed with my own journey to notice their struggles?

You can sit here and put off your dreams for tomorrow. You can choose not to take that risk today. You can tell your kids "maybe next time." But if you keep evading your potential, if you don't strive to be better, then one day your chance to leave a mark will pass. As the grains of sand escape the shattered hourglass, time elusively slips away from us. The end is nearer than you think.

I challenge you to imagine your death at the beginning of each day. Stephen R. Covey said, "Begin with the end in mind." His meaning: Plan each day by thinking about what you would like to achieve by the end of each day. My own idea takes this deeper: Begin each day with your death in mind. Start from there. Prioritize your days. Do things that matter to you, that give you energy and purpose and help you find meaning in life. Without a meaning and a why for life, we are nothing but dust in the wind.

Marcus Aurelius said, "When you arise each morning, think of what a precious privilege it is to be alive, to breathe, to think, to enjoy, to love." Each day truly is a gift. Don't squander it, and please don't discover what your life is about right before you die. Don't regret yesterday. Live fully and be present today.

Part II

The 10 Transformation Lessons

Life doesn't just throw adversity your way, it hurls it like a fastball aimed at your head. The question isn't whether you'll face these breaking points, but how you'll respond when they crack your foundation.

In Part I, you witnessed my journey through hell, drug dealing, jail cells, suicidal despair, and finally, a cancer diagnosis that should have broken me for good. But here's the truth I discovered: those very moments that should have destroyed me became my greatest strength. What I couldn't see while drowning in my own mistakes was that each catastrophe was forging something unbreakable within me. Those adversities weren't punishments, they were preparation. They built the resilience I'd need to stare cancer in the face and say, "Not today, motherfucker."

The 10 Transformation Lessons you're about to discover aren't theoretical bullshit from some guru who's never tasted dirt. They're battle-tested strategies born in blood and sweat, lessons I carved out while clawing my way back from rock bottom. I wrote this book because I'm sick of hearing life advice from people who've never really been broken. When someone tells you how to rise from the ashes, you better make damn sure they've been burned first.

Each principle acts as a stepping stone from victim to victor. They'll show you how to rebuild your self-image from scratch, harness fear as fuel, embrace failure as your greatest teacher, and develop the mental toughness to do what others won't. Whether you're facing career disaster, health crises, or the slow suffocation of a mediocre existence, these lessons will transform how you face every challenge.

As we dive into each lesson, you'll see exactly how they played out in my life through more raw, unfiltered stories, business failures that cost me everything, confronting death during chemo treatments, and fighting to be fully present with my kids while cancer whispers it's deadlines. You'll witness both my darkest moments and unexpected victories, like standing on stage to finish a speech I once ran from, or pushing through a workout after treatment when most would collapse. More importantly, you'll discover how to apply these same transformational lessons to your own life, right now, today.

It's time to stop letting your past dictate your future. It's time to transform from someone who survives adversity into someone who thrives because of it. The breaking point isn't where your story ends, it's where the real one begins.

14

Transformation Lesson 1. Master Self-Image

> *"You have been criticizing yourself for years and it hasn't worked. Try approving of yourself and see what happens."*
> —Louise Hay

I know that a lot of my troubles early on stemmed from poor self-image. I let what I thought others saw in me determine my worth and value. This negative self-perception cost me years of happiness and pushed me toward destructive choices that I still deal with the consequences of today. Even now, I'm not perfect, this is work I commit to every single day. When we don't believe in ourselves, we seek validation in all the wrong places, whether through popularity, risky behaviors, or pretending to be someone we're not. It's a dangerous road that only leads further away from who we truly are and what we're capable of becoming.

Nobody is going to attack you more than the man or woman in the mirror. From the moment we gain self-awareness, we start picking apart every flaw, real or not, we think we have. It's like we're hardwired to focus on the negative aspects of ourselves, magnifying them until they become all we can see and we literally lose sight of our positives. This constant self-criticism of ourselves is like a disease . . . a very destructive disease.

In this chapter we will learn a little about self-image and the impact it has on our lives. Mastering your self-image is crucial not just for your happiness, but for every aspect of your life. From relationships to career success, how you see yourself colors everything you do. I'll share some of my own journey with self-image and the hard lessons I learned. Trust me, if I can learn to love

> "Nobody is going to attack you more than the man or woman in the mirror."

my gigantic schnoz, you can learn to embrace whatever it is you're beating yourself up about. By the end of this chapter, you'll possess practical tools to start rebuilding your self-image from the ground up. It won't be easy, and it won't happen overnight, as this stuff takes time and in fact will be a never-ending practice, but I promise you, it's worth every ounce of effort. And so like Michael Jackson says, start with the man in the mirror and make it happen.

*****

Puberty arrived at our house like an unwanted houseguest, and my brother David was its first victim. Hair began to grow on his body and his nipples became inflamed and sensitive. This is the stage where we would run around our house and punch him right in the tit so we could watch him scream in agony. This brought us much joy and laughter.

TRANSFORMATION LESSON 1. MASTER SELF-IMAGE

David's voice cracked, and he began to smell like shit all the time. However, his life really changed when his nose began growing farther and farther away from his face, extending far out past what we humans would call a normal nose. And so we dubbed it "The gigantic schnoz." Many others, but especially me, would pick on him about it. I'd make fun of his nose any time we quarreled. I'd rag on him about it. He knew he had a big nose, but when people pointed it out and made fun, it hurt him that much more. It made him even more insecure about this part of himself. People in David's situation often enter a new phase in which they fall deeper into the learned habit of not liking themselves. Harsh, daily self-judgment becomes a daily ritual.

    I became relentless with the nose jokes, each one crueler than the last. Big Nose, Super Schnoz, Mount Nosevius, I had an endless supply. David would try to laugh it off, but I could see how each nickname landed like a punch. His shoulders would hunch, his smile would tighten, but that only encouraged me. I was untouchable, or so I thought.

    One ordinary morning, I was brushing my teeth, half-asleep and thinking about nothing in particular. I turned my head to the side, caught my reflection in the mirror, and froze. There it was, protruding from my face like a cruel joke from the universe. A nose that could rival David's, maybe even surpass it. The toothbrush clattered into the sink. "When the fuck did this happen?" I whispered to my reflection, but the giant schnoz in the mirror offered no answers. My mother's words from months ago suddenly echoed in my head with painful clarity: "Jono, both your father and I have rather large noses. Do you honestly think your nose will not get big?" I dismissed her warning with a casual "No way, not me!" Now, staring at my reflection, I realized the universe had turned my arrogance into a permanent fixture on my face.

The hallways of middle school suddenly became a nightmare. It was during that same lonely period when I had no friends that I now had to deal with this new insecurity, and when I say huge, I mean my nose felt absolutely massive. Every passing glance seemed to linger a second too long. In class, I heard whispers: "Big Nose, Birdman." The very names I'd once wielded like weapons against my brother were now being hurled back at me. Each one struck like a knife in the gut. Karma was rearing its ugly head.

Then of course there was Zach from the "Right Between The Eyes" chapter, before we had our big falling out. He made it his mission to announce to everyone that I had a huge nose. His favorite names for me were "Beak Boy" or simply "Bird." I'd laugh off each insult like it was no big deal, pretending it didn't bother me, but in reality, every comment cut deep. Much like what happened with my brother, I became so self-conscious about my nose that it consumed my thoughts every time I interacted with people. I'd catch myself wondering if they were staring at it, judging it, preparing some new nickname that would follow me for years. That constant awareness was exhausting, draining whatever confidence I had managed to scrape together.

My nose bugged me so much I contemplated getting a nose job. That was just not something me or my parents would be forking over any cash for, so thankfully it never happened. I am who I am, and if I can't learn to love myself for who I am, then I can never learn to love anyone else. No matter what I accomplish in life, it will mean nothing if I can't love myself first.

And so, in the end, I got a taste of my own medicine, just like my mother said I would. I also learned early on that we must not judge others' imperfections because we are far from perfect ourselves. I knew I was short and timid, but when my nose grew overnight, that's when I was forced to confront the power of self-image and the effect it can have on our well-being, whether it be in a negative way or positive. You see, I couldn't hide my nose, so I had to face my (self-made) problem head on, and this was mentally draining and debilitating.

When you are too worried about your looks or how others judge your appearance, how do you think you will ever have the extra mental energy left over to accomplish anything good in life? Things only got better for me when I was able to finally stop worrying about the nose and the other little things that make me who I am, and when I stopped saying "I hate my stupid nose" and replaced it with some positive self-talk. That was when I reached a turning point in my life. Ditching all that pointless worrying and that endless, denigrating chatter in my head made me feel like a weight had been lifted off my shoulders. I felt liberated, if you will. And you know what? It felt damn good.

Of course, this didn't happen overnight, and I still had many years of personal development left. I'd have to deal with many more struggles to really learn how to love myself for who I was.

Don't Sacrifice Yourself for a False Boost in Self-esteem

And so here I was again trying to find significance through instant gratification. Here I was again trying to be somebody I was not in hopes of hiding my imperfections. I pulled up to a Chevron gas station in a crummy part of town. Not to get gas but to meet an acquaintance. He was neither a friend nor an enemy, just somebody I couldn't trust. However, he was returning a favor, if you even want to call it that. About a week earlier I had started using performance-enhancing drugs (PEDs, or steroids), yet another one of my great decisions. Now it was time for more. This being my first ever cycle of steroids, I needed an extra hand so I could learn how to shoot the juice into my butt cheek. Since we had nowhere else to go, we chose a scummy Chevron bathroom. Damn, I mean we could have gone to a rich part of town and used their cleaner Chevron bathrooms. I guess that would have raised a red flag though, right? Two men looking totally out of place in the parking lot and then using the bathroom together in the "good" part of town, that would be "call the cops" strange. And so we did what we did in the scummy bathroom. I was only 19 years old at the time, young and dumb.

This guy owed me a dose and a needle that he brought with him. He hopped in the back seat of my truck and began to fill the needle with the juice to the required amount. But here was the problem: this guy wasn't trustworthy. He was shady and broke, and when you're shady and broke, you will do anything to save money and get over on people. I had no idea if he was reusing that needle or if the juice he was pulling from the vial had been sitting around well past its

TRANSFORMATION LESSON 1. MASTER SELF-IMAGE

expiration date. Did he even wipe down the seal to disinfect it? Apparently not. He didn't have alcohol and cotton swabs in his pocket. At the time, I was fine with all this. Like I said, young and dumb.

After getting the needle filled, we headed to the gas station bathroom to do the deed. We decided the bathroom was safer than the truck, imagine someone walking by and seeing me on all fours with my pants down while another man hovered over me with a needle aimed at my bare ass. Not exactly the kind of public display I was going for. As I bent over and exposed my hairy butt to this guy I barely knew, he proceeded to inject the juice. It didn't hurt, as the butt cheek is a very thick muscle. I did, however, begin to sweat profusely. I'm not sure why this happens when shooting certain steroids, because it was only this particular cycle that would do this to me. Yes, this was not my last cycle. I'd do three more cycles in my life until I realized what the heck I was doing to myself!

Being young and ignorant, and thinking you know what's best, will almost always lead to poor life decisions. When your self-esteem levels are low, you chase significance with the wrong intent in mind. Some people tell extravagant stories of nothing but bullshit lies, some people need to show off their material things, and some will fire steroids into their ass.

So what does this story have to do with self-image, you ask? I thought that if I could create the perfect body, then maybe the fact that I felt I was too short, too shy, and had a big nose would become irrelevant. A perfect body would completely change my self-image. Did It work? Absolutely.

Well, at least for the short term it did. It felt good and I looked good. PEDs are no joke. They work. I was able to bench press 275 pounds for eight reps, and the gains came extremely fast.

Think again, short-term gain, long-term pain. Maybe, just maybe, what I did back then altered my DNA or genes just enough to create the cancer I was diagnosed with years later? I believe it is a possibility. I also know that because I'm so small and the weight was totally abnormal for my size, I damaged my joints. And they suffer to this day because of the choice I made to use that stuff. And for what? Instant gratification. I treated myself like shit in hopes to cover up the root cause of my pain. The fix was temporary, and the unfortunate aftereffects long lasting.

Time to Unshackle Yourself

Once you acknowledge you have self-esteem issues, you're ready to unshackle yourself from the relentless grip they have over your mind, and ultimately, your success in life. I know many people who say they don't worry about self-image, but you can tell by their daily actions and the things they say unconsciously that a positive self-image is practically nonexistent. You must first become aware of your issues in order to get better. Lying to yourself will only add to the problem. Your lack of self-respect and your constant bullying of yourself is a disease that must be stopped. However, the only one who can stop this is you. You have the power to change your mind, to rewire the negatives, and to properly wire in the positives.

Low self-esteem is simply another form of adversity, but it can be a tough one to crack because it doesn't stem from

TRANSFORMATION LESSON 1. MASTER SELF-IMAGE

an easily identifiable external source. It comes from within. When we lack in this department, it leads to a very unfulfilled life. We wallow in negative self-perception and doubt everything we do. We become self-critical to no end. I felt all this stuff growing up and even more so later as I thrashed about in my young adult life. My negative self-perception was truly overwhelming and debilitating. It constricted me with fear and kept me from pursuing my goals. I had zero belief in myself, and so made excuse after excuse for not trying those hard things that would have made my life better and spurred me forward to start working on my goals.

Low self-image also leads to chronic stress, something I felt my whole life. Stress is a killer. It may just be another one of the reasons I have to fight now for my life from this dreadful illness. Low self-image drains us of fortitude, and so we lack the energy needed to fight our way through adversity. If you suffer from low self-esteem, you must begin to work on this now. I will say it again because this is huge: begin to work on boosting your self-esteem and the way you perceive yourself today, right now. As you begin to repair and strengthen your self-image, you will reverse all those horrible side effects listed above and turn them into positive ones. Imagine what you could do with your life if you worked hard in this area, without PEDs and modalities that produce a feeling of false confidence in the self. What if you stopped judging your imperfections and started focusing on your perfections? What if you didn't give a damn about what anyone thought of you? Think of the energy you'd have left if it wasn't being drained by your own personal judgments. If you want a deep, fulfilling, and meaningful life, then begin right now with yourself, because you can't have the life you want if you can't master yourself. That's why mastering your self-image is the very first lesson. It's the foundation, the very first step to building mental toughness. Without that mastery, you'll find it difficult to ever conquer adversity.

Transformation Action Steps

The most powerful thing you can do for yourself and your life is to simply begin loving yourself right now. Love yourself for who you are, including your faults, your strengths, and everything else. Love yourself for what you are, *exactly* the way you are, even if there are things you want to change. Here's how to do this:

Write it, Think It, Say It: Train yourself to habitually think positively about yourself. Replace "Damn, I have a big nose!" with "Damn, I've got a killer sense of humor! And my resilience? Off the charts." Learn to love who you are, just as you are. Tell yourself you are valuable and significant right where you are. The lens through which we view ourselves colors our entire world. By shifting focus to strengths and reframing negatives as positives, we transform both self-perception and how we interact with others. Follow this three-step formula: Write something positive about a trait you've been criticizing in your journal. Think about this positive statement throughout your day. Then say it aloud, hearing yourself speak these words is powerful. This practice will reprogram your mind with a positive self-image. Be patient, it takes time, but the effects compound, and I guarantee your life will change if you commit to this practice consistently at least three times per week.

TRANSFORMATION LESSON 1. MASTER SELF-IMAGE

Mirror, Mirror on the Wall: The next time you look at yourself in the mirror, say something nice about yourself. Get in the habit of doing this every time you pass a mirror, no exceptions. This stuff is extremely hard to do at first because we feel stupid doing it. At first I sounded like some cheesy self-help infomercial, "Hey there, handsome, nice nose!" but eventually it became as natural as telling yourself what a piece of shit you are. Only way healthier. Funny how we are okay criticizing ourselves negatively, but when it comes to saying something positive about ourselves, we feel stupid. Totally ass-backwards. These days, I actually look forward to a chance passing of a mirror so I can grab the chance to say something positive about myself. It's quite the mood boost!

> "The most powerful thing you can do for yourself and your life is to simply begin loving yourself right now."

Stop Judging: The man who judges others will always assume others are judging him. We think, "I do it, so they must do it." When we are in the habit of judging others, we are telling ourselves, either consciously or not, that it's totally normal to judge people, including yourself. But it's not! There is no need to do this. It's just a compulsion which we can learn to ignore. All judging does is bring us right back to where we started and right back to beating ourselves down with negative perceptions of who we are. And so the continuous loop carries on.

Reframe It: You wouldn't talk to your best friend, your mom, or your kids the way you talk to yourself. So when you catch yourself talking negatively about yourself, reframe it this way and ask: Would I tell my daughter she's ugly? Would I tell my best friend they're not worthy of good things? No. You wouldn't. So talk to yourself the way you'd talk to a loved one. This is powerful.

Micro Moves: Pick one small, achievable goal each day or week that aligns with improving yourself or your life. It could be as simple as making your bed every morning, reading for fifteen minutes, or passing on a bad habit. The key is to choose something you know you can accomplish. When you achieve these micro-goals consistently, you're proving to yourself that you're capable and reliable. This builds self-trust and confidence, which are crucial for a healthy self-image. As you stack up these small victories, you'll start to see yourself as someone who follows through and gets things done. Remember, it's not about the size of the goal, it's about convincing your mind that you're the sort of person who **consistently shows up for yourself.** Over time, these micro-wins will snowball into major shifts in how you perceive your abilities and worth.

Begin here, and in time you will gain a power you never knew you could acquire. It will be like breaking out of the chains that once held you back. This lesson is absolutely non-negotiable if you want to overcome adversity and build a great future for yourself and your loved ones. If you suffer in this area, it is *imperative* that you do this hard work. There's no doubt I went down the wrong road because of first having a negative self-image, which in turn led me straight to the gates of hell. These practices have the ability to save your life, leading you from your current unsatisfying existence to a much brighter one. So if you're serious, get started. No more delays! It's time to put in the work.

15

Transformation Lesson 2. Conquer the Victim Mentality

> *"Defeat is a state of mind. No one is ever defeated until defeat has been accepted as a reality."*
> —Bruce Lee

I've come to recognize that my suicide attempt was my victim mentality at its peak. While some may disagree, I believe it represented an inability to face life's adversities head-on. Breaking free from seeing myself as a victim has been one of the most challenging but transformative journeys of my life. We use it as a crutch, as an excuse, because being a victim is comfortable. It provides a reason for avoiding the hard work of facing ourselves and our mistakes, our breaking points. It's the easy way out. However, I will tell you this, you'll never find your true potential if you reside in the victim mindset. That mindset gives you a never-ending series of excuses, an endless supply of reasons not to change. This mentality is sneaky and it prevents you from seeing yourself as you really are. Maybe you don't even know you are acting like a victim and need your eyes opened so you can see what you are doing to yourself.

In this chapter, we're going to face self-pity head on and emerge stronger, more resilient, and empowered. You'll discover how I navigated the stormy seas of a cancer diagnosis while trying to launch a business, and I'll tell you about the hard-won lessons I learned about the pitfalls of victimhood.

> "Being a victim is comfortable. It provides a reason for avoiding the hard work of facing ourselves and our mistakes, our breaking points."

But this isn't just my story. It's a road map for your own journey of transformation. You'll learn how to recognize the subtle ways the victim mentality might be holding you back, and gain practical tools to shift your perspective and uncover the hidden opportunities that lie within your greatest challenges. By the end of this chapter, you'll have strategies to conquer adversity, silence your inner critic, and embrace a mindset of unstoppable resilience.

*****

Today was the big day. I was launching a green drink supplement blend, my brand-new product. "This needs to work now more than ever before," I said to my marketing specialist as I sat in front of my computer on a video call. I didn't want to tell him why I was suddenly deadly serious about making my new business work. My cancer diagnosis was none of his business. "I'm authorizing you for another ten grand. Do whatever you think is best."

"Okay," he said, somewhat taken aback by my sharp attitude. "We'll make this worth your while, Jono! This product is going to sell like hotcakes."

"It better!" I said, a bit too forcefully. I quickly hung up the phone, feeling hopeful that things would work out. They *have* to, right? Right!?

It's hard to explain, but I felt confident that because of the cancer bomb that was just dropped in my life, the business gods were going to side with me and ensure that I would acquire customers and start making sales. I guess I just needed the universe to balance things out for me a bit.

I started shoveling over the money. A thousand here, a thousand there . . . Week after week, my budget was spent on ads and other marketing tactics. I was sure this had to work, convincing myself that the universe owed me one. And there it was, the victim mentality creeping back in. I'd been down this road before, years ago when life had me at my lowest and I nearly checked out for good. This time was different, but no less dangerous. I'd been given a dreadful cancer diagnosis, and instead of facing it head-on, I was using it as an excuse, expecting the world to cut me some slack.

So, in all actuality, yes, I *was* a cancer victim. And, yes, cancer had indeed taken over my life. So since I was the victim of that takeover, I felt I deserved to be compensated before I died. Scratch the record! *Wrong!* Life just doesn't work that way. The universe doesn't care what has happened to you or anyone else in your life. You can't just say, "Hey, world, guess what? I have cancer, so everyone needs to buy my product so I can make a bunch of money to feed my family and get my kids set for their future before I pass. Please?"

I said please, didn't I? Nope, it doesn't matter, no one cares, and I'm just not the type of person that would use the victim status as a way to get sales. I've seen it done in the supplement industry. Someone will basically say that their product is why they are healed from whatever disease they had. That they got through it with their magic pill or powder. So they sell it with that story attached and business booms by the selling of that false hope. If I could honestly say that something worked that well, then of course I would, but nobody can say that for sure, especially for one single product. It's such a dirtbag way to make money. It's unethical, and since they are trying to sell you snake oil, karma will bite them back.

I was becoming the ultimate victim. I was already a victim just by the thought and belief that I deserved to gain from being diagnosed with cancer. The ultimate victim believes they are owed something. They feel sorry for themselves and think that life should just go their way, but the truth is no one owes me shit. The same goes for you. Nobody owes us anything.

On the launch day of my product, I heard crickets. Very loud crickets. After launch day and spending thousands more on ad campaigns, I continued to hear those crickets. *Bleep, bleep, bleep.* No sales inquiries. No "Billy M. has purchased your product" emails. Nothing. It was beyond demoralizing. It was heartbreaking. And instead of using the failure to boost myself forward, I made everything worse by becoming a poster child for the victim mentality with my bad attitude.

Nothing was working, but instead of adjusting my marketing tactics or just pulling the plug on the product, I

TRANSFORMATION LESSON 2. CONQUER THE VICTIM MENTALITY

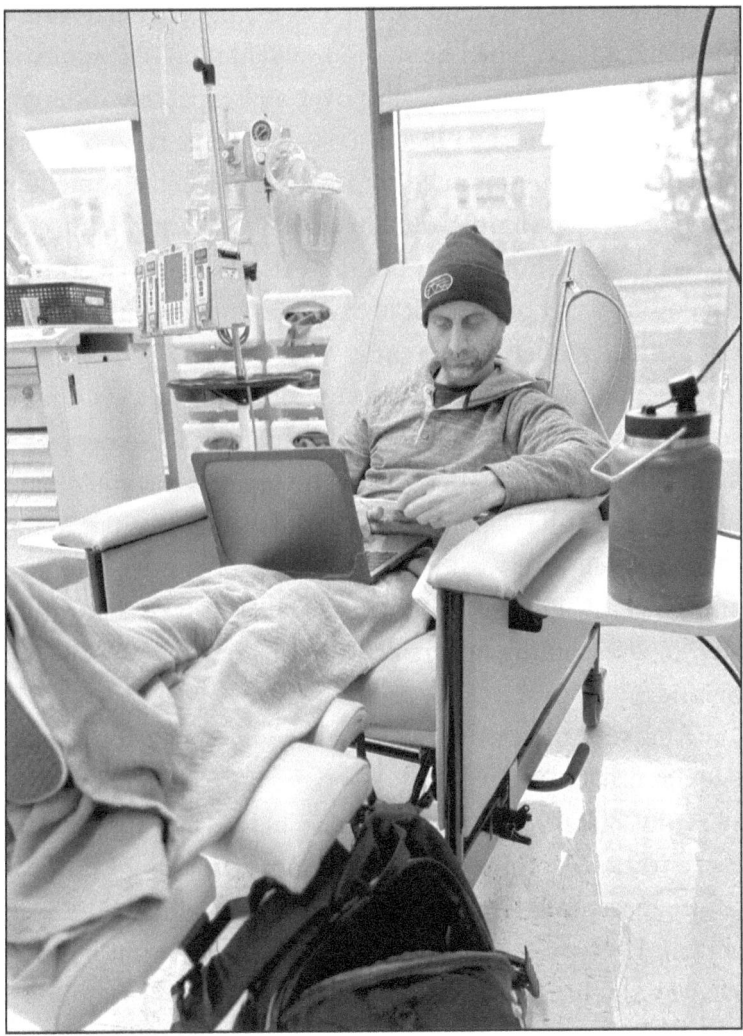

Writing my story while the chemo flows through my veins. We can choose to be victims of our circumstances, or we can choose to face adversity head-on and craft the life we envision. *photo courtesy Ali Gilardi*

continued to mope around, beating my head against the wall in frustrated insanity. You'd think I would have heeded Albert Einstein's advice, when he said, "The definition of insanity is doing the same thing over and over and expecting different results." But I failed to listen. Instead, I kept repeating my mistakes, which continued to get me nowhere. I somehow thought being a victim would be enough, that my victim status would somehow bring me rewards. It's pathetic, and it's the coward's way out of a lot of things, even life—but that was my mentality, once upon a time.

Eventually, I got fed up with my situation, and ever more so with myself. I knew I had to once again strap on my boots and suck it up. No matter where you are or what you're facing, you can still make progress if you're willing to put in the effort and tell your weak-ass self to suck it up, drive forward, and go get it. But you will never be able to take that initial step to overcoming adversity without first leaving self-pity behind.

And so I began the twice-weekly, five-hour round trip back and forth to UC Davis Sacramento Cancer Center to start my chemo treatments. I also began putting in even more work to get my product moving. First thing I did was fire that worthless marketing team and take over the task myself. Remember: When you are first starting out in business or anything that requires hard work and grit, nobody, and I mean nobody—will care as much as you, nobody will put in the work like you, nobody will be more determined than you, and nobody is going to hustle harder than you to make your vision a reality. I had boxes of product piled high in almost every inch of my one-year-old daughter's room.

TRANSFORMATION LESSON 2. CONQUER THE VICTIM MENTALITY

Her crib was hidden inside a scene from Minecraft, brown boxes stacked on top of each other. With the product's expiration date approaching in a little over six months, I finally got it on Amazon.

Sitting in the chemo recliners, connected to an IV line receiving my weekly chemicals, so strong you can smell them as they enter your body. I remember smacking my lips and tongue to the taste of metal as the chemicals coursed through my veins. I used this time to research tricks on Amazon and figure out how to master their ad system.

Hell of a marketing strategy, huh? Selling health supplements while being pumped full of chemicals that made me feel like absolute garbage. My marketing slogan should have been "Buy my health product! Results are not guaranteed if you're simultaneously being poisoned like I am!"

Sick and exhausted from hours in the chair, my wife would drive the long-haul trip home, and I would use this time to respond to customer questions and review algorithms. Despite my weakened body and spirit, I was giving it my all, and it was working.

After putting in a huge amount of hard work, I finally got my product selling rather quickly. My Amazon product page soon boasted over one hundred ratings at four and a half stars. Almost every review was positive. I was adding handwritten thank you notes and a free shaker bottle with every order. People were loving it, and the money was coming back to me.

Here's what it took to turn the corner: **I had to remove my head from my ass.** I had to tell my weak self to stop being a victim and start grinding for the things I wanted in life. I had to show my children that no matter what you're faced with in life, weakness is your enemy.

> "I had to remove my head from my ass. I had to tell my weak self to stop being a victim and start grinding for the things I wanted in life."

In *Rocky V*, Rocky Balboa is getting rocked in a street fight by Tommy Gun, a boxer he mentored throughout the movie until they had different views on where Tommy's career should be at. Rocky's head is ringing from a bare knuckle hit straight to the dome. His vision is going blurry. He's losing it. Tommy is cheering himself on with his hands raised above his head, believing he has won the fight. Just as we think Rocky Balboa is done and can't go on, he rises up and says, "Yo, Tommy! I didn't hear no bell." I get chills from this scene every time. It's the true warrior spirit. It's about doing what you know needs to be done despite the suffering you're in. I kept busting my ass to move that product despite the hell I was going through. It was painful, but it felt so good.

Are you tormented like I was by a victim mentality? Let me help—and I'm going to be straightforward about it. Get off your ass and go get it! Stop being less than your best. You only have so much time left, even if you have a perfectly clean bill of health! The victim mentality is the way out of ever trying to work hard and succeed at anything. It's the perfect excuse to quit your dreams and desires. The victim has the perfect opportunity to eat shitty food, lay around all day watching TV, because, well, "I deserve to do nothing and should be given everything." The victim says, "When's my turn?" Pathetic.

TRANSFORMATION LESSON 2. CONQUER THE VICTIM MENTALITY

You are the only one in your way. This is the cold, hard truth and it's no different for the cancer patient. It's actually quite easy to fall into the victim mentality when you are diagnosed with cancer. There are a lot of victims out there, and if you or I choose this route, we will surely die with a broken heart, because nothing is coming to us. Life doesn't care what you have been hit with. Cancer is no different. Cancer doesn't give a fuck and neither does any other disease or circumstance.

To acquire anything great in life, you must put aside any notion of victimhood and simply go fucking get it. The universe doesn't care if you had a rough childhood or if you were abused. It doesn't really matter if your dad was a piece of shit or your mom was an alcoholic or a drug addict. It makes no difference if you lived in poverty or you were born with a silver spoon up your ass. It's all the same. The universe doesn't care that I was diagnosed with cancer and told by some doctor who doesn't really comprehend my will to live that I only have five to seven years left. I should have asked my doctor if he was including weekends and holidays in that estimate, but I figured his humor was probably as dead as he thought I would be. Nope, it doesn't give two shits about your life problems and never will.

When you abandon the victim mentality, you unlock the power to overcome any obstacle life throws at you. You and I must push harder than ever before to grab what we so desperately want from this life. We must go out and be the person we want to be and create the life we desire, because in the end, freedom begins the moment you stop letting your struggles define you.

Look to marvelous people like Nick Vujicic, an Australian-American Christian evangelist and motivational speaker. He was born with no arms and no legs and is now famous worldwide for changing lives and hearts. Or what about John Nash, the mathematician who overcame schizophrenia with the power of his mind, as shown in the movie *A Beautiful Mind*. Think about someone in your life who has had it rough but has pushed through anyway despite their adversity. They refused to be a victim! What's stopping you from doing the same?

Being a victim means you will remain down in a poor mental and physical state. But once you have banished any thoughts of victimhood from your mind, you will discover a hidden level of consciousness, like in the old Super Mario games we used to play as kids, when you jump down the green tube. This new level of consciousness is a rare state few will ever see and in it you will find what you seek. You will unlock a life of extraordinary potential, one where you define the terms. Your illness, disability, life circumstance, or whatever other excuse you can come up with is no longer valid. You will find new energy, physical prowess, and mental acuity. Your life's purpose will clarify, and you will become an unstoppable force, able to overcome any setback. Ryan Holiday titled his book "The Obstacle Is the Way" for a reason. I completely agree. Dealing with your adversities head-on *is* the way, and it will, I promise, take you through that green tube to the hidden level of life.

Transformation Action Steps

I want to share with you a simple three-step process to defeating the victim mentality once and for all. It's the process I used to overcome my self-defeating mentality, and I still use it on those occasions when some little voice within me tries to convince me to be a victim. The steps are: Identify, Acknowledge, and Correct Course.

Identify: First, you need to spot your victim mentality. Be brutally honest with yourself. What's your go-to excuse for not taking action? Maybe it's some shit from your past, your current struggles, or that classic move of blaming others for your problems. Whatever it is, drag it into the light. Remember, it's not what life throws at you that defines you. It's how you punch back.

Now, what's that one thing you're always bitching isn't "fair"? Found it? Good. Now forget that word even exists. "Fair" is for kindergarten. You're a grown-ass adult dealing with real-world problems. You're not a victim. You're a survivor who's been through hell. Time to break the cycle and show that circumstance who's boss.

Acknowledge: Okay, you've identified the victim in you. It's time to catch yourself in the act. Pay attention to that voice in your head. When you hear yourself whining, "Life's not fair, I can't even afford gas for work," stop right there. Recognize it for what it is, victim thinking. Then flip the script. Say something like, "Alright, this gas situation sucks. But I'm the one who's gonna fix it. I'm the one who needs to make a change in my life."

Correct Course: With a pen and paper in hand, begin to come up with as many ideas as you can on how you can fix your problem. The list of ideas might include things like: I can ask for a raise. I can cut back on those afternoon coffees or energy drinks to save a little extra money each month. Maybe I can create a little extra income through a side job. Be totally honest with yourself or this won't work. Piling more deception onto a victim mentality will just dig a deeper hole. Once your list is finished, figure out which options you're going to pursue and then go get them done. Remember, you are not a victim, and even a few small course corrections can start to build real momentum and may be all you need to change the direction of your life and start a whole new chapter for yourself.

Now get out there and make it happen. The world doesn't owe you shit, but you owe it to yourself and your loved ones.

16

Transformation Lesson 3. Guard Your Environment

"The key is to keep company only with people who will uplift you, whose presence calls forth your best."
—Epictetus

We are about to enter the woods of one of the most fundamental laws in human nature, which is that who and what we surround ourselves with, our environment, goes a long way toward making us the people we are. Like a tree that draws its strength from the soil and sunlight around it, we too are shaped by the invisible forces of our surroundings, the people we spend time with, the conversations we engage in, and the attitudes we absorb, day after day. Most of us float through life unaware of just how deeply these environmental influences penetrate our thoughts, beliefs, and, ultimately, our potential.

In this chapter, we'll explore how our environment molds us in ways both subtle and profound. Through my personal journey, you'll see how the voices around us can either nurture our dreams or slowly poison them at the root. More importantly, you'll discover that while we can't always control our circumstances, we can choose how we respond to them and who we allow to influence our path forward.

What follows is not just a story about environmental influence, but a wake-up call about the power we have to shape our own destiny by consciously choosing our surroundings. The lessons here were learned through experience, and they might just change how you think about success, failure, and the company you keep.

*****

San Francisco, California, the Golden City. In 1999, I found myself working as a laborer for Peacock Construction, a position I secured through a family friend. While it might have been an ideal job for someone taking a break from college to figure out their future, I was coming from a different place entirely, fresh out of one of my stays in the county jail with no direction and no plan.

They had me working in the Embarcadero district, the pulsing heart of San Francisco's money zone. The city's essence was everywhere: cabs honking at lost tourists, messenger bikes weaving through bumper-to-bumper traffic, steam rising mysteriously from underground grates. The distinctive ding of trolley bells echoed through the streets as suits with briefcases rushed past me

> "Most of us float through life unaware of just how deeply these environmental influences penetrate our thoughts, beliefs, and, ultimately, our potential."

TRANSFORMATION LESSON 3. GUARD YOUR ENVIRONMENT

toward their glass-and-steel towers, all of us packed together in America's second-most densely populated city.

I had been working on the construction of the new Morgan Stanley office. I was grunting around, sweeping floors and doing all the heavy lifting, like bringing in all the raw material from the trucks outside. It was backbreaking work, something I'm so glad I no longer rely on. This type of work is great when you are young but horrible as you age.

One day, after a couple of weeks on the job, I was having lunch on the second floor with a carpenter, a young kid who was set on being a carpenter for the rest of his life. This is great if that is what you love to do, but I, on the other hand, had questions remaining in my head. I was curious. I was still very unpredictable in my life decisions, clearly. As we sat on our lunch boxes staring out the huge window at the city life before us, I asked him what he thought about all these people in suits and ties who were going into the office buildings, sitting in chairs all day, and making big dollars without hurting themselves physically. "They are all stuck-up, rich assholes." His reply made me laugh, it was so to the point and totally judgmental. "Yeah, but their biggest workplace injury is probably a paper cut or carpal tunnel," I joked. "Meanwhile, we get off work looking like one of those bums out there on the streets, and nobody can tell the difference. When I hop back on the BART to go home, nobody wants to sit by me cause I stink so bad. I get my own row every day, only perk of the job." I pretended to dust off my clothes and sniffed my shirt, making a face. "Pretty sure I've got more drywall in my hair than we put up today." He just grunted, not finding the humor.

THE BREAKING POINT

But in a way I thought it would be cool to be walking around in a suit making big money, not hurting my body. I could just go to the gym or go for a run to get my exercise. I then asked him how you become a stockbroker, and all he had to offer was this: "That job is for privileged rich kids who were born into it. It's not for guys like me and you." I know at this point in my life I totally internalized what this guy said—I mean, he was a carpenter right? Above me. He must be right. And so his words froze me out of ever thinking about pursuing a career as a broker wearing a suit. I had no idea that his beliefs about what was possible didn't have to become my own limitations. It stings to write about this moment because I can see now how his mindset, not his character or his skills as a carpenter, shaped what he thought was possible. There's nothing wrong with being a carpenter, or aspiring to become a foreman. That's a respected path that requires real skill and dedication. But when someone believes their current circumstances define the full range of what's possible, not just for themselves but for others too, that's where limitation lives. I wasn't questioning his worth or his work. I was unknowingly absorbing his fixed view of the world, one where certain doors were simply closed to people like us.

I eventually moved on from the SF job and got a new foreman in the Silicon Valley area, where the firm was building offices for all the fresh, major start-ups in the dot-com era. Again, I was in awe of how this other set lived, how much cash they brought in, their clean clothes and their nice cars. One day, I asked my foreman, Ronnie, what he thought about all this. He shut me down and said, "You didn't go to school. You will never have a chance of becoming anything like these

TRANSFORMATION LESSON 3. GUARD YOUR ENVIRONMENT

people." Ouch. Unfortunately, I absorbed that as well and kept grinding away, bringing solid oak doors up flight after flight of stairs because they were so big and heavy they didn't fit in the elevators. This work was getting old and a rising sense of discontent filled my day-to-day thoughts.

As the days passed, I felt less and less happy with the construction work and all the negative people around me. I started missing my old life, the fast money, feeling important, hanging out whenever I wanted, and going to the gym in the late morning because I could sleep in. The memory of that easier lifestyle was tempting, especially after long days of hauling materials up stairs for little pay. Like an old friend calling me on the phone, my past was trying to pull me back down into habits I knew were no good for me.

I was regularly working eighteen hours a day, and at one point I had needed to work a few twenty-one hour days. Now, as a young person, working hours like this is no big deal. Also, if you are working on a passion, working hours like this are okay. But when you are working for peanuts and you're working on someone else's dream, building up someone else's goal, it begins to wear on the man who feels he was meant for more.

I remember one night I was driving one of the company's dump trucks back to the shop. I was literally falling asleep at the wheel when I took the wrong exit and found myself headed into San Francisco. This meant I had to go over the Bay Bridge, into the busiest parts of the city, find a place to turn around, and get back on the bridge. Oh, and don't forget the line at the bridge toll. I was in a total road rage. Slamming my fist in the dash and cursing myself to hell. I was also no longer sleepy, for the moment at least.

As I lay in bed that night thinking about Ronnie's negative words, I felt a little more depressed, but suddenly I got a spark in my mind. I had a great idea. So I went back to work the next day and when I saw Ronnie, I approached him with a big smile on my face. "Hey, Ronnie, I know what I'm going to do with my life," I said.

"Oh, yeah? What's that?" he replied.

"I'm going to start a construction company just like this one, just like Mr. Peacock." I was riding high with this idea. I really thought it was possible for me.

Ronnie took one look at me, did a sort of choke laugh, and said, "Mr. Peacock is living a fantasy life, and that isn't a life for guys like me and you, so forget about it. Carpentry is a good job." My smile quickly turned upside down and I walked away slowly.

Wow. I was surrounded by naysayers and men who had all given up on their dreams. They didn't even want to hear talk like that. I think it made them feel insecure because, more than likely, they thought the same things at some point in their lives but never tried to go for it. They gave up and remained stuck where they were. In their minds, if they couldn't do it, couldn't escape to something better, then neither could you. Again, this was absorbed into my soul. I took it to heart, and not in a good way. I believed what they were saying and didn't dare to dream.

However, these deflating encounters did produce one positive thing. I came to realize that when passion strikes you at some point in your life, whether it be in the middle of the night or while you're on the job hauling lumber up flights of stairs, it's important to only share your dreams with positive and encouraging people. That way, your dreams will not be shot down out of the sky before they reach their desired destination. At that age, I had no chance to ever reach my destination. Big dreamers need inspiring and supportive people in their lives. I didn't have those people. Not even close.

Eventually, I was fed up with the long hours, the bullshit, and the negative attitudes. I didn't want to build up someone else's life. I wanted to be significant. The problem? I was too influenced by what I heard from the adults and the folks who were above me. At this point in my life, everyone around me was a dream crusher. They influenced me to think and dream small. I didn't like that feeling. So, I had a plan. I would find my significance. Resolving to do this gave me hope, and lifted my depression a bit. But it soon led to an even bigger problem: When you are insecure and lacking in confidence, your significance may be found in the wrong place.

Be Aware of Your Surroundings

Human beings can be like sponges, soaking up everything from their environment, both good and bad. And if your environment is mostly bad, filled with negative people, like mine was—then you are in for a world of pain unless you learn how to filter the negative out.

So how do you filter out the bad? Practice increased awareness in every single area of your life: health and fitness, work and business, the way you think and feel, how you treat others and yourself, who you choose to surround yourself with. It matters. If you are not surrounding yourself with highly successful or highly positive people who push you forward toward your goals, you'll have no chance to reach your wildest dreams.

Negative people will suck you dry emotionally, as their perspective on life is highly contagious. Their limiting beliefs will become your limiting beliefs. They will erode your desires and drive in life. Their fears will become your fears, and your goals will take a back seat in life, much like theirs did at some point in their own lives. If they couldn't do it, then you better believe they will ensure you can't either. Why? Because if you do succeed, then they will look and feel totally insignificant, and they can't bear the thought of that. Still, understand that negative people don't even realize half the time that they are killing your visions and dreams. So go easy on them, and learn to forgive. It will make your own path easier.

I was buried alive by negative people, and their voices in my mind playing on repeat kept me from trying anything great and from thinking too big. These thoughts pushed me back down the road of despair. And so, I looked up to the only influence I knew at the time, thugs, outlaws, rappers, all talking about the glory in drug deals and robberies. Movies like *Scarface* and *Goodfellas*. Their misdeeds were glorified, and I consumed so much of it that I became it.

Do you think you will be able to lose weight if you are surrounded by overweight people who sit around eating fast food and playing video games all day? Or, what if you just want to be happy? Do you think you can learn to be happy surrounded by a bunch of negative, unhappy assholes all day? It's kind of like money, spending it is easy, but making it takes work. Similarly, absorbing negativity requires no effort, while building and maintaining a positive mindset demands daily commitment. Just as money flows out much faster than it comes in, negative thoughts can infiltrate your mind in seconds while positive habits might take months to establish. To reach your goals, it's best to surround yourself with people who've already attained their dreams, an achievement you so desperately want.

The story above about my life in construction is a perfect example of how I was influenced by my surroundings. I'm not saying it was the only factor in my failures early on, but it had a huge impact. Negative in, negative production out, and the closer these people are to you, the harder it will be to go in the direction you feel is courageous. In the great and highly inspirational movie *The Pursuit of Happyness*, Will Smith, who plays the real-life character Chris Gardner, says this to his son, after crushing his son's dreams and contemplating his own negativity: "Don't ever let somebody tell you you can't do something. Not even me, alright? You got a dream. You gotta protect it. People who can't do something themselves, they wanna tell you you can't do it. If you want something, go get it. Period."

Boy, if I could have only seen past all the bullshit I was told. Or just had that one positive person to say encouragingly, "That's a great idea! Go for it, Jono!" Those early years were a significant detour for me, but I'm on the higher path now. Once I learned to encircle myself with only positive, uplifting people, my whole life changed. A perfect example early on was when I began my swimming pool and repair company. Struggling in the beginning to make ends meet and grow the business, I realized I needed to surround myself with like-minded folks. I spoke with guys who were running large companies and doing extremely well. I went to pool conventions to learn and network. My whole attitude and outlook changed. Connecting with positive people motivated and inspired me. The negativity fell away and was replaced with an optimistic mindset. Soon enough, my business exploded.

> "Once you realize you have the power to choose your influences, everything changes."

Look, at the end of the day, your environment isn't just about where you live or work, it's about who you let into your mental space and what voices you allow to shape your dreams. I learned this lesson the hard way, wasting years listening to dream killers and naysayers who were just projecting their own fears onto me. But here's the thing: once you realize you have the power to choose your influences, everything changes. It's like upgrading the software in your brain. When I finally started hanging around successful pool company owners instead of bitter foremen, my whole world expanded. Those same dreams that seemed impossible suddenly became blueprints for my future. So take it from someone who's been there, surround yourself with people who make you believe in "why not?" instead of "why bother?" Because the truth is, your dreams are too valuable to trust them with people who've given up on their own. Take control of your environment, and watch how quickly your life transforms from surviving to thriving. Show me your circle, and I'll show you your future, we can only rise to the level of those around us.

TRANSFORMATION LESSON 3. GUARD YOUR ENVIRONMENT

Transformation Action Steps

My journey from the construction sites of San Francisco to running a successful pool business illustrates a fundamental truth: our environment shapes not just who we are, but who we believe we can become. The voices of those coworkers could have permanently limited my potential, just as the guidance of successful business owners later elevated it. While my path involved many detours and setbacks, it taught me valuable lessons about managing our surroundings that can help anyone seeking positive change. The strategies that follow are not groundbreaking if you study any successful human being, you'll find they follow these rules as well. However, for me, they are literally battle-tested approaches that emerged from my own struggles to break free from limiting influences and create an environment conducive to growth.

Check Your Environment: You cannot begin to make the proper changes until you know where the problem lies. Let's face it, your current environment might be working against your goals. This is especially true when you're first starting your journey of self-improvement. Family members with negative attitudes and fixed mindsets can create significant obstacles. Friends who are comfortable with mediocrity or even poverty might resist your desire for change. When you begin pushing for something better, you'll often find your existing environment isn't equipped to support your growth, and might actively work against it. And so if you choose this path of growth and becoming a better version of yourself, you may just find yourself alone at times. Just know this is part of the process.

Begin by taking a good, hard look at your environment as a whole, individuals as well as the things you consume and what occupies most of your time and mental space. This could include family members, friends, coworkers, or mentors, even what you watch on TV. A great example is the news, and I'm not talking about Ron Burgundy's news. I'm talking about the fear-mongering primetime news stations that are only after making you feel bad, mad, and just plain unhappy. For each item, document your emotional and mental state after interacting with them or it. Do you feel energized and motivated to pursue your goals? Or do you find yourself questioning your abilities and ambitions? Do you find yourself suddenly being pessimistic? Pay attention to subtle cues, does somebody's response to your dreams remind you of my construction crew colleagues, ready to shoot down any aspiration that exceeds their comfort zone?

Let Them Go: Here's the hard part. Sometimes we have to move on with our own lives and leave behind the people and things that we may have loved. If I kept hanging out with the same crowd back in my drug dealing days, I would either be dead or in prison for life, there's no doubt in my mind. I had to ditch some friends who did not line up with my change in lifestyle. They didn't understand, and still to this day I receive DMs from a few of them, wanting to hang out and reminisce on the old days. What the hell for? I see them, the lives they are living—and want no part in it. So let go so you can reach up. This may be harder as we get to people closer to us. Family, for instance. They won't understand you either, and we can't just ditch them all together unless they are pure poison to our lives. If you love them but your lifestyles do not line up, it's time to distance yourself. Spend less time with them. When you do spend time with them, you gotta protect your mind and your dreams. When the conversation goes sideways, change gears or say you gotta go to the bathroom, and do not re-engage in that convo again.

What are you choosing to watch on TV? Ask yourself, Is this serving my best self? More than likely it's not. It's time to walk away from it and choose only the things that serve your greater purpose. I know this can be devastating, as it's become a habit, indulging in those feelings of madness we get from watching the news manipulate our minds into believing everything and everyone is out to get us. Even the simple comforts we get from watching a great show, like when *Game of Thrones* was hot, need to be taken into consideration. I'm not saying you have to stop watching those awesome shows altogether, but you do have to minimize them, and not consume them at all until you have finished your daily goals and feel good about your progress. I still watch movies and shows, but I limit them to a Friday or Saturday night, and absolutely none to start the day, as that just sets the wrong tone. A perfect day of mediocrity. Learn to let these people and these things go and your mind and future will thank you for it. You will notice a difference in yourself rather quickly.

A Fresh Start: Create a fresh start. Beginning anew requires confronting the comfort zones we've built around ourselves. While the prospect of change is scary and hard, as it was for me, almost taking my life over it—you must ask what matters most to you. Ask yourself, What are the things and people I want in my new, positive, supportive environment? This is the time to start filling your mind with content that serves your growth. When I decided to make my swimming pool business successful, I immersed myself completely in that world. I sought out industry experts, devoured relevant books, and learned everything I could about the business. This hands-on education meant I failed often—even destroying peoples' swimming pool equipment as I figured things out. There was simply no room for distractions or influences that didn't serve that ambition.

Many people struggle with where to begin, especially when they don't have direct access to mentors in their chosen field. The solution lies in books. They have been transformative in my own journey toward becoming a better person. Books have literally saved my life. They provide the foundation, introduce new ideas, reshape mindsets, and offer insights into every aspect of life and success. Start by reading in the areas of interest to you. Supplement this with podcasts, YouTube videos, and audiobooks. In today's digital age, there's no excuse for not accessing the knowledge you need to improve in any area.

Another good place to begin is to become actively engaged in your new community. Join professional organizations, attend industry events, or participate in groups like Toastmasters, which has significantly enhanced my communication and speaking abilities. This steady progression up your chosen ladder isn't random, it's the direct result of selecting the path you want to take and surrounding yourself with the positive influences that will help you climb.

Remember, the ascent you choose is truly your decision. But that choice becomes meaningful only when you start to create an environment that supports and strengthens your growth. Your future depends on the choices you make today. Looking back at those construction site days, I let their words define me. Their limitations became my limitations, their ceiling became my ceiling. The difference between staying trapped in that mindset and eventually building a successful business wasn't just about skills or knowledge, it was about finally recognizing how deeply those negative influences had shaped my reality, and then choosing to make myself a fresh start by building a different environment. When I think about how many years I lost believing "that's not for guys like us" or buying into the gangster mentality, it reinforces why these changes are so crucial. Every time you distance yourself from a negative influence, every quality book you read, every growth-minded person you connect with, you're building a new foundation that can support bigger dreams. The path to creating this new environment might feel lonely at times, and the changes won't always be comfortable, but remember: the environment you create today becomes the reality you live in tomorrow. I know this firsthand because I lived in both worlds. Make sure you're creating an environment worthy of your potential, because I can tell you from experience, it will shape everything you become.

17

Transformation Lesson 4. Develop Self-Control, the Ultimate Adversity-Busting Superpower

> *"The ability to discipline yourself to delay gratification in the short term in order to enjoy greater rewards in the long term is the indispensable prerequisite for success."*
> —Brian Tracy

Self-control, in my opinion, is the ultimate superpower in our modern world of temptation and instant gratification. Why do I like to call it the ultimate superpower? Well, it's quite simple actually. Think about how different your life would be if you had the self-control to routinely, almost effortlessly, do the things you know you must do, like exercise each day or sit down and read a book. Then, of course, you'd also want to have the ability to refrain from doing the things you know you do *not* want to do, such as eating too many bad foods (or just overeating in general) or watching too much mindless

TV. Can you envision living your life with this potent superpower? The many bad choices you wouldn't make, and the countless good choices you would?

In this chapter we will see why self-discipline matters and how it can transform your life from a sugar-coated mess to a lean, mean, goal-achieving machine. You'll get a front-row seat to the struggles I had with self-control, which at that time were mainly related to my diet, from scarfing down donuts for breakfast to finally kicking my junk food addiction to the curb.

But the purpose of this chapter isn't to tell you about me (I'm just an example), it's about arming yourself with the tools to become the master of your own choices. We'll explore why our society makes it so damn hard to stay on track, exactly how to go about building your self-control muscle until it's as strong as Popeye the Sailor after he downs a can of spinach, and why waiting for life to deliver you a wake-up call, such as a serious illness, isn't an option. By the time you're done, you'll be ready to tell that whiny voice in your head that's begging for another slice of pizza to take a hike. So, are you ready to unlock your inner badass and become the person you've always wanted to be? Good! Let's do this.

*****

Every day was the same. I'd drag myself out of my bed as late as possible, quickly get dressed, hop in one of the work trucks, and head off to do my pool service rounds for the day, still in the process of waking up. The business was doing well overall, but the ever-revolving set of employees we had made things tough. The turnover was absurd. I was always

TRANSFORMATION LESSON 4. DEVELOP SELF-CONTROL

out cleaning pools myself, fixing my employees' mistakes, and working tirelessly to keep customer complaints at bay.

We were consumed with constant employee issues and a daily stream of customer demand and complaints. I was stressed out and very unhappy in my work. I was at the point where I just wasn't feeling it anymore. If you are ever experiencing this in your job or your business, don't feel bad about it. Things change, and one's perspective evolves, and something that may have fit the bill at one stage of your life may no longer work for you later on. The key is to begin the process to make the desired change you would like for yourself. Remember, an unfulfilling life leads to poor decisions and poor habits in other areas, like diet, lifestyle, and relationships. And look, The human spirit has an incredible capacity for reinvention, I've done it several times, and so can you.

Heading off to start the day, I would first hit up the closest 7-Eleven to get breakfast. Usually, this breakfast would consist of a package of chocolate-covered mini donuts, a bear claw, the occasional stick of beef jerky, and a Red Bull or two to wash it down. This was a great way to start my days, right? I was probably already hitting over 100 grams of sugar just with this "breakfast." And what about the caffeine hit? I justified it because I wanted to get the job done as fast as possible, and Red Bull gives you wings! Well, those wings last for a few hours, then they fold up and you're left paralyzed with zero energy to finish the day.

Similarly, with all the sugar, I'd start my days rather quickly and efficiently, but it was only a matter of time before the sugar wore off, which was usually around lunchtime. Perfect. Time for some McDonald's or Burger King, ah, so many yummy choices. Boy, do they make our lives easy these days. What a great time to be alive, right? I would supersize everything and wash it all down with a gigantic Coke. That soda alone has over 100 grams of sugar. On with the day!

One particular day, while working in the hills of Northern California, I discovered just how badly my diet was destroying me. It started with a low gurgle in my stomach. Then heat surged through my body and up to my face. Sweat beaded on my forehead. My gut twisted into knots. Suddenly, I had to go. Bad. Really bad.

When you're working on someone's pool in their backyard, thirty minutes from the nearest gas station restroom, this is the ultimate nightmare. I squeezed my cheeks together so hard I thought I might pass out, but it wasn't working. The pressure was building and I was running out of time.

I half-ran, half-waddled to my truck, trying to look as normal as possible in case my customer glanced out the window. I grabbed a bucket, dumped out my 7-Eleven bag and grabbed some tissue, and headed straight for the pool equipment shed. I dropped the bucket, lined it with the bag, stripped my pants, and squatted down right there in my customer's shed. Relief flooded through me. Then reality hit. My customer was home. Every once in a while, he'd come out to chat about the pool or complain about something. This was bad. Really bad. I quickly cleaned up, tied off the bag, finished the job as fast as humanly possible, and left with my bag of shit literally in hand.

Sorry for such a detailed story, but this is what my stomach did when I consumed processed, sugary garbage all day

TRANSFORMATION LESSON 4. DEVELOP SELF-CONTROL

long. My body was screaming at me to stop poisoning it, but I wasn't listening yet.

The rest of the day would drag on. Some days, I might still have another fifteen to twenty pools to service after lunch. I'd do my best to get through it, but I was usually so burned out and exhausted, all I wanted to do was tell all my customers to F-off so I could go home and relax. That would have been interesting. The look on some of their faces would have been priceless. Some of those entitled bastards deserved it. But I never went there, no matter how bad I wanted to. I knew what was at stake and at the end of the day, I was a professional.

My day would finally come to an end, and I'd be wiped out. Plus, if it was wintertime, I would be soaking wet and freezing cold. And if it was summer, I would practically melt, despite working around swimming pools all day long. Swimming in a customer's pool would have felt refreshing, until they'd come outside and say, "What the hell are you doing?" So this daydream never became a reality. I did, however, fall in a couple times, but let's keep that between us.

After finishing up with the last service, I'd head to my supplier and get all the items I'd need to complete the next day. Still tired, I'd make a quick stop at another 7-Eleven, because I told myself I had such a rough day that I deserved more sugar and tasty processed foods. It's my reward for all the hard work I put in. And so I'd load up on some beef jerky, maybe grab a pack of Skittles or a Snickers bar, and I might even grab one of those tasty hot dogs they've got turning on the hot metal rollers. Of course, I couldn't forget another Red Bull so I could finish my day at home awake. There would almost always be customer calls to make and fires to put out all evening long, so the Red Bull would help get me through the worst parts of all that stressful business.

Dinner would roll around and it would usually consist of carbs and meat, zero veggies and zero fruits. Just a big plate of carbs, maybe pasta, or how about a pizza? "Sure." I'd wait about an hour or two, and then guess what time it was? Dessert time! Half a gallon of cookie dough ice cream should do the job quite nicely. Then I'd sit on the couch, watching the latest episode of Game of Thrones with my wife and enjoy myself. My dopamine was on high and everything was gonna be just fine. I was pretty much the Jon Snow of nutrition, I knew nothing. And unlike the White Walkers, my expanding waistline wasn't going to wait for winter to come.

> "Most of us find it damn near impossible to control our urges not to spend money on the 'next best thing.' "

I look back at those days now and think, "What in the heck was that?!" I was literally killing myself every day with my food and lifestyle choices. I had zero self-control. Add the fact that I was totally unhappy with my business and the direction I was headed, and my lack of self-control in that one area started seeping into other areas of my life. Soon, any bit of discipline was impossible to find. I was out of control and heading for disaster with my health.

Now, I've never been a large man or ever considered obese, but I definitely had a gut that made doing my job just that much harder. Bending over was a strain, and since I wasn't finding the time to exercise, my back was also in constant pain. I have a bulging disc from motorcycle wrecks and snowboarding accidents (among other things!) in my twenties. Eating like this and not taking care of myself contributed to a harder existence, mentally and physically. If my work wasn't so physically demanding, I would have been in way worse shape, maybe even pushing obese.

Then of course, much like scarfing down a fat slice of cake, we often can't control our spending habits. That shiny new object makes us feel like a million bucks in the moment, only for us to realize a few minutes or days later the feeling has passed, and we're stuck with the bill.

Back when I was still in the drug trade, living in my first apartment, yeah, the one with that old antique twisting staircase, my girlfriend and I went on a shopping spree to furnish our new pad. Flush with easy cash from the street, we hit up Best Buy, Costco, and the local furniture store like we were on a mission. We had zero regard for how much we were spending or if we really needed the nicest entertainment center and the finest French flax linen. Hell, we probably couldn't even spell *linen* at the time. We got the biggest TV, the plushest couch, and all the little shiny things we thought we needed to feel like we'd made it. We were throwing dollars around like confetti. The funny thing is, I never even got to plant my ass on that nice, plush couch we bought as the handcuffs went on before it could even be delivered.

Looking back, it's embarrassing how easily we fell for the trap of thinking stuff equals happiness. But here's the thing: most of us find it damn near impossible to control our urges not to spend money on the "next best thing." We're like kids in a candy store, except the candy is flat-screen TVs and overpriced gadgets, and the store is our entire consumer-driven world. It's pathetic how we can't put off racking up our credit card balances and depleting our savings just to feel good right now or to say to our friends I got the eighty inch TV.

But what happens when we make the conscious effort to practice self-control? When we save our money, pile it away for a rainy day, or invest it wisely on things that don't bring an instant reward? You know exactly what happens. Something called "short-term pain, long-term gain." Read that again.

Most recently, my wife and I decided to work on a rental property. It needed a lot of work, money, and time, as well as self-discipline, to devote our resources to this project instead of blowing our cash on a trip to Hawaii or taking the kids to Disneyland. So we buckled down and got it done. We shut down the need for pleasure right now to reap the long-term benefits of creating another income stream. Disneyland can wait till next year and there is nothing more memorable than a cheap camping trip into the woods, which is what we ended up doing with our kids. Everyone had a good time at a fraction of the cost.

When we choose to educate ourselves instead of scrolling on our phones for hours, we're choosing self-discipline. We're choosing our goals, ourselves, and the vision we have for the future. Not some fleeting feeling derived from the latest shiny object.

Theodore Roosevelt said, "With self-discipline, most anything is possible." It's self–control that keeps us strong and in the fight. It's self-discipline that's going to keep me alive! It's time we grew up and faced the music. Just like saying no to that extra slice of pizza, we've got to learn to say no to unnecessary things like wasting time scrolling or overspending on things we do not need. Your bank account and your mind will thank you, and trust me, you don't need the bigger boat or the faster car to feel significant. Real significance comes from mastering yourself, not from mastering the art of swiping your credit card.

> "The rewards of discipline create a powerful, healthy cycle. The more you practice it, the more you crave it."

We are all lacking in self-control. We are food junkies, sex addicts, alcoholics, workaholics, druggies. We spend far too much time glued to our phones and TVs, often at the expense of our relationships. And exercise is the last thing on our minds. We are all in this together, and we all need to learn how to control ourselves or we will remain weak, unhappy, and unfulfilled. Real strength reveals itself in moments of perfect self-control. The woman who can sit down at a restaurant and say no to dessert while her friends indulge in lava cakes and ice cream is a strong-minded woman. Beware: some of your "friends" will make you feel bad for choosing the right thing. A man who can say no to a beautiful woman who is practically throwing herself at him demonstrates total self-control and respect, both for himself and the woman. Stopping yourself from having one too many drinks while everyone else gets wasted is hard, but there isn't anything more powerful than having the ability to do what is right and to administer total self-control in the heat of the moment. As I stated earlier, it is the ultimate superpower. And nothing is better at helping you bust through adversity.

In a world that is flooded with in-your-face easy choices, we must train our self-control muscles. I struggle with this daily. Mastering it completely is not an easy task, but I've become very good at it with time. No, you can't have your cake and eat it too. Throw that shit in the garbage. Discipline requires making choices, the right choices, over and over. And once that habit becomes ingrained, there is no finer treat.

Because I got sick, I trained to improve my self-control. It's unfortunate that I had to get sick to get my act together, but I'm practicing daily to get better. I invite you to do the same, now, before life forces your hand.

Start actively working on your life right now to find what makes you happy. The discoveries and improvements you make will snowball into other healthier habits. Find joy in the power you can display to pass on the extra beer or refrain from buying the latest iPhone, because the rewards of discipline create a powerful, healthy cycle. The more you practice it, the more you crave it. Building self-control will create confidence within you and a feeling of "I can't be stopped. Whatever I want in this life, I can get!" Self-control truly is the master virtue. Master it, and you will get the sense that you can master anything.

Transformation Action Steps

Practice self-control daily in the areas you find the most weakness. The following steps are designed to help you master the art of self-discipline. Each step is meant to build upon the previous one to maximize your success. From controlling your thoughts to creating friction against bad habits, and from setting clear goals to managing your stress, these techniques work together to fortify your willpower. Remember, intelligent planning and having daily structure goes a long way toward making self-control easier.

Control Yourself: We must learn to tame that wild beast we call our mind, and there's only one tried and true way to accomplish this: you must be hyperaware of your thoughts at all times. This awareness is the key to preventing you from taking action on your worst, most self-sabotaging habits. You know, those stupid little habits you regret afterwards, like staying up way too late or scarfing down that extra piece of cake after you've already had plenty. So when a thought pops in your head that's pushing you toward that salty bag of chips or that unnecessary purchase, ask yourself, "Do I really need this? What purpose does it serve? Nope!" So quickly chase those self-destructive impulses out of your mind.

Next, remind yourself how good you feel after you make the right decision, the self-disciplined decision, as opposed to the weak and wrong one. By switching the channel in your mind, you begin to change the narrative of your thoughts. It's after you have said no to the chips and after you declined the purchase of a seventy-five-inch TV, because you thought your sixty-five was too small, that you feel good about yourself and your confidence in your ability to control your mind grows.

Create Friction: In other words, make it hard to do the things you don't want to be doing. Let's say you have a problem with the foods you keep jamming in your mouth, like I did. The first step is to remove all bad food from your home. That creates friction. Why? Because if it's not there, you can't have it, and you'd need to make the effort to go out and get it.

Similarly, you want to *reduce* friction for the things you do want to be doing. Let's say you want to replace the bad food in your diet with healthy options. If you're on the road a lot like I was, use your self-control to get up a bit early and make yourself a healthy breakfast and pack yourself a lunch. When you see the quick stop or the drive-through at McDonald's, you'll be inclined to pass it up because you've already got a delicious lunch sitting next to you on the passenger seat. You've *reduced* the friction to eating right and staying on course with your diet. Bonus tip: It's very critical to begin a mantra or some positive self-talk. As you drive by McDonald's, say, "Nope, I only eat good, healthy foods." Say it with conviction, and say it as often as needed, and eventually over time you won't even notice those places anymore. Your body will thank you for skipping those mystery meat ingredients. Now when I see a fast food restaurant, I'm actually disgusted that I ever ate that shit. You can get there too.

Focus on Weak Spots: I have a daily habits section on my planner for the week. If I'm struggling in a certain area, I will write down the habit that needs improvement and check it off each day. Just writing it down provides the motivation to keep yourself in check, and by checking off that goal each day, you are exercising those crucial self-control muscles. Each check means you're closer to getting where you want to be.

Structure: This one is huge for me. When we lack a well-planned, well-structured day, we are setting ourselves up for failure. When we structure our days and plan them out as best as we can to keep us busy and productive, we are less likely to become bored and go on the prowl for bad things. Having your day well-planned, and then executing that plan bit by bit as the day progresses, gives you a strong sense of satisfaction. It propels you through the entire day, like you've got a rocket strapped to your back.

A good example of this is me when I have my writer's hat on. Sometimes I find being a writer is extremely hard. If I try to write for a full eight hours, I will have many moments where I just don't know what to write any longer and I will go raid the fridge and cupboards. Fortunately, we no longer have bad foods in this house, but my mindless foraging can lead to overeating (overeating healthy foods is still overeating). That is why it's so important to keep the mind busy and ourselves productive throughout the day. By the way, an added bonus when you pursue each day in this manner is you get *a lot* of shit done. And that is rewarding.

Stress Management: It seems to be an ironclad law of nature that when you're stressed, your self-control weakens. I was stressed out all the damn time when I was working those pools. Whether it was a customer yelling at me or an employee not doing his job, the business had me on edge all day long, which led to, you know what, bad choices and shitty foods.

Since then, I've developed ways to manage stress and maintain self-control. My single best tool for overcoming stress is exercise. Try to start your day with a workout that gets the blood flowing and the sweat dripping. This ensures you start your day on good terms, and you can't help but feel really good about yourself having done this first thing in the morning. It's also a major confidence booster. Now of course there are the times when someone or something gets under your skin and you feel the stress ratcheting up inside you. When this happens, stop everything you are doing, close your eyes, and take some deep breaths. Slow everything down, your mind, your body, your breathing, and come back to neutral. Know that this stressful moment is only temporary and it will pass. Maybe even try to laugh about it. When you can laugh off your troubles, you have mastered the art of stress management.

Suffer: Lastly, and this is probably the most important step of them all, you've suffered through a lot up to this point in your life, and now it's time to suffer just a bit more. You must be willing to endure through the pain of waiting for that anticipated reward, of not getting that instant gratification, because when you can push past that little episode of wanting something right now, you are flexing that self-control muscle hard. And once you get through the struggle of walking away from that shiny object, that is when you are rewarded with the feeling of winning and knowing you can do this shit. The by-product of that is more energy for the things we want to be seeking in life. It's the forcing ourselves not to take that hit or bite that burger that matters. That's where we find out how powerful we can be. That's when we come to understand we can overcome just about any adversity life throws our way.

18

Transformation Lesson 5. Master Your Fears

> *"He who is not everyday conquering some fear has not learned the secret of life."*
> —Ralph Waldo Emerson

Fear. It's a force that can paralyze us, keeping us trapped in our comfort zones and preventing us from reaching our full potential. Fear can be the most daunting obstacle we face as we confront life's many challenges. Its great power can force us to cower and beg for mercy from our shitty circumstances. But what if I told you that conquering your fears is the secret to overcoming adversity?

This chapter is about exploring fear and the grip it can have on our lives. It will take you through my journey from a sweating, panic-stricken inmate forced to speak in front of hardened criminals to a man who voluntarily stepped into a room full of strangers to improve his public speaking skills. This wasn't just about mastering public speaking, it was about developing the courage to face any challenge life throws our way. We'll discover how confronting our deepest anxieties can lead to profound personal growth, equipping us with the resilience to overcome even the toughest obstacles.

*****

I grew up tongue-tied, literally. I didn't speak in school until the fifth grade, and even then, finding the courage to speak was almost impossible. I was so shy that instead of asking to go to the bathroom, I'd just piss my pants. Imagine being that kid, reeking of urine with no ability to explain why you smelled so bad. Making friends was out of the question.

As I moved into middle school and high school, I began ditching class whenever I knew presentations were scheduled. You know the kind, standing up in front of the whole classroom while everyone stares at you. Pure nightmare. I figured failing was better than facing my fears.

I remember sitting in history class watching a fellow student deliver her report. She was so confident and I thought, *how is that even possible?* Surrounded by rows of students, with portraits of dead presidents hanging on the walls, I was already feeling the panic rise. Those painted presidential eyes seemed to stare right at me. George Washington's dead gaze particularly triggered my anxiety. Was he silently judging me? Was he about to laugh at my pathetic, nervous self?

I was third in line to give my presentation. My armpits were already soaked with sweat, my heart beating in my chest like a drummer boy in Washington's Continental Army. What the hell was I going to do? In desperation, I rolled up my report, stuffed it in my backpack, and approached the teacher to ask if I could use the bathroom. "Ok, just be back in time for your report," he whispered. "You've got about ten minutes." Hey, at least I could ask to use the bathroom now, that was progress.

I nodded, walked back to my desk, and watched as the teacher swiveled in his chair to focus on the current presenter. That was my chance. I grabbed my bag and slipped out the door without making a sound. Close call. I would not be giving a report that day, or any day, if I could help it. Until, of course, that inevitable moment when there's no escape. We've all been there.

Back when I was in jail, I was taking the drug rehab program my wonderful lawyer Ronnie told me to take so I could get out sooner. I hated that class. I wasn't a drug addict, and on my first day the instructor had me go to the front of the class and tell everyone who I was and why I was there. I had to stand up in front of at least twenty hard-ass inmates and speak.

The moment filled me with dread. I walked up to the front of the classroom, turned around, and saw a room full of orange jumpsuits, and the men inside them were staring back at me with an *I don't give a fuck* attitude. Their faces said it all: "Who the fuck is this kid?" The instructor stood off to the side in the back corner, expressionless, arms folded across his chest. I introduced myself, and at the same time I began to sweat. First it started at my armpits, then it made its way to my forehead. As I was talking and sharing my story, I felt a bead of sweat rolling down my nose. *What the fuck? I never sweat! Why am I sweating so bad right now?*

As I told these men about my charges, one of them said, "All those charges and you only got a year. What are you, a snitch?" I returned fire because I couldn't be weak or times would get hard in the slammer, harder than they already were. "I'm not a fucking snitch!" Now I was really sweating, and pissed off too.

The guy who called me a snitch was a Northerner. One of northern California's Latino street gang members. So this little quarrel I had with him could have been bad. Thankfully, one of the older members of that gang, who I happened to know quite well, stood up for me pretty fast and he was able to calm the waters. Bullet dodged.

I continued with my talk, but rather than get comfortable, my fear grew. Now I began to lose my vision. *Oh shit, I'm literally blacking out!* I struggled to finish my talk, as I was now suffering from tunnel vision. Literally, I felt as if I was looking at the class through the wrong end of a periscope as things darkened and squeezed in on me. Everything was blurry, and I didn't have a lot of confidence in my balance. I ended my little speech as quickly as I could and partially blind, I slowly walked back to my seat crashing into it much like a drunk would his couch after an all night bender. It was a total nightmare, and I vowed never to speak in front of anyone again. Shaking off the fear of speaking in front of people would be very hard to do after that experience. The trauma of that day lingered.

I eventually passed the course and earned a certificate, though not without resistance. The instructor made it clear he would only grant it if I continued attending class. Not going to happen. The mere thought of standing in front of those men again made my stomach churn. I knew he'd make me present again, and I had absolutely no intention of subjecting myself to another round of that torture.

TRANSFORMATION LESSON 5. MASTER YOUR FEARS

Once I realized the drug rehab class wasn't my ticket to an early release, there was no incentive strong enough to drag me back to that nightmare. So I chose the safer path, isolation and avoidance, a strategy that would follow me well beyond the walls of that hell hole and into the decades that followed.

Roughly twenty-two years later, there I was again, facing that same deeply rooted fear that went back my entire life. I was sitting in my truck in front of our local library on a cool October evening, watching the minutes tick closer to the start of the Toastmasters public speaking club meeting. When things are hard, we humans love to come up with amazing rationalizations to avoid the struggle all together. Most of the time, it works. But I was determined that tonight was going to be different, right?

> "Life is too damn short to be a victim to your fears."

I had finally worked up enough courage to go to a public speaking club. Directly facing my long-time fear was how I planned to stomp on this struggle that has always held me back. It was me telling my weak self to step aside, sir, because there's a new me that's taking over. I was sick of cowering, sick of hiding and keeping myself down. Life is too damn short to be a victim to your fears.

With the start of the class just fifteen minutes away, I was sweating. Again. My palms, armpits, and face were all lightly coated with damp sweat. I was hot, even though it was forty degrees outside! I swear, you could have cooked an egg on my forehead.

Worst-case scenarios flooded my mind. What if this time I actually black out completely and fall over in front of the class? We all tell ourselves stories that scare us, stories that make it seem like it will be so much worse than it actually will be.

I was scared to death, but I am in good company. Most of us are afraid of public speaking. Seventy-five percent of people are afraid to speak in public. They even say people would rather be in the casket than deliver the eulogy at a funeral. I beg to differ on that one. Ask them that question again when their mortality is on the line and I guarantee they'll answer differently. I would quickly trade my incurable cancer for speaking in public, naked to ten thousand people, if I could.

Looking back, I have to chuckle a bit at my train of thought, sitting there in my truck, permitting fear to master me. I recall telling myself how everyone in there was going to be better than me. They were all going to be suit and tie, high-end, smooth-talking business people. Who was I to practice my speaking skills with folks of such elite caliber? I was going to make a fool of myself. Impostor syndrome kicked in hard. There are times when the last person you should listen to is yourself, and this was one of them.

Most of the time, we do a great job of talking ourselves out of what we need to be doing. And, thankfully, I knew that's what I was doing to myself, simmering in my own fear. I'd come a long way by this point, and I had developed the self-control to see it through. I knew it was imperative for me to get up and go do it.

The great writer and lecturer Dale Carnegie said, "Do the thing you fear to do and keep doing it. That is the quickest

TRANSFORMATION LESSON 5. MASTER YOUR FEARS

and surest way ever yet discovered to conquer fear." I have never seen someone reach their goals sitting in their house or car, just waiting for their goals to reach them. It just doesn't happen. We all want better lives, but we are rarely willing to do the work to reach the destination we desire. And so there I was at forty-three, about to face one of my deepest fears, and what I believed had been my Achilles heel my entire life. It was time to do this work, to overcome this obstacle in my life. Lacking the ability to speak up for yourself, to ask for what you want or need in life, is something that holds a great many of us back from our desired lives, and from our destiny.

As I sweated it out and offered myself all the excuses in the world, I eventually settled on this: *If you don't do this right now, you will suffer in silent agony for the rest of your life. Jono, you are going into that library, and that's the last I will say about that!* With that, I got out of my truck, slammed the door shut, and walked into the library. As I was walking toward the door, I also told myself, *This will not be harder than when you did this in front of a bunch of hard-headed convicts who would more than likely beat your ass for saying the wrong thing. What's the worst that could happen here? They sentence me to three minutes of impromptu speaking? I survived jail, surely I can survive saying "um" too many times.*

The funny thing was that once I got in there, I realized everything I told myself was dead wrong. The people were welcoming and the atmosphere was positive and encouraging. I ended up really enjoying myself. I went in as a timid man and came out with my head held high, seeing just how far we humans can go if we push ourselves through the fear and find our confidence. You will not find me on my deathbed regretting the evening I drove away from a speech club when I should have just gone in, sweat and all.

Mastering your fears takes time, and there will be ups and downs during the process, but we just have to keep pushing until eventually we get better. But we must take that first, all-important step forward. Nothing great ever came from letting fear hold us back from our goals. We can't be happy living timidly, afraid to walk into a freakin' library! I am a changed man because of the action I took that night to get better and move beyond the bad decisions that I had made in my past. While my heart still races every time I step up to speak, I've somehow learned to love public speaking. Crazy, right? Who would have thought the guy who once pissed his pants rather than ask for the bathroom would end up voluntarily grabbing the mic?

> *"An individual develops courage by doing courageous acts."—Aristotle*

What is something you've always wanted to try but have been too fearful to give it a chance? What steps could you take to do this thing, knowing that if you do it, you will open your

Speaking to a group, something I never thought I could do. I now do it with ease because I pushed through my fears. *photo courtesy Robert Pitari*

TRANSFORMATION LESSON 5. MASTER YOUR FEARS

mind to a whole new consciousness, a world of opportunity? Not only will you become more resilient, you will expand your comfort zone, increase your self-esteem, and inspire others with your courageous acts of blasting through your fear. I say, do what makes you nervously sweat. You can always shower afterwards.

My confidence has skyrocketed in all aspects of my life outside of Toastmasters. I've found my courage. My kids' school events, where there once used to be a lot of uncomfortable situations and awkward silences with other parents, no longer feel uncomfortable. I know who I am, and I also know this: we are all equal, and by learning to become confident in communication, by doing those fearful things, you will realize this and your whole life will change.

From ditching presentations to nearly fainting in front of inmates to confidently winning speech competitions—proof we can overcome anything.

Remember, nobody is better than you! Let me repeat that for you, because I really want it to stick. Nobody is better than you! Nobody has your unique array of personality, talents, skills, joys, failures, and life lessons. So why let something as petty as a mere emotion like fear hold you back? The world needs you. There has never been and will never be anyone like you. There is no one who can match you, and no one more deserving of all the world has to offer, no matter what your past might try to tell you. If you get nothing else out of this book, let me leave you with this hard-fought and dearly-won truth: The world is better off with you in it. So don't hold back!

Transformation Action Step

It's time to face your fears and strengthen your courage muscle. We'll always have fears, even the most courageous of us, because each time we conquer one there will be another. We all share fears, but your fears are not my fears. So rather than try to address your specific fears, my goal here is to give you the tools to step into your fear, journey through it, and blast out the other side. So, put on lots of deodorant, grab a water and a towel, and let's go sweat out your fears:

Identify Your Fuel: To get out the door, to step into that classroom, or to tell your boss you need a raise, you need the fuel to push you through that wall of fear, much like I needed the fuel to walk into the library that evening. It's impossible to do this if your reasons are not strong enough; you'll just come up with more excuses and turn your back on the very thing you know you must do. And so, find your fuel. Find your unassailable reasons. Remember your past, remember your struggles, remember the adversities you've overcome. That pain you went through, the hardship you are faced with now. Focus on these things deeply. See them in your mind. Even allow them to get you a little mad. There's nothing wrong with a little touch of madness to give you the fuel you need to step forward.

One way I master my fears today is by looking back at all the pain I experienced from not being able to communicate in front of people, the insecurity that ruled so many of my life's choices. The near blackouts in front of hardened convicts, ditching class to avoid presentations, even pissing my pants as a shy kid, I don't run from these memories. Instead, I feed off them in the present and allow them to guide me forward. I use all those painful experiences to my advantage. Because I know life is short and one day I won't have the opportunity to grow anymore. And I don't ever want to say to my kids, "It's too late for me."

> "There's nothing wrong with a little touch of madness to give you the fuel you need to step forward."

So I encourage you to do the same: ride your past adversities and your current challenges right through your darkest, deepest fears and emerge triumphant, your fears conquered, your objectives achieved, and you a stronger person for it all.

Take Action: Now that you've identified your fuel, it's time to chart your course. Fear often seems insurmountable because we see it as one giant obstacle. The better way to think of it is as a journey comprising my steps. I had to acknowledge that I was not going to just walk into a public speaking club and suddenly be great at speaking in front of others. That was the end goal, not the beginning. So the mountain loomed very large at first. I told myself that just stepping foot in the door was the first step, speaking up was the second, and that eventually I would go on to do a speech and so on. I could see the mountain summit, but the hike up was going to take awhile.

The key is action. When we take action on those first steps, we begin to gain momentum and gradually, patiently, we become more courageous. Our stride lengthens and we get closer and closer to our goal. And remember, the goal isn't to eliminate fear entirely (that's impossible), but to build your capacity to act despite it. Each small victory will build your confidence and momentum. Be specific with your plan, set deadlines, and commit to taking at least one step forward each week.

Reflect and Celebrate Progress: After each attempt to face your fear, take time to reflect on what you learned and how you felt. Recognize your courage in taking action, regardless of the outcome. Celebrate your progress, no matter how small. This builds confidence and motivation to continue pushing your boundaries.

The satisfaction I took from that first move I made into that library was tremendous, and the gratification from overcoming fear and taking those first initial steps in pursuit of other goals in my life, are truly worthy of celebration. I want you to do the same. Mastering fear is never easy, because fear is one of the many forms of adversity, and overcoming adversity always requires grit and effort. But the rewards for doing so make the effort more than worthwhile. So celebrate!

19

Transformation Lesson 6. The Art of Failure

> *"I never thought of losing, but now that it's happened, the only thing is to do it right. That's my obligation to all the people who believe in me. We all have to take defeats in life."*
> —*Muhammad Ali*

Winning feels good. It bolsters our confidence and validates our hard work, practice, and learning. But life isn't a constant string of victories. The reality is, we're going to lose and we're going to fail. If you haven't yet misfired or had something go seriously wrong in your job, business, craft, art, sport, or health, brace yourself, it's coming. However, this book was written mostly for those of you who have been down the road of failure before. But even if you have not suffered through many losses, you will still learn invaluable life lessons that may save your ass from making the wrong decisions. Either way, learning from loss is key to your growth in your journey through life.

THE BREAKING POINT

Life is a blend of winning and losing, succeeding and failing. It's in that beautiful struggle between triumphs and setbacks that we discover who we truly are and find the strength to keep pressing on. In my experience, the losses seem to happen more frequently. But there's a purpose behind all this losing and failing. In this chapter, I'll share some of my significant life failures and explain why I've come to see them not as setbacks but as opportunities. We'll explore my son's first jiu-jitsu tournament that didn't go as planned, and the gut-wrenching experience of losing my life savings while simultaneously being diagnosed with cancer. These stories will show you how to see your past failures as guiding lights and recognize your inevitable future losses not as something to fear, but as signposts that you're headed in the right direction.

What many of us don't realize is that there's an art to failure. Like any skill, failing well can be learned and mastered. Sounds odd, I know, but when done properly, failure becomes a powerful tool for growth and innovation. It's not about flouncing around aimlessly after a setback, but rather approaching failure with intentionality, seeking to extract its lessons and use them to propel yourself forward. This artful approach to failure can maximize its benefits, turning what seems like a negative experience into a stimulant for positive change. So let's tackle one of life's biggest adversities: failure and loss.

*****

The stakes feel different when you're watching your six-year-old step onto a competition mat for the first time. After just three months of jiu-jitsu training, my son's instructors had recognized his potential and encouraged him to compete. When he agreed, we embarked on a three-and-a-half hour journey to Stockton, California, where he would face his first real test in front of hundreds of spectators. This wasn't just any competition, it was what I'd call a "life competition," a moment where confidence, skill, and character would be tested far beyond the confines of his regular training environment.

From a six-year-old's perspective, the arena was gigantic. Twenty-two competition mats spread across the floor, with lower and upper decks for seating, and a jumbotron looming overhead. This overwhelming spectacle churned anxiety in all our stomachs. The event dwarfed any tae kwon do tournament I'd ever attended. Watching his wide eyes take in the massive venue, I knew he must be feeling the nerves, I certainly was. One thing was certain: this moment would leave an indelible mark on his memory.

The stage was set, emotions running high for both of us. After two hard-fought rounds, he got his butt kicked by submission twice, eliminating him from the tournament and any chance of getting a medal. His competitors were clearly more experienced, as the stripes on their belts suggested. Each loss intensified his emotions, and as he tried his hardest to hold back tears, he walked off that enormous stage defeated, crushed, and heartbroken. My heart ached watching him sit in silence with his head down. A failed attempt stings, but how you bounce back is what matters.

After a quiet ride back to our hotel, he asked me a question that cut straight to my core: "Dad, why does it hurt even though I'm not hurt?" This dug at my heartstrings and set my emotions on fire. This was my time to shine as a father, and I wouldn't let it slip away.

Looking into his eyes, I said, "My son, that is your heart that hurts. It hurts to lose. Losing is one of the hardest parts about life. Whether you're losing a jiu-jitsu match, a relationship, a good job, a business, or someone you loved dearly who has passed on, it will all hurt your heart. Some losses are worse than others. However, this teaches us so much more than winning ever could. You will grow from this."

He looked up at me doubtfully, but I continued. "You will learn resilience and become stronger in your heart from this. Losing teaches us to be better people. It humbles us. I'm proud of you for showing your bravery today. Proud of you for stepping out on that stage despite whatever fears you may have had. You took care of business, and now you'll be ready for the next fight with greater awareness and determination. Never forget I love you always, no matter what. Besides, I lost a lot in the beginning when I did tae kwon do, so you can be just like me."

An hour later, he snapped out of his slump and was having fun in the hotel pool and spa. I was still hurting for him, but he was clearly going to be fine. We can learn so much by watching how kids respond to losing and failure. It's remarkable how they don't stay down for long. They move on. They learn and grow. They live in the moment.

Watching him splash around and do cannonballs in the pool, I learned powerful lessons as a father. His resilience struck a chord in me and inspired me to be better, a better dad, husband, friend, and even a better failure and loser. As Vince Lombardi wisely said, "Losing doesn't define you, it's what you do after you lose that defines you."

TRANSFORMATION LESSON 6. THE ART OF FAILURE

So what did my son do after? He went straight back to jiu-jitsu class the following Monday, more determined than ever and hungry for redemption. Fast forward to today, my son is now the proud owner of numerous medals. His dedication has paid off, in his most recent tournament, he went undefeated. Those victories felt so much sweeter because of what he had to overcome to achieve them.

At a tournament in Santa Cruz, my son witnessed the pain and tears in one of his opponent's eyes as they stood on the podium. As they stepped down, the heartbroken boy walked toward his father, tears streaming down his face. In that moment, my son remembered his own experience with defeat. He stopped his competitor, put his arm around the boy's shoulder, and said, "You did so well in the second fight.

My son Gio, after his first competition, defeated, and also humbled. The lessons are deeper in failure and loss, which makes the eventual winning even better as he smiles on the podium, undefeated with a gold medal. *photos courtesy Ali Gilardi*

I thought you won because you were like a different fighter the second time we fought. It was super hard for me to defend myself. You should be proud of yourself." This interaction seemed to comfort the boy's father even more than the boy himself, sparking an encouraging father-son conversation about resilience.

When you lose, when you face adversity, you gain in other areas, but these gains don't come automatically. To realize them, you must commit to adopting the art of failure as an ingrained practice in your life. You must remain open to the growth that failure offers, or you might glean nothing from your high-value losses.

Fortunately, my son embraced growth from failure, as most kids naturally do. One of his greatest developments was empathy. Seeing the hurt in his competitor's eyes, the same hurt he had experienced on his own journey of losses, helped him develop a heightened sense of compassion. He connected with the boy's emotions and felt compelled to support and uplift him, even if he didn't know he was doing that at the time. His actions were truly honorable.

As Jocko Willink says, "You got beat, you got tapped out, GOOD!" A few hours of pain for a lifetime of knowledge, that's the gift of losing. It builds character, resilience, and heart. Losing and failure are life's ultimate teachers.

So, the next time you fail or lose, no matter how devastating it seems in the moment, remember this: losing isn't actually losing. If you keep an open mind, you're actually winning, despite what the score says. You're gaining invaluable knowledge, confidence, skill, and resilience. The ability to not just handle but profit from a loss gives you more chances

TRANSFORMATION LESSON 6. THE ART OF FAILURE

to succeed and overcome, as you become less concerned with outcomes and less anxious about failure, allowing yourself to make calm and steady progress.

Why do you think it's so rare for an NFL team to go completely undefeated, to win every single game in the season, plus the playoffs, then the Super Bowl? The reason is simple: You don't learn enough by winning all the damn time. You don't get humbled. You don't learn to adjust and pivot your game plan. And the worst part about constant winning is that you start to think your shit doesn't stink. When you and your team are walking around with oversized heads, the loss will eventually come, and maybe then you can snap back to reality. That's why the 1972 Miami Dolphins remain the only team ever to achieve a perfect season, it's an extraordinary feat precisely because failure is such a valuable teacher.

Brush It Off and Move Forward

I vividly recall sitting on my bed, my head aching, my body slumped over in misery. My entire life savings gone! Gone... Every last bit of it, just gone. There was no going back. No saying, "Hey! I want my money back, please?" Nope! It was just gone.

At one point, I so desperately wanted my supplements project to work out that I bet big. How big? To the tune of everything in my savings. A lot of the money we made selling the swimming pool company had just vanished. I never thought that I would be one of those guys who throws away their life savings into a business, only to lose it all. I thought that if I found a way to get the sales flowing, I could just duplicate that method and continue to grow my sales. I was basically the next Jeff Bezos in my head, minus the actual success, business sense, or backup plan. Wrong! I paid the ultimate price for my ignorance. I should have sought experience first, a safe set of hands to guide me through the growth process. Lesson gained. The painful loss provided me with the knowledge to progress forward, and it will do the same for you, if you listen.

I went into that new supplement business blind as a bat. It was an area in which I had zero knowledge. I refused to ask questions about how hard it was going to be and just assumed I'd start getting sales and I'd just woo all my customers with my impeccable charm. Wrong again. I lost all of that money and eventually squandered the rest of our reserves.

It was also at this point that I was diagnosed with cancer. Talk about the universe kicking you while you're down. Business failure and now a health failure, a double whammy that made me question everything. Boo hoo, poor me, right? But did I really want to give up on everything? My dreams, my life, my family? Never! I was NOT done. I will never be done. Done is the victim who throws in the towel and goes back to the easy thing. That just ain't me.

Did it suck losing my life savings? I'm sure you know what my answer is, so I'm not even going to bother writing it. Lesson learned. Getting busted in the drug trade business was another failure that taught me a lot, a different kind of life school that came with its own painful tuition. The suffering from these failures strengthened me, making me more resilient to face a life that would inevitably, unavoidably, produce more failures down the road.

TRANSFORMATION LESSON 6. THE ART OF FAILURE

Over time, I've stacked so many failures in all areas of my life that I've become partially immune to their sting. This resilience has allowed me to keep moving forward in a positive way, knowing it will all come together if I just bounce back with the right mentality.

The point of this chapter, and my real message to you, is this: failure is the way forward. I had to spend my life's savings to learn that my supplements business wasn't viable. I felt bitter about the loss, but as time passed, I came to realize I had received a priceless education that isn't offered in any school. The lessons I learned from every aspect of that adventure would carry over to every future business venture I undertook.

Thousands of dollars worth of the supplement I crafted, tossed into the garbage dumps because of the expiration date. Failure hurts, but I learned a lot.

Getting an incurable blood cancer diagnosis sucked beyond words, but it kickstarted my path toward a much healthier way of living, not just for me, but for my entire family. My daily actions and habits now set them up for success in ways they never would have experienced otherwise. I'm always looking for the good in such a calamity, and this is definitely one. My kids are going to watch me bust ass for what I believe in right up to the very end.

If I had never made such a dramatic change in my life, my kids would have seen me mentally bullying myself, eating lots of candy, ice cream, and energy drinks, rarely working out, and watching way too much mindless television. I would have led my kids right into the same trap I fell into. Sure, I was still striving for my goals back then, and I had many ambitions, but I was nowhere near as focused and disciplined as I am today. Every minute of every day, everything matters, and it all compounds, positively or negatively.

We have all failed in our lives and we will have many more failures along the way. Most of us go through life trying our best not to fail at things, because wanting to succeed is natural. But if we take failure avoidance too far, it only means we're not trying anything new or hard. Without failure, there is no growth. And if you haven't lost in any way during your time here on Earth, you better begin to do things that just might lead to a nice big fuck-up so you can start to learn the art of failure.

As adults, it's easy to get stuck in ruts and calcified in our behaviors. We avoid hard things and new things because we're scared of failure. But think back to when you were a kid. Did you avoid everything because you were scared to fail at it? As an infant, did you keep trying to learn to walk or did you give up? Now, as an adult, you still crawl all over the place, right? No!

What about riding a bike? Didn't you keep trying to learn how to ride a bike, even though a fall could be painful? Broken arms and road rash are not fun. And of course, anyone

TRANSFORMATION LESSON 6. THE ART OF FAILURE

who's learned to swim had to get over the initial fear of drowning. When we were kids, it seemed like nothing could stop us. The art of failure came naturally to us. We were going to fail, fail, fail until we succeeded or drowned. And we grew tremendously from our failures. There was simply no other way.

Eventually, as we started to grow up, schools told us failure is bad. Our parents said failure is bad. We began to avoid it at all costs. "Play it safe," they said. But here's the truth, safe isn't working a job, only to get laid off because the business is failing. Safety is a facade we chase. Learning to fail as an adult is harder. We have more responsibilities, kids, school, bills, and our jobs. We feel more restricted because we can't risk our livelihood since other people depend on us. I get that. I'm not going to put my kids at risk. I need to pay my bills.

You know what we can do, though? Risk failure on the side in ways that won't jeopardize your family. I call this "side failure", the act of doing something you may be interested in, like a side business or a new hobby, and being willing to accept the risk of not succeeding. When I started writing this book, it was a "side failure" project. If it flopped, my family would still eat. If it succeeded, bonus. This approach is a great way to get better at the art of failure without substantial risk.

Maybe you start a class doing martial arts or learn how to grow a garden. And guess what? You're going to fail, especially in the beginning. You'll get kicked in the face and your crop will die. But through these smaller failures, you're going to find out if this project is actually worth your time and passion. If you find that this side failure isn't working out or just isn't worth your time, stop and find something else on the side and start failing in that. If you find that you are enjoying this project despite the failures and setbacks, well then, like John C. Maxwell says, "Fail early, fail often, but always fail forward."

I love Maxwell's quote because it so succinctly expresses what this chapter is all about. The art of failure comes down to this single, simple thing: When you fail, make sure you are still progressing forward. As long as you keep going and don't stop, you will move forward, and suddenly you won't be failing anymore. You'll be growing as a person. If every day you keep watering the ground the seeds of failure are planted in, who knows what will blossom?

Transformation Action Steps

Many of you picked this book up because you have dealt with adversity before, so failure and loss are not new concepts but familiar companions on your life journey. You've been knocked down, perhaps multiple times, and you're still here. That resilience is your superpower. The lessons below are about leveraging your past experiences to fuel your future growth.

Identify and Learn: When I look back at my life and take stock of all my past wins versus my failures, the tally racks up much faster on the latter side of things. But that is actually a good thing, because those failures have formed a wealth of knowledge I now get to pull from. What I want you to do is get your journal out and begin identifying and listing all your past losses and failures, small and large. Please don't become discouraged by this exercise, and take your time with it. Just think of it as a vast reservoir of hard-won experiences you can tap into.

TRANSFORMATION LESSON 6. THE ART OF FAILURE

After you have identified your past blunders, begin to write down the things you have learned from them. Think deeply on this and take your time with it. Really examine what happened and why. Are there any recurring themes or patterns to your failures? One of my recurring patterns early on in business was not seeking proper guidance from those who had already been there. I always had a "I can do it myself" attitude, which while commendable in some ways, ultimately set me up for failure. You can find patterns in just about any failures you've had, be they in the areas of health, work, or relationships. Try to identify at least one or two lessons for each item on your list

Lean into Growth: Now that you learned something from your failures, you need to apply and use these lessons going forward. Relationships are hard, and I've dealt with a wide range of different interpersonal disasters and picked up a lot of lessons while I was at it. One of those lessons was communication. I had to become a better communicator. After being able to identify this problem area, and my pattern of poor communication, I educated myself on better communication skills and I became hyperaware of how and what I said and how I listened, because you can't be a good communicator if you cannot listen. I've made huge strides in communication, not only within my marriage but in all my relationships.

And so what failures do you need to work on to improve your outcomes? You lost your job? What skill can you build to ensure this does not happen again? How can you increase your value or your worth as a person for your next career?

Moving Forward: Now that you have learned to see your past failures as opportunities for growth, you will begin to

THE BREAKING POINT

make huge strides in life. Being diagnosed with cancer was a huge smack in the face for me. However, I'm choosing to use it to my advantage, when possible. I'm always asking myself, "How can I get stronger and healthier, despite this hefty health failure." After every setback or mistake, I always assess what went wrong and why it happened. I then adjust, learn, and grow. For instance, if my blood work is off in a certain area, whether it be a low white blood cell count or my glucose being too high, I begin to analyze all the factors that may have led to this failure. What did I eat? How was I feeling in the days and hours leading up to the blood work? I will identify what went wrong and then adjust my wellness regimen from there. We must use all failures as our guiding lights to move us forward in the direction we'd like to go.

> "If you want it badly enough, you will do whatever it takes to fucking get it, despite the inevitable pain, struggles, and failures you will encounter on the way."

And so, approach each day and each setback with a growth mindset. Get good at the art of failure by transforming your losses into wins! I think the law of success is simple: If you want it badly enough, you will do whatever it takes to fucking get it, despite the inevitable pain, struggles, and failures you will encounter on the way. When you run into a point that tries to break you, ask yourself, "What can I learn here?"

20

Transformation Lesson 7. Fight Your Way Out of the Gloom

"There is hope, even when your brain is telling you there isn't."
—John Green

I've spent years wrestling with depression's demons, battles I never thought at the time I could win. This is an area where I'm not only very passionate but where I've unfortunately gained a lot of hard-fought expertise. Through these struggles, I've developed valuable lessons and tools that I'd like to share with you.

In the journey of life, we all encounter moments that test our resilience and challenge our spirit. Adversity has the ability to break you faster than you can blink in a sandstorm. Whether it's a physical setback, an emotional blow, or an unexpected twist of fate, these trials can plunge us into the depths of despair and creep up on us like a goblin in the darkness of a bitter night. This chapter explores the raw reality of facing such challenges and provides a road map for fighting your way out of the gloom that threatens to swallow you up.

And so, drawing from personal experiences and battles with depression, we'll touch on a series of tools I've personally used, both in the past and present, to overcome misery and life's setbacks. You will learn how to accept what is outside your control and how finding meaning in life is all you need to move forward and beyond. You'll see that while life's hardships are inevitable, succumbing to them is not. Prepare to arm yourself with tools to not just weather the storm but to emerge stronger on the other side.

*****

The rain was softly tapping on my head as I stood in the darkness, glaring through the hospital's emergency room windows. With each passing minute, I became more and more soaked, frozen in place like some creepy stalker waiting to commit an unlawful act. But I wasn't stalking anyone; the only person I was hurting was myself. I was teetering on the edge between life and death, torn between walking through those sliding doors to get the help I desperately needed, or making a run for it to drown my sorrows in some cheap bottle of booze. My heart ached as my mind bounced back and forth: "It's not going to be okay, just go inside and get the damn help you need" versus "Screw this life. Let's go get wasted and find the courage to end it all."

Dread and despair had wrapped around me like a boa constrictor from the darkest depths of some South American jungle. There was no escape as the tension got tighter and tighter, squeezing out what little hope I had left. I'd lost everything that once defined my life, my home in Antioch, my

TRANSFORMATION LESSON 7. FIGHT YOUR WAY OUT OF THE GLOOM

boat, my motorcycles, money, all the toys that made life feel worth living. Now I was barely scraping together rent money, living in a shitty dark apartment, missing my dog Blue, and drowning in the aftermath of a breakup. The pressure kept building as the boa squeezed tighter. I began to cry, or maybe it was just the rain now streaming down my face. Who the hell could tell anymore?

I began to walk slowly away from the emergency room. Making my way around the tall building, I searched for some kind of clarity in this mess I had created in my mind. Each step felt purposeful, even if that purpose was just a distraction. I came to a fence with a sign: "No Trespassing. Violators Will Be Prosecuted." I hopped over without a second thought. Maybe there was a way around, but I didn't give a shit. It was probably just some delivery yard anyway. Plus, breaking the law felt good for a moment, a small act of defiance that pulled me out of my head and focused me on the now. One foot in front of the other, I made my way around that whole damn hospital, eventually ending up right back where I started, wallowing in my pathetic misery.

Standing there again, staring into the lit-up emergency room, I tried to summon back that pure misery from before. But something had shifted. I knew what I had to do. I turned and walked back to my truck, a soggy mess of a broken man, cranked the key, and drove in silence straight to my shitty-ass dark apartment. Somehow, those dark thoughts of wanting to remove my soul from this planet had loosened their grip, at least temporarily. I stripped down and crawled into bed, where sleep quickly became my sanctuary. Safe, at least from my mind and its relentless thoughts. *Maybe I just won't wake up.*

THE BREAKING POINT

The gloom sneaks up on you bit by bit. It weaves its way around your fragile mind like a parasitic worm, corrupting every good thought you've got. Pushing it away becomes damn near impossible, and the deeper that parasite burrows, the harder it gets to shake those dark thoughts. As we slip deeper into that pit, it becomes critical that we act fast, get inside that brain of ours with a pair of tweezers, and start picking out bits of that nasty disease that's made itself at home. At the time, for me, that pair of tweezers was the walk I took around the hospital, the small thrill of breaking the law that felt invigorating and hijacked my mind from its death spiral. My heart was beating, and my blood was moving just a little bit warmer through my veins. It felt good to focus on something real, something immediate, pulling me away from my misery and out of my wretched mind.

This was just months before my real nightmare I shared with you in the first part of this book. Looking back, maybe walking into that hospital would have been the better choice, but it probably would have just been another Band-Aid, a temporary fix for a corrupted state of mind. What could they have really done to clean up the mess inside me? I'm the type who has to learn through trial by fire, through getting burned so badly I never want to touch the flame again. Eventually, I'd learn the valuable lessons that would keep me standing through life's twists and turns, and of course horrible situations like my cancer diagnosis. But first, I had to go deeper into that darkness before I could learn to climb back up. Those pitch-black nights taught me something crucial: survival isn't about avoiding the hits, it's about learning how to take them and get back up swinging.

TRANSFORMATION LESSON 7. FIGHT YOUR WAY OUT OF THE GLOOM

Years later, as I've stumbled through life's inevitable setbacks, both small and large, I've become better at handling the situations that try to take me down as swiftly as a black belt in jiu-jitsu. This doesn't mean I don't experience the emotions that come with each challenge. I still feel the pain, wrestle with the questions, and work through the solutions. We're human, after all, and these emotions need to be felt. We are not robots and bottling them up, waiting for the day we get shook only to eventually explode, can be disastrous, a hard lesson I learned many moons ago.

It's from our darkest times that we gain the knowledge and strength to face today's nightmares. And we are always being tested. These lessons would be put to the test sooner than I expected.

One day, not long after I'd begun to feel like I was regaining control of my life, I was walking through our walnut orchard after a run, headed for my house. I was feeling good. My heart rate was up, my mind was clear, and my shoulder, still on the mend from a brutal surgery and months of grueling rehab, was finally giving me some relief. I was on the road to recovery and nothing could derail me! Yeah, right . . . My phone buzzed, and as my eyes hit the screen, my heart skipped a beat. Notification from my doctor's office. *Yay! My favorite thing.* Not! My monthly blood work came in and it wasn't good news. The red text took up most of the page as I quickly scrolled. Red text equals bad news. My heart rate skyrocketed. That bastard cancer was on the rise. Apparently it didn't get the memo that it wasn't invited back to the party. There was a faint trace in my blood work. This was the first sign of it in two years. This meant I was coming out of remission. In that moment, all the strength I had built was like dust in the damn wind again!

That same day I got the update on my phone about my blood work, my family and I were leaving to head up to Dunsmuir Railroad Park Resort in Northern California with our travel trailer. My brother was celebrating his fortieth birthday, so we were going into the great outdoors for some family fun. Getting outdoors is pure medicine. Being amongst the trees and nature will help you in a silent and beautiful way. I'm blessed to be so close to such beauty in Northern California.

The kids were already in the truck, everything was packed, and the trailer was hitched and ready to roll behind us. But at that very moment, I didn't want to go. I sat in my room slumped on the side of the bed, chin to chest, crushed and heartbroken. My wife entered and was confused about what the heck I was doing. She sat down beside me and asked, "What's wrong? What are you doing? We are all ready to go."

> "Dwelling on the negative is a pivotal state of mind we must become hyperaware of or we risk falling in defeat.

I paused long enough so I could try to get the news out without bursting into tears. "It's coming back." The pause wasn't long enough. I sat and cried with my wife for a few minutes as she said some encouraging things. Having an optimistic life partner in your corner helps beyond measure. But I still had to feel the pain before I could move forward and onward!

And so, I drove up in silence the whole way, thinking about why I got such a bad hand in life. Dwelling on the negative is a pivotal state of mind we must become hyperaware of or we risk falling in defeat. I knew that once we got to our destination, I'd have one of two options: hide out in the trailer for the weekend, staying in a down state of self-pity, or suck it up and have fun with my family. I chose the latter. I chose to make memories with my family. At first, it was hard, but soon things turned around and the pain I felt inside began to subside. I began to enjoy myself and just take in the beautiful place we were at. I was beginning to win the war inside. Remember, like my walk in the rain many years ago: It's in the sidetracking of the mind that we can buy the time to push past the negative state we are in. A critical moment.

My daughter Olivia and I. With love and moments like these, life's sufferings seem to fade away. *photo courtesy Ali Gilardi*

One morning on the trip, I woke up early and rode my bike up a trail through thick pine and redwoods that eventually took me right alongside Castle Crags, which is a granite rock formation that takes on the look of an old mystic castle. The ride got my heart rate up and some sweat flowing. I reached an opening that seemed like a great spot to take a break for a moment, and as I sat there and looked at this impressive granite formation, I felt a deep feeling of strength inside me. I am not sure if it was the burst of energy I felt from the workout or just the raw beauty of what I was seeing. What I do know is that it was an extraordinarily powerful sight, and I took it all in, breath by breath. I found my peace on that mountainside.

That morning at Castle Crags taught me something profound. When life hits you with a flurry of punches and you feel like throwing in the towel, you have two choices. You can let the darkness win, or you can fight your way back to the

Exercise in wild places remains my most trusted remedy for depression and tough days. It's where I find both my strength and my peace.

light. I've done both in my life, and I can tell you which path leads to freedom.

In my darker days, I was the guy who hung out in cemeteries, talking to headstones, thinking death must be easier than living. "It must be so easy to be dead. You guys don't have to worry about shit," I'd say. The weakness would ooze out of me. I was actively digging my own grave, both figuratively and literally. Wherever you focus your energy and thoughts, that's where you end up. Remember: Stick to the same depressing-ass narrative, and you'll remain in the same depressing-ass life. So simple, so true!

Life has a way of teaching you, if you're willing to learn. Through all my setbacks, I've learned that acceptance isn't weakness, it's the first step toward strength. While you can't always control getting cancer, you *can* control how you respond to it. You can't always prevent life from knocking you down, but you *can* choose whether to stay down.

That day in the mountains, sweating from my bike ride, staring at those ancient granite formations, I understood something essential: Pain is inevitable but suffering is optional. I had finally figured it all out. I had built a life worth living, my wife and two beautiful children brought me joy and the fuel I needed to keep putting one foot in front of the other no matter what I was going through. Simple things like the power of exercise and appreciating each sunrise were tremendous for me. I had meaning and purpose; I found that being grateful for each day, grateful to be alive, was the perspective I was missing when my cards were bad.

Think about the people who are watching you, because when you stand and face your struggles head-on and show them what resilience is, you are inspiring them in the most profound way one can. You are providing hope for anyone who may be facing any of life's battles and cruel twists.

"Take risks. Fail. Pick yourself back up again. And always, always remember this: there is no adversity capable of stopping you once the choice to persevere is made."—Jason Kilar

My days are numbered. Your days are numbered. We don't know when our number will be called, but we do get to choose how we spend the time we have. Will you spend it in the darkness of depression, consuming and acting in ways that only strengthen it, or will you fight your way back to the light? Will you let adversity define you, or will you use it to become stronger?

Transformation Action Steps

Yes, bad things happen that can bring us to our breaking points. The key is to put the pieces back together as quickly and efficiently as possible before the cracks deepen and harden. For when they do, it takes much more effort to repair what's been broken and find our way to wholeness again.

Acceptance: Some things in life we can control and others not so much. Marcus Aurelius advised long ago, "Some things are up to us, and some things are not up to us." Getting cancer may not have been up to me, but learning to accept it was. Squandering years of my life on meaningless poor actions could easily be something I allowed to get me down. However, I choose to accept these things.

TRANSFORMATION LESSON 7. FIGHT YOUR WAY OUT OF THE GLOOM

Freeing yourself from a negative mindset begins with accepting what you cannot control and making peace with past events. Resisting unchangeable circumstances often deepens depression, so it's essential to acknowledge your current state without judgment rather than fighting or denying it. This acceptance becomes your foundation for positive change. The next step is transforming your internal narrative. Instead of saying "I suffer from depression," reframe it as "Each day I become happier as I find more joy and meaning in my life." As you shift your perspective, you'll notice changes beginning to unfold. This mental transformation will free you from the burden of worrying about things beyond your control, leaving you with more energy for constructive actions.

Restart with Meaning: During my own struggle with severe depression, I found myself alone, a lot. I didn't want to be around anyone. I didn't have a family yet. In that solitude, I discovered an unexpected source of meaning: my swimming pool business. Although I didn't recognize it immediately, that venture became my lifeline. By pouring all my energy into building that business, I found a sense of purpose that focused my mind in productive directions and pulled me out of depression's grasp. The work energized me, providing a profound sense of satisfaction that naturally led to increased happiness.

A crucial point: having something you're passionate about is essential in warding off depression or climbing out of a low period. For some, this passion may align with their career. If you find yourself in a job you dislike, it might be wise to consider an exit strategy, as job dissatisfaction can negatively impact other areas of life. However, not everyone needs to find meaning in their primary occupation. Many people can find purpose outside their careers, whether through hobbies, artistic pursuits, or other creative endeavors. The key is to identify what brings you joy and gives you a sense of purpose. When you're feeling down, engaging in these meaningful activities can be a powerful antidote to negative emotions. Whether it's your work, a side project, or a personal passion, having something that drives you forward can be the difference between succumbing to misery or rising above it.

Remember, meaning doesn't have to be grandiose. It can be found in small, everyday pursuits that bring you satisfaction and a sense of accomplishment. The important thing is to recognize what gives your life purpose and to actively engage with it, especially during challenging times.

Exercise: Early in my life, when I got in a slump and I felt the demon approaching, I'd just freeze, hole up in my house, and wallow in self-pity. I would let it consume me until it fully took hold. That was until I became so fed up with this habit that I could no longer bear residing there anymore. I've always been into exercising, but I'd stop when life wasn't going my way. I eventually concluded this was precisely the wrong thing to do.

We must force ourselves to exercise when the cards are not in our favor, as it is one of your best tricks to crack depression. And it's something you can start right now. A high-intensity workout has the remarkable power to bring you back. When life is beating you down with suffering and negativity, I promise if you get that heart rate up, the sweat flowing, and the breath going, you will begin to feel better.

TRANSFORMATION LESSON 7. FIGHT YOUR WAY OUT OF THE GLOOM

You don't like to work out? Too bad, it's time to begin, so just do something, anything. Start with a five-minute walk if that's all you can manage, then build from there. The important thing is movement, not perfection. The exercise will increase your dopamine levels and your confidence will skyrocket. Even on your worst days, drag your ass outside for ten minutes. When you exercise your body, you can't help but feel extraordinary and be well on your way to saying goodbye to depression. Consistency beats intensity, a daily walk trumps a once-a-month marathon pity party. Get moving, keep moving, and watch your mind begin to follow.

Social Connections: And I don't mean social media connections. I'm talking about real, genuine, human-to-human connections. These vital links to other people were, like exercise, another thing I'd shut down, deliberately isolating myself. I used to think that being alone was the only way through it. That's bad medicine.

Whether you think so or not, we are inherently social creatures, and having positive interactions with loved ones or good friends will boost your mood, keep you distracted from the BS you are trying to avoid, and give you a sense of belonging. Few people truly thrive in complete isolation, so get out there and call an old friend. Create memories with those you love. I know for me that when I'm having a bad day, my children can put a smile on my face faster than a spark ignites a wildfire on a dry summers day. Who can you look to when you need a little pick me up?

Reverse Gratitude: Finding gold in the shit you're not supposed to thank. Everyone tells you to be grateful for sunsets and lattes and your kids' laughter. And you should be. Those things matter. Being grateful for the good in your life keeps you grounded and reminds you what you're working for. But there's another level of gratitude that most people never touch, and it's the kind that actually transforms you. It comes from finding reasons to be grateful for the things that tried to destroy you. I'm grateful for my cancer diagnosis. Not in some toxic positivity "everything happens for a reason" bullshit way. I'm grateful because it taught me lessons I could never have learned anywhere else. It forced me to confront my mortality in a way that made me stop wasting time on things that don't matter. It showed me what I'm actually made of. It gave me a depth of perspective that no amount of comfort or success ever could have. That's reverse gratitude. It's being thankful for the very things you're "supposed" to curse, the betrayals, the failures, the diagnoses, the losses. The experiences that society tells you to be bitter about.

Here's how you practice it: Instead of your typical gratitude journal where you list your blessings, create a reverse gratitude list. Write down the hardest, most painful experiences you've been through. Then ask yourself: What did this give me that nothing else could? Not "what was the silver lining?" That's too passive. But what did you gain from it that makes you, in some twisted way, glad it happened? Maybe the divorce that shattered you also freed you from becoming someone you'd hate. Maybe the business failure taught you resilience that success never would have. Maybe the parent who abandoned you made you determined to be present for your kids in a way you wouldn't have understood otherwise. This isn't about pretending the pain didn't hurt. It's about refusing to let that pain be wasted. It's about extracting value from experiences that tried to break you.

Be grateful for the good, it keeps you human and reminds you what matters. But don't stop there. The things you're "supposed" to be grateful for will keep you grounded. The things you're not supposed to be grateful for will make you who you need to become. So start reverse engineering your gratitude. Find reasons to be thankful for the shit that shaped you. Because if you can be grateful for your worst moments, nothing can keep you down.

Get Outdoors: Find a peaceful place amongst the trees or beside the ocean. Much like when I sat in awe at the sight of Castle Crags, when your eyes see a thing of beauty in nature you can't help but get a shot of stimulating dopamine that will course through your veins and provide a deep sense of satisfaction. The world is full of beautiful things to see. Breathe in the fresh air, close your eyes, and be at peace for some time. Meditate in the solitude. Connecting with the natural world in this way seems to put things in perspective.

Take a Walk in Someone Else's Shoes: Next time you're feeling down, try this: Take off your own metaphorical shoes and look around. Really try to see and feel the struggles others face: the person battling a terminal illness, the single parent working two jobs, the elderly neighbor living alone. There's always someone who has it harder, and when we open our eyes to their reality, our own burdens often feel lighter.

I learned this firsthand at the gym when I met a man in the early stages of ALS. Instead of staying wrapped in my own troubles, I connected. I listened to his story, recommended an inspiring book, and suggested a meaningful show he could watch. The smile that lit up his face, even if temporary, lifted both our spirits. My own problems obviously didn't vanish, but they suddenly felt more manageable.

This isn't about minimizing your struggles; it's about discovering your own strength by witnessing how others face their battles with grace. When you help shoulder someone else's burden, your own load becomes easier to bear.

With chemo, scans, biopsies, and endless lab work ahead, I know the road won't be easy. But when I look at my family, my reason for everything, I can't help but smile. *photo courtesy Dawn Michaela*

21

Transformation Lesson 8. Treat Your Mind Like a Sanctuary

"No problem can withstand the assault of sustained thinking."
—*Voltaire*

Adversity isn't just something that life throws at us. Sometimes, we're the ones creating it through the movies we play out in our head. We become so good at visualizing failure that we forget we have the power to visualize success instead. And that's where everything changes. Imagine if you could harness that same vivid imagination and use it to see yourself succeeding instead of failing. In detail, picture yourself nailing that challenge, crossing that finish line, or achieving that goal you've been dreaming about. Visualization is not just positive thinking; it's a powerful tool that you can use to reshape your reality, much like I have.

I spent decades of my life constantly visualizing disasters. It was just part of the negative conditioning I grew up knowing. Back in the day, rolling down the street with a few pounds of weed, I'd always envision that cop getting behind me and pulling me over. I'd literally play the scene out in my head right down to when they'd put the cold steel cuffs on my wrist. Sure enough, they'd always be close by and lurking. Maybe it's why I was always getting busted, I manifested that shit.

On the brighter side, I did eventually stumble into the positive aspect of visualization. I recall vividly visualizing the success of my swimming pool company. I envisioned trucks and employees and, sure enough, soon I had trucks and employees. At the time, I had no real idea what I was doing with this technique, and I certainly didn't appreciate its power. It wasn't until later in life that I put it all together. I bet you could recall having similar experiences if you looked back on your life. What are the things you visualized positively? How about negatively? What were the outcomes?

In this chapter, we're going to look at some of my stories that help illustrate why I feel visualization is a powerful tool for success and for overcoming your obstacles. You'll learn how to create visions of yourself not only overcoming adversity but envisioning your ultimate success. The visions, these movies, will be so compelling that your brain will start to believe them to be real, and then it will make them happen.

Visualization has been used for ages and is a practical skill used by top athletes, successful entrepreneurs, and all manner of people who wish to overcome their biggest fears. People have even been able to heal themselves through visualization techniques. It's about programming your brain for success, one mental image at a time. Trust me, once you master the

TRANSFORMATION LESSON 8. TREAT YOUR MIND LIKE A SANCTUARY

art of visualization, you'll wonder why you ever wasted time imagining anything else but your amazing potential.

*****

There I was, dressed in brand new jeans and a nice light-blue, pressed, button-down shirt with a fresh haircut. I was looking good on the outside, no doubt. However, what's going on outside doesn't always tell you what's on the inside. Inside my head, in this case. The day had finally arrived and I was entering my first ever Toastmasters speech contest. A little over a year ago, I had been terrified to speak in front of people, and now I was actually entering a speech contest. What a difference a year makes when you put in the effort to get where you want to go.

As I entered the room, I was initially delighted to see the turnout wasn't as big as I had imagined. I think mostly because of COVID, people were still having a hard time getting out and on with their lives. This meant that a lot of the speakers were viewing, and also competing in, the event through Zoom virtual meetings. I didn't like this at all. The competitors on Zoom could literally read their speeches from a script if they wanted to, which makes it easy to not make mistakes and sound perfectly polished. Me, I'm old school. Even though most of the competitors were older than me, I wanted to experience this in-person, on the stage in front of the crowd, do or die.

The day seemed to drag on as this was one of the district's first contests using Zoom video meetings, so there were a few setbacks and technical difficulties that put a huge damper on the day. Despite the technical hitches, sitting in the room watching the competitors on stage and absorbing their speeches made for a good first-time learning experience. Everyone who spoke was so confident and made no mistakes. No major blunders today. Then it was my turn to take the stage.

As they called my name, I rose from my seat in the back. The audience began to clap, and I strolled on up to the stage with the confidence and charisma of a guy who has been doing this for some time. I got up there and shook the announcer's hand and turned to face the audience. Suddenly, I realized I wasn't afraid to be there. I wasn't afraid to speak in front of these people. I was over that part of the fear of speaking. And so, I began.

Everything went well at first, but right at the end of my opening, just when I was about to begin the story and tie things together, I went blank. It was like a fog had drifted over my head and I could no longer think, let alone speak. Five . . . ten . . . seconds went by. Silence. *Okay, no problem, I can still recover.* Twenty seconds. I still couldn't think. My armpits were draining like a faucet and my eyes were burning and beginning to get blurry. Still nothing was coming to me. My mind was drawing blanks.

I looked out over the crowd and saw blank stares looking back at me. They felt my pain. I stared down at the ground, hoping for something to come to mind, anything to get me on track. I'm well past thirty seconds without speaking at this point. I looked to the sky, or the ceiling in this case, nothing. I looked at the camera and saw myself on the screen, a lost and confused look upon my face. I couldn't believe this was happening. I had *prepared* for this speech. Still nothing. I just wanted to scream out the words that I knew were inside my

TRANSFORMATION LESSON 8. TREAT YOUR MIND LIKE A SANCTUARY

head but were avoiding me, like how I evaded the police those years ago on my motorcycle. It was agonizing. Then it happened, and I spoke. "I can't do this." And I walked off the stage and out of the room, crushed and extremely embarrassed. I went outside and cursed myself. I failed, I quit. "*What happened?*" I asked myself, over and over.

Here's part of the answer. During the weeks I spent preparing and polishing my speech, I began telling myself that I hope I don't freeze up and forget what I'm going to say. I painted a picture of this in my head that I could clearly see. That picture was of me, standing stunned on stage, with no words coming to my mind and unable to go on. I had spent more time thinking about this failure scenario than I had thought about doing a great job and completing my speech. Instead of visualizing a positive outcome of successfully completing my speech, I continually visualized failure.

I truly believe I manifested what happened to me that day. I had given that speech a few times at my local club and had gone over it by myself hundreds of times. Everything I visualized would happen, happened. I envisioned failure, and so it was. Our thoughts and what we tell ourselves, including what others tell us about ourselves, are extremely important.

When I was in middle school and high school, I was told I had a learning disability and that I wasn't very smart. When we are young, we tend to believe what older people of authority tell us. I allowed this nonsense to enter my mind and I believed it. I became what they told me I was. And so I saw myself as a dumb-dumb. Young kids are told negative things like this every day. They are given no chance, taken out of the game too early by what others placed inside their heads. Set up for failure or mediocrity. I'll never let my kids face this fate, nobody should, and neither should you. I'd like to think this book has the power to help you overcome what you think you are. John C. Maxwell said in his book, *The 16 Undeniable Laws of Communication*, "We can become only what we see ourselves becoming."

If you play that movie over in your head about something you want long enough, you eventually start making moves that make your thoughts come to fruition. When I was first starting my swimming pool company, I used to envision being so busy with work that I would have no time for anything else. I was seeing a therapist at the time and I remember her telling me, "Be careful of what you see yourself becoming." I shrugged it off and went about my business. Like a movie, I would just keep playing it over and over in my head while simultaneously backing it with affirmations: "I want more work. I need more work. I want my business to be highly successful." I was envisioning what I wanted over and over every single day. You begin to take actions toward what you vision in your mind, and before you know it, you have arrived at the destination you visualized wanting so badly. True to my vision, I quickly became so busy that I didn't have time for much else.

> "You're the programmer. Every time you vividly imagine yourself succeeding, you're writing a new line of code for your future."

This led to questions about my personal life. I started envisioning a family and shifting my mental movie. What was it that I really wanted from this life? It didn't take me too long to

TRANSFORMATION LESSON 8. TREAT YOUR MIND LIKE A SANCTUARY

figure it out. A wife and kids. Lo and behold, a few years later, I had a beautiful bride and two beautiful children.

Unfortunately, once I found happiness, my negativity, which had been shoved to the back of my mind during those wonderful years of growth, kicked in again and I began to have visions of getting sick and dying early. I would tell myself things like, "Watch, I'm going to get cancer." I could practically see myself getting treated for this, and the visions only escalated when I had kids. I began selfishly worrying all the time about these negative thoughts. My mind became the Netflix of disaster scenarios, constantly streaming new episodes of "Ways Jono Might Die Tragically." I remember coming home one night with a friend. We had just done some hard partying celebrating his birthday, and I was wasted. So wasted that I was barfing in the toilet. As I hugged the toilet bowl, I was telling my wife in a drunken stupor for no reason at all that it was cancer causing this. (It couldn't have been the twenty shots of tequila.)

That was how bad I was with the movies that played in my head, and, sure enough, here I am, fighting for my life against cancer, my nightmare came true. Were the visions in my head the primary cause of my diagnosis? I'm super spiritual, but I don't believe my cancer was caused solely by negative thinking. It comes down to many poor lifestyle habits over time.

Now, I spend significant time rewiring and refocusing my brain to create only positive thoughts and visions. I deliberately play optimistic movies in my head, filling my mind with images of being healthy, strong, and powerful. Remember, I am living to the ripe old age of one hundred and twenty! After forty-one years of negative thinking and absorbing harmful messages, removing every negative thought from my pre-wired mind is no easy task. It will take the rest of my life to completely rewire, but I've already made huge strides by shifting my mindset. And it truly all starts with visualizing where you want to go.

Your mind is the most powerful tool you've got. It's like a supercomputer that's been programmed to create the life you want. And guess what? You're the programmer. Every time you close your eyes and vividly imagine yourself succeeding, you're writing a new line of code for your future. You're not just daydreaming, you're actively designing your success. Whether it's nailing that presentation, running that marathon, or conquering that fear that's been holding you back, your visualizations are laying the groundwork for success.

Visualization is not just some magic trick, and what you envision the night before is not going to make tomorrow's adversity you are about to face suddenly become a walk in the park. It's not just a one-and-done type of thing, you must work at it. Some days as you visualize it will be like seeing a movie in 4k resolution, clear as day. Other days it may seem like you are back in the seventies trying to find the sweet spot on the old rabbit ear antenna just to get a half-ass decent picture. If you truly want to shatter your adversities and carve out your path to success, you've got to do more than just dream. You need to visualize your victories, and then put in the sweat equity to make it as real as the movie you are playing in your head. So when it gets hard, keep at it. The more you practice, the sharper your mental picturing will get, which in turn will have a more powerful impact on your real life.

TRANSFORMATION LESSON 8. TREAT YOUR MIND LIKE A SANCTUARY

Remember, every great achievement in history started as a vision in someone's mind. The smartphone in your pocket, the car in your driveway, and the freedoms we enjoy, all began as someone's visualization before they became reality. And make no mistake, each of these visions faced a gauntlet of adversities, doubt, failure, and seemingly impossible obstacles. Think of the Wright brothers and the adversity they faced. Nobody thought they could fly. They were crazy, insane even. But the power of that initial visualization, that unwavering mental picture of success, gave them the strength to push through and turn their dreams into our everyday realities.

So, what's your vision? What future are you creating in your mind right now? Whatever it is, see it, feel it, believe it. Then go out there and make it happen. Your mind is the launchpad, but your actions are the rocket fuel.

Redemption

"I am a calm, poised, relaxed public speaker. When I speak in front of others I am confident, courageous, and brave. And so it is." I speak this to myself in the mirror of a public bathroom. I take a deep breath, hold it in, and breathe out. I walk out and stride down the short corridor into a room full of humans sitting in chairs, silently staring forward. I take my seat. Not one minute later I hear my name called. "Jono Gilardi!" I stand. Again I walk to the stage with confidence, but also with a sense of humbleness. I've been here before. I shake the announcer's hand, turn, and look out over the audience. Deep breath. Some faces I recognize, some I do not. However, the turnout is quadruple as before. Another deep breath. And I begin my speech.

I stand in the same Toastmasters contest venue where my public speaking nightmare unfolded two years ago, when panic gripped me and I abandoned my speech. Now I've returned to rewrite that story.

Going back for redemption is scary and even more nerve-wracking than the first time. When you are in the same room and some of those same faces are watching you, knowing you had failed miserably not too long ago makes the emotions intense. I almost did not want to be there at all. However, this time was different. This time I had done my visualizations, over and over again. Even right before I walked out on that stage, in that bathroom I was visualizing myself completing this speech. I did this three or four times before heading for the stage.

Good friend and great mentor Robert Pitari and I after my redemption contest I took first in. *photo courtesy Al Cathy*

I only had one goal, and that was to complete the speech. I didn't care if I fumbled my words or said things that didn't make sense—all that mattered was completing the speech. I held that vision of completion in my mind's eye. I played it like a 4K movie, because, well, that was easy. I've been in this room before.

After about seven minutes, I hear myself speak my closing statement. *Done! I had done it.* I made it all the way through and it was good. Sure, I was not perfect. But who is? Perfection is a lie we tell ourselves, almost like an excuse as to why we can't go on. "I'm not ready yet, it's not perfect."

The applause resonates through the room, each clap affirming my accomplishment. I take a deep breath and walk to my seat. My friend Karen says excitedly, "You finished." I flash a smile so wide and fierce it feels like my face might crack. An expression of victory that would make the Joker himself proud.

About thirty minutes later they are announcing the awards. I couldn't care less as I had already won my battle, so who came in first, second, third—who cares? And the announcer speaks, "First place we have Jono Gilardi." I'm floored. I'd come for one thing and that was redemption, to finish. I left in first place. Today was a great day.

Was this feat possible because of visualization alone? Of course not. Many factors contributed to my being able to finish, including taking action and doing lots and lots of preparation. But visualization is the catalyst that transforms preparation into performance. When you can see your success vividly in your mind before it happens, you've already conquered the hardest battle—the one within yourself.

Transformation Action Steps

We've all been there. We've all told ourselves things aren't going to work out. We've even watched ourselves fail in our mind's eye before we've even *attempted* the task at hand. Isn't that pathetic? Why do we inflict this type of negativity on ourselves? Much like I saw myself freezing up in the first speech contest, you've probably seen yourself never getting through that important presentation at work. Or maybe you've said you were going to catch a cold, and lo and behold, a day later you're reaching for the tissues.

Adversity isn't just something caused by external factors beyond our control. We have the power to create our adversities. Nobody is immune to this self-sabotage if they're not aware they're doing it in the first place. The good news is that while nobody can control what the outside world throws at us, we have surprising control over what goes on inside our crazy ass heads. To break this cycle of negativity, we must begin to visualize better outcomes for ourselves, our future, and our goals, thereby lessening the potential for self-inflicted adversity.

Visualize: To this day, when I go to give a speech, I still get sweaty and nervous. My heart pounds like a jackhammer on concrete, relentless and thunderous in my chest. But not always. Sometimes I'm able to give talks with no uncomfortable side effects. So what do I do differently in those cases? I practice positive visualization, and it has worked wonders. It can do the same for you. Here's what you can do:

Find a quiet place where you can be alone for fifteen minutes with your journal. I know if you have kids like me, this may be as challenging as finding a unicorn in your backyard, but just do your best. Begin by closing your eyes and slowing your breath. Now, choose one area where you'd like to improve or where you want a better outcome than you've been imagining. This could be a goal, an aspiration, a job interview, or even an exercise workout you've been dreading.

Grab that journal and start writing about the objective you'd like to complete. A couple of lines is fine; we're not writing a novel here. Now close your eyes again and begin visualizing yourself completing this objective. Picture every detail of the process, from start to finish. See yourself conquering that interview or completing that ten-mile run you've been putting off. Visualize yourself victorious, walking away with a confident smile on your face. See it play out just like a movie would. How does this make you feel? Open your eyes and write about this little mental journey you just took. Focus on how it feels to achieve this success: the surge of emotions, the sense of accomplishment, the pride swelling in your chest. Write it all down and revisit what you noted often. Let these words be your personal cheerleader when doubt creeps in.

> "Your mind is like a muscle, the more you train it to visualize success, the stronger it becomes at making those visions a reality."

If you're struggling in a certain area, commit to this visualization exercise at least three times a week. Before you know it, you'll find you don't need to do it anymore, and what was once a daunting adversity has become something you accomplish by second nature. It truly is an amazing feeling to transcend such a difficulty, to look back and wonder why you ever thought it was so hard in the first place. After you've gained control of that particular area you were working on, choose another obstacle to conquer and begin the process again. Your mind is like a muscle, the more you train it to visualize success, the stronger it becomes at making those visions a reality.

I know for some of you, visualization might sound stupid or not worthy of your time. Trust me, I felt the same way once. However, now it's not just a part of my life, it's a fundamental tool that has reshaped my approach to challenges and supercharged my ability to overcome obstacles. You just have to be willing to do it regularly in order to start seeing the benefits. It's like having a secret weapon that turns your thoughts into your biggest allies rather than your worst enemies, and the more you do it, the more battles you will win.

> "It's simply about being better than your own baseline, performing better today than you did yesterday, and applying this principle continually and consistently."

Leverage Your Past Victories: One last thing to supercharge your visualizations: leverage your past victories. You've faced a lot of trials and tribulations in life, and you've overcome a ton of those adversities. You have wins under your belt, and you can use them to build your confidence for the new challenges you're now facing. Tap into past adversities that you've conquered and apply that invigorating feeling of triumph to your existing visualizations.

Begin by visualizing any past adversity that you have overcome. Vividly see yourself as you crossed that finish line in a race. For me, when I complete a speech successfully, I'm flooded with deep feelings of joy. I can see the smile on my face so clearly in my mind, feel the surge of accomplishment coursing through my body. I take this powerful feeling of winning and inject it into my visualizations of future challenges. This gives my mental rehearsals a true sense of victory, imbuing them with the deep, visceral feeling of actually overcoming that adversity.

And don't just take my word for it, this stuff is actually scientifically studied. Research shows that combining visualization with physical practice can improve athletic performance by as much as 45%. A survey of Olympic athletes revealed that over 90% use some form of visualization technique. Brain studies have confirmed that visualizing an action activates the same neural pathways as physically performing that action. This is why many sports psychologists consider visualization "a way of conditioning your brain for successful outcomes," it's essentially a mental rehearsal that programs your mind and body for success. What works for elite athletes can work for you too, whether you're facing a speech, a job interview, or any other challenge in your life.

The science is clear, visualization works, and it can work for you too. By consistently practicing these visualization techniques, you're not just daydreaming, you're actively rewiring your brain for success. You're building a mental toolkit that will serve you in facing any adversity life throws your way. So close your eyes, take a deep breath, and start visualizing the success you deserve. Your future self will thank you for it.

22

Transformation Lesson 9. The Habit of Hard!

"If something's worth doing, it's worth giving it your best, or in some cases 'beyond' your best."
—Haruki Murakami

You've learned eight transformation lessons so far. You've worked on your self-image, shifted your victim mindset, developed self-control, and faced your fears. But here's the truth: none of that means anything if you're not willing to do what's hard. Because transformation isn't comfortable. Growth isn't easy. And becoming the person you're meant to be requires you to embrace the one thing most people spend their entire lives avoiding: doing hard shit.

Doing hard things is about pushing beyond your perceived limits. It's grinding out an extra mile after you've already run thirteen. It's about embracing discomfort and challenge, even if the challenge is your worst adversity yet, because you know growth lies beyond your comfort zone. It's the willingness to do what others won't, to push when others quit, to stand when others fall. And when you commit to doing hard things every single day, something remarkable happens: you become someone extraordinary. You become above average by default, not because you're trying to compete with anyone else, but because you're refusing to accept mediocrity in yourself.

Why is it that we Americans are always seeking comfort and ease when what we should be doing is seeking discomfort and doing hard things? We want the easy life, the good life, with no pain and no struggle. We want the quick pick to win the millions. We don't want to struggle our way to greatness. So why would anyone ever want to deliberately do hard things? Why would anyone ever want to deliberately create for themselves adversity? The simple answer to that question is this: Nobody ever got anywhere good in life by taking the easy path. Nobody ever created something extraordinary in comfort. And nobody ever got through adversity without pain. Walt Disney did not create Disney without a persistent focus on doing the many hard things he had to do to fulfill his vision, and nobody ever cured themselves of disease by just sitting back on their couch in comfort, eating pizza and drinking soda pop.

So, what is "hard"? Hard is doing the things that suck, that make you sweat, that make you grimace in pain. It's the things that make your brain hurt because you studied so hard. It's getting knocked on your ass over and over again and getting up to keep on trying to do whatever it is you're determined to do. It's being told by a doctor you don't have much time left, and instead of believing him, you decide to take matters into your own hands and do everything possible to thrive. It's

TRANSFORMATION LESSON 9. THE HABIT OF HARD!

doing hard shit day in and day out with a hardcore belief that you will prevail.

This chapter is all about forcing yourself to do the hard things in order to make life, including even your adversities, flow like water around rocks in a stream, effortlessly navigating the obstacles in its path.

You see, when you do hard things, you're not just making life difficult for the hell of it. You're forging yourself into something stronger, more resilient. You're building a stronger body to face tomorrow. You're building the mental toughness to face any challenge life throws at you. You're becoming the kind of person who doesn't back down, who doesn't quit when things get tough (and things *will* get tough), who achieves greatness. That is the kind of person I strive to be, as should you.

*****

Let me take you through a typical Saturday for me at the time of this writing, so I can show you why doing hard things keeps me going. By forcing myself to do hard things, beyond what I'm already forced to endure on this day, I find myself with more energy, strength, and vigor for life. Because it's the doing of those hard things that gives me the confidence to move past the struggle with poise and resilience. First, I wake up at five in the morning and make some French-pressed black coffee and pop my twenty milligrams of Dexamethasone.[8] I meditate and do my affirmations for about ten minutes. Then I grab my journal and do my pen to paper affir-

---

[8] Dexamethasone: a corticosteroid used to fight inflammation and, in my case, cancer. Side effects include weight gain, sleeplessness, osteoporosis, and increased susceptibility to infections.

mations plus my morning gratitude. I always write down three things I'm grateful for. I try to do this stuff every day, but sometimes things just don't work out properly. But guess what? That's ok. We are not perfect, and don't let anyone tell you they are. That's just what they want us to believe on their social media channels.

After I complete these tasks, I read a few pages from whatever personal development book I'm reading at the time. I then take a quick cold shower for a mental boost because I now have to drive two hours and forty-five minutes to UC Davis Cancer Center, where I get my chemo. The chemotherapy usually takes about an hour. From there, I jump back in the car and begin my two-hour-and-forty-five-minute drive home. So much fun, right?

> "It's the doing of those hard things that gives me the confidence to move past the struggle with poise and resilience."

Now, at this point, I must hold it together, try my best not to get down or complain, because this schedule really does suck. Plus, gas is not cheap these days. However, the way we choose to perceive our struggles is all that matters. I choose to perceive it in the best way possible. Look, I can choose to bitch and moan, or I could choose to embrace this time and find the positive aspects about the long drive and the chemicals I get pumped into me. The drive? *Awesome.* I choose to educate myself by listening to either audiobooks or certain podcasts that will build and grow who I am. If you're stuck in your car for long hours every day, think of it as a peaceful interlude, your opportunity to educate yourself. So use it wisely.

TRANSFORMATION LESSON 9. THE HABIT OF HARD!

I return home anywhere between two and four p.m., depending on what time my appointment was. I'm tired, I usually feel a little nauseous, and my whole body usually feels pretty funky. So what do I do? Lie down and watch some shows? Maybe eat some crappy food? Nope. Still in a fasted state, as I have not eaten since the evening before, I will eat some healthy protein. I'm always hydrated because I usually drink a gallon of water per day. And now I'm off to the gym,

Cold plunge in the creek behind my house. There's something powerful about choosing discomfort, whether it's ice baths or any hard thing you'd rather avoid. Each time you override that voice saying "no," you're building real mental toughness. *photo courtesy Ali Gilardi*

where I will do high-intensity interval training that usually consists of the use of assault bikes and assault treadmills. If you've never used either of these, you should try them out. They give you a beast of a workout. I'll also do three to four different types of ab workouts, some box jumps, and mix in some kettlebell work. I usually go through a circuit like this five times, and finally, when the sweat is flowing and my heart rate is pumping and I really feel like I'm going to puke, I end the session and go sit in the gym's sauna for ten minutes.

Finally, I return home and make myself a clean, healthy meal to finish my wonderful Saturday. I've earned whatever comes next, which usually consists of spending quality time with my wife and two kids. Can't forget about the family, as they are why I do what I do each day.

Remember this at the end of the day: Don't forget to spend time with those you love. It's easy to be a selfish parent these days, with all the technology, phones, iPads, gaming systems, and streaming services to distract both you and your kids. You have a choice: You can just sit the kids in front of a console and walk away, or you can spend quality time with them, creating a relationship and a bond that will last a lifetime. And if you guys are into video games, then play with them. They will never forget that.

And so my long Saturday comes to an end. I don't slow down and I will never give up. This cancer thing they say I have doesn't control my life. It does not control my mind and tell me things like I should take it easy because I deserve to. No! All it means to me is that I need to put in twice as much work as everyone else. Ten times the sweat, ten times the pain, ten times the blood, and ten times the discipline in all areas.

TRANSFORMATION LESSON 9. THE HABIT OF HARD!

I'm never going to give up on myself or my family, and that requires me chasing after everything that is hard in life so I can be healthier, stronger, and wiser. So I can ultimately live a long, full life. So I can be here for the long run.

> "The struggles you face today are forging you into the person you need to be for tomorrow's challenges. Every time you choose the hard path, you're investing in your future self."

I believe we all need to experience an unfavorable hand at times. This will allow us to see life from a different perspective and fuel us to a higher potential. It's those of us who have been down who have a much easier time chasing after the hard things in life. The struggles you face today are forging you into the person you need to be for tomorrow's challenges. Every time you choose the hard path, you're investing in your future self.

Choosing to do what needs to be done is hard, but it's what must be done. There's no other way to put it. All other things aside, handle your business. If you're in the fight, then fucking fight. Choose hard over easy, because it's easy to live easy:

- It's **easy** to watch shows every night of the week. It's **hard** to actually sit down and read a book with the intent to learn something new instead.
- It's **easy** to sleep in. It's **hard** to get up an hour early and work on yourself or go to the gym.
- It's **easy** to run a mile. It's **hard** to run five, ten, or maybe even fifteen.
- It's **easy** to have a cheeseburger and fries plus dessert. It's **hard** to choose the super healthy foods that provide you with the energy you need to crush your days.

- It's **easy** to be the victim because your adversity is hard, but it's **harder** to rise above it and rewrite your story.
- It's **easy** to plop your kids down in front of a video game or movie and ignore them all day. It's **hard** to give them your time, to play, listen, and do things together that create a bond and connection. To be a great mother or father, and ensure they get the best possible chance at life, while still doing everything you need to do to create the best in yourself.
- It's **easy** to stuff ourselves with food all day. It's **hard** to fast for two, three, four, or five days.
- It's **easy** to retreat in life, to throw in the towel, to refuse to actually put in the work to make whatever goal you have come to life. It's **hard** to fight back every day until your objective is complete, and then move to your next target.

When you don't have an aim in life, you will find that life is actually harder. Sitting around and watching a show you enjoy is not actually progressing your life. All you're doing is sacrificing long-term gain for short-term pleasure. When your time comes, you will find that all the time you spent evading the hard has left you weak and unprepared. You will realize, with deep regret, that it was actually the hard you should have been doing all along.

Some days I wake up and say, "Fuck, do I really have cancer?" I feel so alive and vigorous that sometimes I can't believe I do. But the treatments and the pills I've taken on the daily over the past five years were not just a dream; they were a nightmare, in reality. It all happened and *is* happening to me. I never really thought I'd find myself in that fucking chemo recliner. I'm not in fantasyland. I have to accept this fact daily. I do so by choosing what's hard over what's easy at every bend in the road.

Hard is mastering **Self-image**. It's about not becoming a **Victim**, no matter what the circumstance. It's **Guarding** your **Environment** from toxic influences, meaningless distractions and the people who drain you dry. It's developing the **Self-Control** to refuse the french fries. It's staring down your **Fears** and facing them head on, because even if you **Fail** or **Lose**, you can still say, "I learned a lot." It's pushing past the **Gloom** of adversity because you don't stay down for long, and then moving on and **Visualizing** your success rather than envisioning the negative. It's disciplining yourself each day to do what is **Hard!**

Every transformation lesson in this book has required you to choose the harder path. And when you do that consistently, when you make it a daily habit, you're not just surviving, you're becoming someone who refuses to settle for anything less than extraordinary. You're becoming more than you were yesterday, and that's what it's all about.

We must do the things we find hard, torturous, time-consuming, and sometimes meaningless if we want to find the strength for the struggle. Remember: greatness isn't born in the spotlight but in the shadows of relentless, unseen effort.

Elbert Hubbard once said, "Self-discipline is the ability to make yourself do what you should do, when you should do it, whether you feel like it or not." So get off Netflix and go work out. Take the cheeseburger out of your mouth and eat a salad. Pour that can of soda down the drain and drink more water.

Nobody is going to give you the results you want. You have to achieve those results on your own.

Theodore Roosevelt was a weak and sickly child and plagued by life-threatening asthma. However, young Teddy threw himself into a strict regimen of harsh physical exercise as a way to conquer his frailty. Eventually, he beat back his asthma. He once stated, "I wish to preach, not the doctrine of ignoble ease, but the doctrine of the strenuous life, the life of toil and effort, of labor and strife; to preach that highest form of success which comes, not to the man who desires mere easy peace, but to the man who does not shrink from danger, from hardship, or from bitter toil, and who out of these wins the splendid ultimate triumph." Be like Teddy. Live a strenuous life for good.

This is what happens to us when we do the hard things in life:

- Our dreams become reality. It's true! When you do hard things, you have the self-discipline to tackle the adversity standing in the way of your goals and the life you want.
- The more you challenge yourself with these hard tasks, the better you will become at killing procrastination. We love to procrastinate on hard tasks, which is why procrastination is the ultimate dream killer. But once you learn to kill it, say "*Fuck it*" and just get it done right now. Procrastination doesn't stand a chance before your focused determination.
- You will never regret doing the hard shit; you will always regret the many days you spent doing absolutely nothing. When someone asks you what you did

today, what would you like to be able to tell them? That you accomplished nothing? Or that maybe you ran thirteen miles, just cause. That you finished a book that's been sitting on your shelf for months. That you created something, anything that didn't exist before today.
- Who's watching you right now? Someone close to your heart, your spouse, your coworkers, your family, your kids? My kids will see me doing the hard shit till the day I die, because when you are doing those difficult things, people take notice. You are inspiring those around you with your positive examples of doing the hard. Even if it's just one person, lead by example.

Is having cancer hard? Sure, I'd be lying if I said my life was a walk in the park. It's not. It's an everyday battle with the mind and the body. However, I could make it "easy" by simply becoming the victim. Sitting here now writing this, I've had a little over two and a half hours of sleep because the Dexamethasone keeps me up at night. I could choose to shut the computer down, save it for another day. Go lie in bed, grab a bowl of some grade A bullshit snack, and flick on the old TV. Take a nap, do some complaining and some sympathy searching. Cry to my wife a little and get out of having to pick my kids up from school and take them to their after-school activities. I could just allow myself to waste away faster by treating myself like shit; the cancer would then definitely get the advantage. But all those things would be easy. They would be effortless. They would not be hard.

That's not my path. But you know that already. I don't want easy to be your path either. We're all mortal, and by choosing the hard path, we're doing what's right not just for ourselves but for those around us. Whatever your past and present hardships, I challenge you: What are *you* going to do today? What choice will you make? Will you take the easy road or the hard path? It's your decision. Mary McCarthy once said, "We are the hero of our own story." So ask yourself, what would the hero in your story do?

Transformation Action Steps

It's time to instill the habit of hard. Are you ready to build your mental toughness so that when adversity strikes, you are fortified to face the challenge head-on with resilience and bravery? If you dig deep, I *know* you'll find what it takes to come out on top. This step is simple, but done each day it's hard. Let me share with you this simple truth: if you do something hard every day, you are going to see significant gains in your life. After some time, you may not even recognize yourself. Your confidence will shine and your discipline will be solid as rock. Let's begin.

Discovery: Take fifteen minutes to brainstorm and write down all the hard things you've been avoiding or putting off. These could be related to health, career, relationships, personal growth, or any area of your life. Maybe it's doing that first workout you've been putting off. Or passing on the after-work pizza with coworkers. Maybe it's forcing yourself to wake up an hour earlier each day. Or maybe it's something momentous, like gathering the courage to walk away from a poor relationship. Today is that day.

Remember, every day is a new day to try a new hard thing. I love cold plunges, and I've been doing them for years now.

But you know what never changes about that cold water? It's always fucking cold. Every day I don't want to get in it, but every day that I stand next to it, I know that I am about to do something hard, and that inspires me. When you have that "this is going to be hard" feeling, you know you're on the right track. (By the way, if you have not tried cold exposure yet, it's time to start. It does not matter what mood you are in, you cannot help but feel amazing after a freezing cold ice bath.)

Prioritize and Select: Now that your list of hard things is complete, I want you to arrange the items in order of priority. Then pick your top hard thing that would have the most significant impact on your life if you tackled it consistently. Write down what the end result would be if you persistently did that thing for a month. How would it change your body or your mind? Use the power of visualization, as discussed in Lesson 8. What about your energy level? Would your daily habits be improved? Or your performance at work or in the gym? How about your relationships with loved ones?

Craft the Task: Now that you have that one hard thing, write in your journal what tactical changes you would need to make in your life if you committed daily to doing this task. How might you have to reconfigure the structure of your day? Doing hard things is hard, and it can be a struggle just to find time to do the thing you have in mind, so as you write I want you to think of all the obstacles that could hinder you from completing this task each day. Much like planning for the inevitable, I want you to devise a plan so that failure, excuses, and whatever else comes up will mostly not stop you. Failproof the hard as much as you can.

Commit: You've done the hard work of introspection. You've identified your challenge, visualized the obstacles, and imagined the triumph. Now comes the real test: the commitment. For the next thirty days, you're going to do this one hard thing. Every. Single. Day. No excuses, no cop-outs, no "I'll start tomorrow." Your commitment starts now.

But what if you picked something like going to a speech club or a new class that meets only once a week? Obviously, you can't do this every day. So, beyond committing to attending the club or class each week for the next thirty days, I want you to spend the off days educating yourself in that craft, reading the books, watching the educational videos, and so on.

Remember, this isn't just about the task itself. It's about who you become in the process. Each day you follow through, you're not just completing a challenge, you're forging a stronger version of yourself. You're building the mental toughness that will carry you through life's toughest battles. There will be days when you don't feel like it. Days when life throws curveballs, when you're tired, when it seems easier to quit. These are like the days after my long drives to and from UC Davis Cancer Center for my chemo injections, when I'm exhausted, and I finally arrive home and all I want to do is throw in the towel and lie down, but instead I gear up and head to the gym. These are the days that matter most. These are the days when champions are made.

Now imagine yourself thirty days from now. Feel the pride, the confidence, the sheer badassery of knowing you did what you said you'd do. You faced your fears, pushed through discomfort, and came out stronger and more resilient, ready to face anything that opposes you.

This is your moment. Your chance to prove to yourself what you're truly capable of. Don't let it slip away. You've got one shot at this life. Don't waste it wishing you'd been braver. Do the hard things now, so your last thoughts can be "Fuck yeah, I lived." So make the commitment. Right here, right now. Write it down, say it out loud, tell a friend. Make it real.

The Journey Never Ends: Congratulations! You've completed your first thirty-day commitment to doing something hard. If that something was a habit or lifestyle change, such as exercising every morning or reading for thirty minutes before bedtime, keep doing it. Don't stop! Make it a permanent part of your life. Notice how much easier it is now compared to when you started?

But you're not done. In fact, you're only just beginning the process of reshaping your life into something awesome. Now it's time to start another thirty-day challenge for yourself. Go back to your list and pick your next task or objective. Add this on top of your first hard thing (which should now be an ingrained habit) and begin again the steps from above. Repeat this process over and over, and one day you'll find you crave the challenge of doing hard things more than anything else. Your old foe, adversity, has become your best friend.

> "You've got one shot at this life. Don't waste it wishing you'd been braver. Do the hard things now, so your last thoughts can be 'Fuck yeah, I lived.'"

23

Transformation Lesson 10. Fuck Average!

> *"All I know is that I never want to be average."*
> —Michael Jordan

Throughout history, we've witnessed the astonishing capacity of the human spirit to rise in the face of overwhelming challenges. When backed against the wall, we discover reservoirs of strength we never knew existed. This isn't coincidence, it's biology and psychology working in harmony. When confronted with true adversity, our survival instincts activate, flooding our systems with determination and clarity. The comfort of mediocrity suddenly feels irrelevant. We see with perfect vision what truly matters, and the excuses that once held us back dissolve. Adversity becomes the catalyst that propels us toward our greatest achievements. It's not that we need suffering to excel, but rather that hardship strips away the nonessential and reveals the extraordinary potential that existed within us all along.

You've made it to the final chapter of this book. If you've been doing the work, really doing it, then you've already made a choice, whether you realized it or not. You've chosen to be more than average.

Think about it. The person who commits to shifting their victim mindset? That's not average. Most people cling to their victim story their entire lives because it's easier than taking responsibility. The person who works on building unshakeable self-control? That's not average. Most people give in to every impulse and craving that crosses their path. The person who deliberately reshapes their self-image and confronts their limiting beliefs? That's definitely not average. Most people never even question the mental programming they've carried since childhood.

Every single transformation lesson in this book has required you to do something uncomfortable, something most people won't do. That's the point. This entire book has been about choosing the harder path, the path that leads to growth, fulfillment, and extraordinary results. That path? It's the above-average path. And you've been walking it this entire time.

But here's what I need you to understand: being above average isn't about competing with the ultramarathoner, the genius entrepreneur, or the self-made millionaire. It's not about being better than everyone else. It's about being better than *your own* baseline. It's about refusing to accept mediocrity in your own life. It's about showing up today better than you showed up yesterday, and doing it again tomorrow, and the day after that.

TRANSFORMATION LESSON 10. FUCK AVERAGE!

This chapter is going to tie everything together. I'm going to share with you the moment when I discovered this truth, when the word "average" became the wake-up call that changed everything. And I'm going to show you why committing to an above-average mindset isn't just another lesson—it's the foundation that makes all the other lessons possible.

In the face of life's great challenges, we stand at a crossroads. Do we surrender to our circumstances or do we face them head-on, driven by something greater than ourselves? This chapter will take you through the early stages of my cancer diagnosis and reveal why I chose to seize control rather than accept mediocrity. We'll explore the powerful link between adversity and extraordinary achievement. Prepare to have your perceptions challenged about what's possible when facing overwhelming odds.

Whether you're confronting a health crisis, a professional setback, or any other personal challenge, these pages will arm you with tools to not just endure the storm, but to emerge stronger and more resilient than ever. Remember: true growth often emerges in our darkest hour. In the crucible of adversity, we must decide. Will we retreat to the comfort of a basic life and accept gnawing unfulfillment? Or will we forge our way through the depths of darkness to create an above-average life? You get to decide. Are you ready to seek more and become more?

*****

Back when I was first diagnosed with an incurable blood cancer, my wife and I were lost. We were so confused. We needed to find out what this meant. What it meant for my family and me. And so we began our search. We had Zoom calls from our home in California to doctors in New York City, specialists in Minnesota, anyone who might have answers about what it meant. We drove to Sacramento and to Palo Alto, and flew to Arizona, to talk to some of the country's top specialists in the particular cancer I have. We weren't looking for a second opinion; we were hunting for a tenth, a fifteenth, however many it took. We refused to accept the first answer, the easiest answer, or even the most convenient answer. Every doctor, every specialist, every expert who might know something more than the last one, we tracked them down. The flight to Arizona? Covered by Big Pharma. Free of charge. We were relentless, desperate, and determined to find the best possible options for our family. We would not settle. Not with this. Not with our lives on the line. One thing I learned early on in this process is that cancer is big business.

We also made a trip back to my old hometown in the San Francisco Bay Area. You know that feeling you get when you reapproach your old stomping grounds. Memories come flooding back. However, this time, even though I wanted it to feel good, I was consumed by the reality of my situation and the reason for coming back to SF, despite the majestic sight of the Golden Gate Bridge, Alcatraz Island looming in the bay's mist, and the gleaming city skyline, I couldn't shake the reality of my situation. Memories of baseball and football at Candlestick Park, the restaurants, and the beaches tickled my mind, but I could not come to feel good about this visit. My mind was focused on my problems, as we neared closer and closer in the thick, bumper-to-bumper traffic to UCSF Hospital.

After arriving, my wife and I made our way to the top floor, the cancer center. We pushed through the double doors only to see a packed house. I got an overwhelming impression of sad and depressed faces. A tear or two dropped to the floor. I mean, how can you be happy when death is so close? You could practically feel the Reaper's vile stench in the room. Much like all those years ago when he sat beside me on that blood-stained couch. The scene was profoundly depressing.

We checked in and quickly seated ourselves near a huge window that overlooked the San Francisco cityscape. Memories again tried to steal my sadness. The sight of Golden Gate Park, where my grandma had taken me as a very young boy, vaguely brightened my mind. I tried to recapture the fun I had there. It seemed like a dream I was having a hard time recollecting, as my stomach began to tell me I wanted to puke.

I was quickly pulled from my daze as I heard someone say my name. "Mr. Gilardi," a nurse called from an open door in the corner of the room. We were led back to your normal-style hospital room, nothing special here. "The doctor will be in to see you very soon," the nurse said. About ten minutes later, in walked the doctor with a smile on her face, a smile I wished I could share. But I was unable to reciprocate. Could you blame me? Following closely behind was her nursing assistant, who was just as cheerful. Maybe they were trying to cheer me up with smiles and positivity.

The doctor began to explain her approach to this incurable blood cancer. How she treated it. What the different outcomes and possibilities were. The different types of drugs, what they do, and what they can't do. She also tells how there are a lot of new drugs and treatments that are coming down the pipeline in the future, and that she is very optimistic about the cancer. Coming from a negative, mostly pessimistic background, I had an extremely hard time feeling positive, despite her professed confidence. And she did confirm to me that, despite all the promising treatments, the cancer is incurable and always comes back. After about thirty minutes, she finally came to the conclusion of her well-spoken introduction.

"Do you have any questions?" she asked my wife and me. At this point, I am so discombobulated from all the info she laid down, plus all the big words she used, that my numbed mind has zero questions for her. My wife, on the other hand, had something deeper she wanted answered. "How long does he have?" "Well," the doctor replied in a quiet, compassionate tone, "the average multiple myeloma patient lives ten years, give or take." My wife, Ali, begins to softly cry. However, I could only think of one thing. Ten years. I did the math—that wouldn't even give me enough time to see my kids off to college. But when you think about tuition prices these days, maybe that's not such bad timing. Seriously though, I could only think... at forty-one years old, ten years puts me at fifty-one. That's not going to cut it. I've got way too much still to live for, my wife and my two-year-old daughter and my four-year-old son. I've got so much I want to teach my beautiful kids still, and I want to watch them grow up, see them succeed, and start lives of their own. I want to travel the world with my wife and make more memories

> "Never forget that life is precious and we must be grateful for each day we get to crawl out of our bed and spend time with our loved ones."

TRANSFORMATION LESSON 10. FUCK AVERAGE!

and have more experiences. Then, of course, what about my personal dreams and aspirations? I've got so much I still want to accomplish in my lifetime. "It's not fair!" I thought.

It was on that day that I began to learn my deepest lesson. Never forget that life is precious and we must be grateful for each day we get to crawl out of our bed and spend time with our loved ones. If we can shift our mindset to see life from that perspective every day, we can then find more happiness in the day to day.

Once Ali and I made it back to our car in the parking garage, I was no longer able to hold back the tears that had been trying to choke me out since the patient room. We held each other for some time and then began our long drive home. My mind was foggy, like so many days in San Francisco. I couldn't see my future anymore; it was blurry and uncertain. We quietly drove out of the Bay Area traffic, skyscraper buildings shrinking behind, and made our way back to Redding. What would I do? How would I survive this?

Now, this did not happen overnight or during the next week or even during the next month; it took several months, but one morning I woke up and instantly had an epiphany. You see, during each one of my many doctor visits, there was one word that just kept coming up. Each one of those doctors just kept saying this word over and over again. What was that word? Average! The *average* American, the *average* cancer patient, the *average* multiple myeloma patient lives ten years. I had to think, well, what is average? Average is basic, it's comfort or mediocrity. What do we know about the average American? I knew the average American was sedentary. We do not exercise nearly enough, but instead sit around television sets and computer screens all day and consume too much negativity. The average American eats way too many processed, sugary foods that add to health problems. The average American has a fixed mindset rather than a growth mindset. The average American is not doing well, if you take a look at the big picture.

    How do you think the average cancer patient fares on top of all this BS? Better or worse? Well, I can tell you from experience, it can be much worse because it's much easier to take the easy path and allow mediocrity to dominate your life, as I did in the beginning. Wallowing in self-pity, I'd think poor me deserved a little extra sympathy, poor me deserved an extra bowl of ice cream on top of the bowl I already had. And back then, I could put back some ice cream. Chocolate chip cookie dough, half gallon in one night—no problem. Oh, and poor me deserved to sit around and do nothing all day and consume negative TV and be a rude asshole to my family. Anything that made me feel good right now was ok. I was all about instant gratification to hide my suffering. You see, I had a special pass. It was that victim's pass we talked about earlier in the book. Not only did I think this pass was legit, so did my family and friends. Anyone, really, could take one peek at this pass, hand it back to me as if I was in line for some sort of victim's fest, and say, "Proceed. You, sir, are definitely a victim." Not ok! That's the victim's mindset. That plays into how the averages are figured out. That's where they get their stats, their data. That's why average is, actually, pretty lousy, when you stop and analyze it. This thought alone was a huge awakening for me.

TRANSFORMATION LESSON 10. FUCK AVERAGE!

I knew I had to change, that I had to become more. You see, what if, by becoming more than average, by applying an above-average mindset to my life, I could change the prognosis on my diagnosis? Could I knock that ten-year life expectancy right out of the ballpark? The more I thought about it, the more I believed I could.

And so I began doing what most people wouldn't think to do because it's too hard and life-altering. For example, when I do chemotherapy, I fast anywhere between eighteen to thirty-six hours before chemo and a similar amount after because there's evidence that fasting allows the drugs to work better and stronger. They can do their job and be less hindered by other factors, most importantly digestion, when one is in a fasted state. I read about this in *The Longevity Diet*, by Valter Longo, PhD.

A big part of being better than average is that I exercise six to seven days a week, no excuses. Unless of course I'm incapable, as chemo side effects can be a bitch at times. But this is extremely rare, as I usually push through any side effects I might have. For example, when I first started the chemo cycle I am on at the time of this writing, it hit me hard. I ended up in the ER later in the day because I lost most of my vision, had a fever, and broke out in a nasty rash. After a couple of hours, I checked out ok and they let me go home. It was at about seven-thirty, feeling like shit and still not able to see well, that I jumped in the ice bath for three minutes and followed that with twenty-five minutes of burpees and then a hot shower. I felt so much better afterward.

I consistently go above average in my work, in raising my kids, and in being the best husband I can. I eat extremely clean

99.9 percent of the time, making rare exceptions for special occasions like birthdays or Christmas parties. I maintain a positive mindset most of the time, always tipping the scale in my favor by stacking above-average efforts across all areas of my life. This is just the beginning; I'm constantly learning, growing, and finding new ways to optimize my health and lifestyle. For me, it's an all-around approach, being excellent in all areas, not just obsessing over one dimension. I could chase trophies or medals in something that pulled me away from my family, but that's not true success. I don't want to neglect my family. Life is a marathon, and despite what the evidence suggests about my condition, I'm in it for the long run. I will never give up. This dedication to personal growth isn't just a phase; it's become my way of life. It's who I am.

Transformation Action Steps

I've now told you how when the worst adversity of my life hit me, an adversity that I will continue to deal with for the rest of my life, I chose the hard path of no excuses. Of using my tough break as a springboard to seek out and live a richer, more fulfilling life than I had ever lived before. I chose to apply everything you've learned in this book—the mindset shifts, the discipline, the self-control, all of it working together.

Ultimately, this is not about me and my story. This is about *you* and *your* story, the wonderful story that is going to unfold for you if you choose to be more than average. You're very close to the end of this book, and it's time for you to find out what you want from this life and how far you're willing to go to get there. It's time to get your head out of your ass and make a decision.

TRANSFORMATION LESSON 10. FUCK AVERAGE!

Think about this for just a moment. What if you applied the above-average mindset to a certain area in your life where you were lacking? Your work, your business, your health and wellness, your goals, your mindset, your relationships? What if you added just a little more effort, got yourself just a little above average? What do you think would happen? I'll tell you one thing is for certain, and that is you will begin to experience more

Excellence in living becomes a form of leadership, inspiring others simply through who you are. *photo courtesy Ali Gilardi*

abundance. If you apply the above-average mindset as a daily habit with good intentions and skill, if you apply it to all the transformation lessons in this book, you are going to flourish! The added effect of the extra effort only means one thing: results!

The best part of applying and becoming above average is that all your hard work and discipline begins to slowly influence others around you. Recently, my nine-year-old son Gio set a two-week goal leading up to his jiu-jitsu competition to improve his performance. His plan was to eat clean and exercise each morning. His determination was impressive.

One night, he had a birthday party at a pizza restaurant. I mentioned to my wife, Ali, that this would be challenging for him, watching all his friends eat pizza and drink soda while he practiced self-control and discipline. This would be difficult for anyone, let alone a nine-year-old. When I saw him that evening, he couldn't wait to tell me that he had prevailed. I was incredibly proud of him. The biggest takeaway is that I never instructed him to do this; it was entirely his plan, his idea, and his discipline, and it paid off. He went undefeated in eight jiu-jitsu matches and earned himself a gold medal.

Would any of this have happened if I were a lazy, average person who ate unhealthy food all day and never exercised or practiced self-control and discipline? I don't think so, especially not for a nine-year-old child. There is no better feeling than when your actions inspire not only your loved ones but also others around you to take positive action in their own lives.

This step is simple. It's a mindset shift. You must commit to the habit of being more than average. Ask yourself, are you willing:

- to take your adversities and learn from them, grow from them?
- to refuse mediocrity, even when everyone around you has accepted it?
- to go the extra mile in your work and watch yourself rise to the top of your profession?
- to become disciplined to do the things you need to do to get to where you want to go?

- to take this life that you get to live and make something special of it before your time runs out?

> "The world does not need any more mediocrity, it has plenty of that already. And the world definitely does not need any more of your average. What the world needs, what your friends, your community, and your loved ones need, is your absolute, unyielding best self!"

Most of all, will you rise above when everything seems to be crashing in around you, when life seems so hard, and it's throwing a torrent of obstacles your way? When you want to give up, throw in the towel, and walk away? Times of adversity are when you need to dig in and find your strength. To go all in. No matter how hard it may seem at times to be and strive for above average, never give up! Because when you apply the above-average mindset, you only have one destination, and that is straight to the top, no matter what adversity you face. **Fuck average.**

Look, I've been saying "above average" throughout this chapter. I've been polite about it. But let me tell you what I really call it, what I say to myself every single morning when I wake up, what I remind myself when things get hard, when the chemo kicks my ass, when life throws another obstacle in my path: **Fuck average.**

Those two words changed my life. They became my rallying cry, my rebellion against mediocrity, my middle finger to the statistics that tried to define my future. When that doctor told me the average multiple myeloma patient lives ten years, something ignited in me. I wanted to obliterate average. I wanted to reject everything about it.

Fuck average isn't just about my cancer. It's about everything. It's about refusing to accept a mediocre marriage, a mediocre career, mediocre health, mediocre relationships, or a mediocre life. It's about looking at the path most people take, the path of least resistance, the path of comfort and convenience, and choosing the harder road instead.

For those feeling overwhelmed by the thought of this, I want you to understand this important distinction: it's not about competing with others. As I said earlier, it's not about trying to outperform the ultramarathoner or the genius entrepreneur. It's simply about being better than your own baseline, performing better today than you did yesterday, and applying this principle continually and consistently.

- Maybe you've been stuck in bed with depression for weeks, and today you took a shower, got dressed, and walked a mile? #fuckaverage
- You've been silent in every meeting at your new job, and today you gave a presentation in front of your coworkers? #fuckaverage
- You just started lifting weights and felt insecure about people watching, but today you pushed past that fear and crushed a personal record. #fuckaverage

Small, steady improvements compound into extraordinary results.

This is my challenge to you: Make "fuck average" your mantra. Let it be the thing that pushes you when you want to quit. Let it be the voice in your head when you're tempted to take the easy way out. When you're at the party and they

TRANSFORMATION LESSON 10. FUCK AVERAGE!

are serving dessert, say in your mind, **"Fuck Average."** Shut it down. Let it be your reminder that you're capable of so much more than settling.

I want to see **#fuckaverage** everywhere. I want you to say it out loud when you're struggling. I want it to become a movement of people who refuse to accept the basic, the mediocre, the "good enough." Because you're not average, you never were. You just needed permission to stop pretending you were.

The world does not need any more mediocrity, it has plenty of that already. And the world definitely does not need any more of your average. What the world needs, what your friends, your community, and your loved ones need, is your absolute, unyielding best self!

So here's my final question for you: Are you ready to say **fuck average** and mean it? Are you ready to live it every single day? Are you ready to join this movement? Because if you are, then everything changes. Everything.

If this book hit you the way I hope it did, I want to see it. Take a picture with it. Post it online with #fuckaverage. Show me you're in. Show the world you're done with mediocrity. Let's build this movement together.

Now go out there and show the world what you're truly capable of.

#fuckaverage

Conclusion: From the Depths We Shall Rise

"God will not look you over for medals, degrees,
or diplomas, but for scars."
—Elbert Hubbard

We've been through hell, spoken to the reaper, and played some bad hands. We've made mistakes and carried heavy burdens, all while trying not to slip. Each of us reaches our breaking point differently, that critical moment when we must decide whether to crumble or transform. We've corrected our course like an old ship captain only to find that the last heavy storm moved us further from our destination. Yet our dreams and goals are just outside the door, and though the scars are deep, each one was a waypoint on a tattered map. Our bodies, our minds, and our stories guide us like the northern star.

Whether we die today, tomorrow, or years from now, we will die with purpose, happiness, joy, and fulfillment because we know in our hearts we left no stone unturned. We embraced many perfect moments that we would have missed by living a life of narrow-mindedness. We loved greatly and learned wisely. Our scars carry deep meaning, each one tells a story, teaching us about every aspect of life. In the end, it's not about what you have to show in credentials or money, but rather how you lived and how you're remembered. And the best way to become someone worth remembering is to live a life of excellence: to be brave, courageous, kind, giving, helpful, and loving, all while enduring your own personal traumas and adversities.

Learn to live for your dreams, not somebody else's. The life you desire can only be carved out by you. Let the mysteries of pain and suffering guide you to your truth and purpose because these things provide you with experience not taught anywhere else. You can accept your circumstances as they are, stay broken, and remain the victim, or you can choose to take responsibility and make the proper changes needed to attain your goals.

The great Buddha said, "What we are today comes from our thoughts of yesterday, and our present thoughts build our life of tomorrow. Our life is the creation of our mind." The breaking point isn't where we fall apart permanently; it's where we discover what we're truly capable of rebuilding. Work to get better every day, so tomorrow you can be that much closer to your goals. But remember, if you are not pursuing them in a state of happiness, then those goals will mean nothing. All your aspirations must begin with joy.

Imagine a life where you loved getting up in the morning, where you didn't need an alarm clock because you were so excited to start the day. You'd walk around with confidence, a smile on your face, joyful to just be alive. You'd dance in the rain with your kids, laugh with your better half over a nice dinner, unleash your creativity, and see the destinations you've always dreamed of. This is the life we discover when

CONCLUSION: FROM THE DEPTHS WE SHALL RISE

we face our mortality. Life is too short to be serious all the time or to waste it on things that don't give you light.

Your life is all you've got. It's short, it's often painful, but it's glorious. Take hold, enjoy the ride, and never let adversity slow your pursuit of greater meaning and fulfillment. When you're down, get up. Live with passion and honor.

Who you become through times of walking through hell is what makes it all worth it. As Jim Rohn said, "What you become is far more important than what you get. What you get will be influenced by what you become."

- Who you become starts at the bottom as you scratch and claw your way to the top.
- Who you become is my seven-year-old son losing his first jiu-jitsu match while the tears stream down his face as they raise his opponent's hand instead of his.
- Who you become is struggling to pay the bills as you work on your dreams.
- Who you become is being afraid, being very afraid, but doing it anyway.
- Who you become is reaching your breaking point, almost ending your life only to bounce back with more determination to succeed than ever. This is the paradox, what breaks us becomes our foundation.
- Who you become is being locked in jail, but coming out on the other side clean, only to realize you were meant for so much more.
- Who you become is losing your life savings in a business startup, but still seeing the good in all you learned from it as you continue to move forward.

- Who you become is being diagnosed with an incurable blood cancer and not allowing it to break you.
- Who you become is screwing up your life to a seeming point of no return, but finding a way to piece it all back together.
- Who you become is who you are after hitting rock bottom.
- Who you become is grinding every day to be better than you were yesterday, because the only person you should be in competition with is yourself.

Who you become is a person with the ability to see regrets as stepping stones, not errors. It's piecing life back together when it seems beyond repair. It's grinding every day to be better than you were yesterday, competing only with yourself. Everything you've been through creates mental toughness and becomes your guiding light, leaving you on uncommon ground to conquer any challenge with grace and poise. Your past hardships make today's obstacles conquerable and self-discipline easier because you know it could be so much worse.

In your life, let your scars tell your story of resilience, growth, and triumph. They are not marks of shame but badges of honor that showcase your journey through life's storms. I now leave it up to you to decide: What is your reason? What is your purpose? Why will you strive for the extraordinary despite adversity? Remember, in the depths of your struggles lie the seeds of your greatest strengths. On the ground where it really does feel good and easy to just remain, you shall rise, stronger, wiser, and more alive than ever before.

Transformation Steps Quick Reference

Transformation 1: Master Self-Image

Summary: Mastering self-image is crucial for happiness and success in all aspects of life. Constant self-criticism is destructive and can hinder personal growth and achievement. Learning to love yourself, exactly as you are, is the foundation for overcoming adversity and building a fulfilling life.

Remember:
- The way you view yourself colors your entire world.
- Self-criticism drains energy and limits your potential.
- Positive self-perception boosts confidence and achievement.
- Changing your self-image takes time and consistent effort.

Transformation Action Steps

Change the Habit: Train yourself to think positively about yourself daily. Replace negative self-talk with positive affirmations. Each morning or night, write three positive things about yourself in a journal.

Mirror, Mirror on the Wall: Compliment yourself every time you pass a mirror. Overcome the initial discomfort you may feel from positive self-talk and embrace the mood boost it provides.

Stop Judging: Avoid judging others. Recognize that the habit of judging creates a cycle of negative self-perception. Break this loop by focusing on acceptance and understanding.

Reframe It: Talk to yourself the way you would talk to a loved one.

Micro Moves: Set small, achievable daily goals for self-improvement. These consistent wins build self-trust and confidence, crucial for a healthy self-image.

The Transformation Mindset: Embrace the power of self-love and positive self-perception. View yourself as capable, worthy, and resilient. Recognize that mastering your self-image is the first step in bouncing back from any adversity.

Mantra: "I am valuable and significant exactly as I am, and I'm capable of positive change."

The work of mastering your self-image is nonnegotiable. It is the foundation for overcoming adversity and building a great future.

Transformation 2: Conquer the Victim Mentality

Summary: Breaking free from the victim mentality is crucial for personal growth and success. The victim mindset provides comfort and excuses, but it prevents you from reaching your true potential. Recognizing and overcoming this mentality is essential for facing adversity and achieving your goals.

Remember:
- The victim mentality is a comfortable crutch that hinders growth.

- No one owes you anything; the universe doesn't care about your circumstances.
- Overcoming adversity requires abandoning self-pity and taking action.
- Your mindset determines your ability to overcome challenges.

Transformation Action Steps

Identify: Spot your victim mentality. Be honest about your go-to excuses for not taking action.

Acknowledge: Catch yourself in the act of victim thinking. When you hear yourself whining or making excuses, stop and recognize it for what it is.

Correct Course: Take actionable steps to address your challenges:
1. Write down ideas to solve your problems.
2. Choose the most viable options.
3. Take immediate action on those choices.

The Transformation Mindset: Embrace the warrior spirit. Like Rocky Balboa said, "I didn't hear no bell." Push through your challenges, no matter how difficult they seem.

Mantra: "I am not a victim. I am a warrior who can overcome any battle."

Keep reminding yourself: The world doesn't owe you shit, but you owe it to yourself and your loved ones to be your best self.

Transformation 3: Guard Your Environment

Summary: Your environment, especially the people around you, profoundly shapes your beliefs, ambitions, and potential.

Like a tree drawing strength from soil and sunlight, humans absorb the attitudes and expectations of those around them. Negative influences can limit your dreams and potential, while positive ones can elevate you to new heights. Happiness and success often depend on consciously choosing who and what you allow to influence your thoughts and beliefs.

Remember:
- People absorb both positive and negative influences from their environment.
- Negative people often project their own limitations onto others.
- Share your dreams only with positive, encouraging people.
- Your circle of influence directly impacts your future success.
- Environmental change often precedes personal transformation.
- Proximity to success increases your chances of achieving it.
- Negative influences can be subtle but deeply impactful.
- Distance from toxic influences is sometimes necessary, even with family.

Transformation Action Steps

Check Your Environment: Take a hard look at your current environment: the people, media, and influences in your life. Document how each interaction affects your mindset and goals. Pay attention to subtle cues that might be limiting your potential.

Let Them Go: Make the difficult choice to distance yourself from negative influences, even if they're close friends or family. Minimize exposure to toxic relationships and unproductive habits that don't serve your greater purpose.

A Fresh Start: Immerse yourself in positive influences through books, industry experts, and professional communities. Flood your environment with content and connections that support your growth and ambitions.

The Transformation Mindset: Understand that your environment is a choice, not a destiny. Take active control of your surroundings to create conditions that support your growth and success.

Mantra: "I choose to surround myself with people who believe in possibility."

Your environment is either lifting you up or holding you back. By consciously choosing positive influences, you create the conditions for success and resilience in the face of adversity.

Transformation 4: Develop Self-Control, the Ultimate Adversity-Busting Superpower

Summary: Self-control is a crucial superpower in our modern world of temptation and instant gratification. It's the ability to do what you need to do and refrain from what you shouldn't do. Mastering self-control can transform your life in profound ways, helping you achieve your goals and overcome adversity. It's about delaying short-term pleasure for long-term rewards and success.

Remember:
- Self-control impacts all areas of life: diet, finances, relationships, and personal growth.

- Lack of self-discipline can lead to poor health, financial troubles, and an unfulfilling life.
- Building self-control is like strengthening a muscle; it takes consistent practice.
- Self-discipline creates confidence and a sense of empowerment.
- Intelligent planning and daily structure make self-control easier.

Transformation Action Steps

Control Yourself: Be hyperaware of your thoughts. When faced with temptation, question its purpose and remind yourself of the benefits of making the right decision.

Create Friction: Make it harder to engage in bad habits and easier to maintain good ones. Remove temptations from your environment and prepare for success in advance.

Focus on Weak Spots: Identify areas where you struggle with self-control. Write them down and track your progress daily.

Structure: Plan your days well to stay busy and productive. This reduces opportunities for boredom-induced bad decisions.

Stress Management: Develop stress-reduction techniques like exercise, deep breathing, and laughter. Stress weakens self-control, so managing it is crucial.

Suffer: Be willing to endure short-term discomfort for long-term gain. Push through the pain of delayed gratification to strengthen your self-control muscle.

The Transformation Mindset: Embrace the power of self-discipline as a path to personal growth and resilience. View each act of self-control as a step toward overcoming adversity and becoming your best self. Remember, mastering self-control gives you the confidence to face any challenge.

Mantra: "I have the power to control my actions and shape my destiny."

Self-control is the master virtue. By practicing it daily, you're building the ultimate tool for bouncing back from any adversity life throws your way.

Transformation 5: Master Your Fears

Summary: Fear can be a paralyzing force that keeps us trapped in our comfort zones and prevents us from reaching our full potential. However, conquering our fears is a powerful tool for overcoming adversity and achieving personal growth. By confronting our deepest anxieties, we develop the courage and resilience needed to overcome any challenge life throws our way.

Remember:
- Fear is a common human experience, but it doesn't have to control your life.
- Confronting fears leads to profound personal growth and increased resilience.
- The stories we tell ourselves about our fears are often worse than reality.
- Courage is developed through practice, not by avoiding what scares us.
- Nobody is better than you; we all have unique qualities and experiences.

Transformation Action Steps

Identify Your Fuel: Find strong, unassailable reasons to face your fears. Use past struggles, current challenges, or future goals as motivation. Focus deeply on these reasons to give yourself the push needed to take action.

Take Action: Break down your fear into smaller, manageable steps. Chart a course of action with specific goals and deadlines. Commit to taking at least one step forward each week. Remember, the goal is to build capacity to act despite fear, not eliminate it entirely.

Reflect and Celebrate Progress: After each attempt to face your fear, reflect on what you learned and how you felt. Recognize your courage in taking action, regardless of the outcome. Celebrate your progress, no matter how small, to build confidence and motivation.

The Transformation Mindset: Embrace fear as an opportunity for growth rather than a barrier. View each act of courage as a step toward becoming more resilient and capable. Remember, mastering your fears is an ongoing journey that equips you to face any adversity.

Mantra: "I am stronger than my fears. Each step I take builds my courage and resilience."

The world needs your unique voice and perspective. Don't let fear hold you back from sharing your gifts and achieving your goals. As you face your fears, you'll discover strengths you never knew you had.

Transformation 6: The Art of Failure

Summary: Failure is an inevitable part of life, but it's not something to be feared. Instead, it should be viewed as a powerful tool for growth and innovation. Mastering the art of failure involves approaching setbacks with intentionality, extracting valuable lessons from them, and using them to propel yourself forward. By embracing failure as a teacher, you can turn negative experiences into catalysts for positive change and personal development.

Remember:
- Failure is not the opposite of success; it's a crucial and necessary part of the journey.
- There's an art to failing well that can be learned and mastered.
- Losing and failing are life's ultimate teachers.
- Without failure, there is no growth.
- Failure is the way forward, providing priceless lessons not taught in any school.

Transformation Action Steps

Identify and Learn: List all your past losses and failures, both small and large. For each failure, identify the lessons learned. Look for recurring themes or patterns in your failures to better understand your growth areas and challenges.

Lean into Growth: Apply the lessons learned from past failures to future endeavors. Identify areas for improvement based on your failure patterns. Educate yourself on what skills are needed to address these areas and commit to developing them.

Moving Forward: Approach each day and setback with a growth mindset. After every setback, assess what went wrong and why. Adjust, learn, and grow from each experience. Use failure as a guiding light to move in your desired direction.

The Transformation Mindset: Embrace failure as an opportunity for growth and learning. View each setback as a stepping stone toward success. Remember, the ability to bounce back from failure is what defines your character and determines your future success.

Mantra: "I transform my losses into wins. Each failure brings me closer to success."

The law of success is simple: if you want it badly enough, you'll do whatever it takes to achieve it, despite the inevitable struggles and failures along the way. When adversity strikes, ask yourself, "How will I bounce back this time?"

Transformation 7: Fight Your Way Out of the Gloom

Summary: Life will inevitably present challenges and setbacks that can lead to depression or feelings of hopelessness. However, by adopting the right mindset and taking proactive steps, it's possible to overcome these difficult times and emerge stronger. Principle 7 focuses on strategies to combat depression, deal with adversity, and maintain a positive outlook, even in the face of significant challenges.

Remember:
- Adversity is inevitable, but succumbing to it is not.
- Past struggles can be a source of strength for current challenges.
- Nothing lasts forever, including pain and suffering.
- Physical health and mental health are closely linked.
- Choosing to perceive setbacks positively is crucial for overcoming them.
- Creating positive memories can help transcend pain.

Transformation Action Steps

Acceptance: Acknowledge what you can and cannot control. Accept your current state without judgment.

Use acceptance as a starting point for change rather than a destination.

Restart with Meaning: Identify activities or work that gives you a sense of purpose. Engage in meaningful pursuits, especially during challenging times. Find joy in small, everyday accomplishments.

Exercise: Commit to regular physical activity, especially when feeling down. Use high-intensity workouts to boost mood and confidence. Maintain consistency, no breaks, no excuses.

Social Connections: Reach out to friends and loved ones. Create and nurture genuine human-to-human connections. Spend time with people who lift your spirits and support your growth.

Gratitude: Keep a daily gratitude journal. However, you need to find the "reverse" gratitude in the things you're not supposed to be grateful for. That thing that got you down? Find the good in it.

Get Outdoors: Spend time in nature regularly. Find peaceful places that inspire awe and tranquility. Use natural settings for meditation and perspective-gaining.

Take a Walk in Someone Else's Shoes: Look beyond your own struggles to see and understand the challenges others face. Connect with those battling harder circumstances, and let their resilience inspire your own journey forward.

The Transformation Mindset: Embrace challenges as opportunities for growth. View each setback as a chance to demonstrate resilience and strength. Remember, your ability to overcome adversity defines your character and inspires others.

Mantra: "I choose to find strength in my struggles and joy in each day, no matter the circumstances."

Your days are numbered, so approach each one with the awareness of knowing you will die one day. Choose happiness and strength, showing resilience in the face of adversity. Your attitude and actions can inspire others and create a lasting positive impact.

Transformation 8: Treat Your Mind Like a Sanctuary

Summary: Your mind is a powerful tool that can either create or overcome adversity. By harnessing the power of visualization and positive thinking, you can reshape your reality and achieve your goals. Transformation 8 focuses on using visualization techniques to program your brain for success and to overcome obstacles.

Remember:
- We often create our own adversity through negative visualization.
- Visualization is not just positive thinking; it's a powerful tool to reshape reality.
- What you consistently visualize tends to manifest in your life.
- Every great achievement started as a vision in someone's mind.
- Visualization must be backed by action to be truly effective.

Transformation Action Steps

Visualize: Find a quiet place for fifteen minutes with your journal. Choose an area of your life you want to improve or achieve a better outcome in. Write briefly about your objective.

TRANSFORMATION STEPS QUICK REFERENCE

Close your eyes and visualize yourself, in detail, completing the objective. Write about the visualization, focusing on the feelings of success. Commit to this exercise at least three times a week.

Leverage Your Past Victories: Recall past adversities you've overcome. Visualize these past successes vividly. Tap into the feelings of triumph from these past victories. Inject these powerful feelings into visualizations of future challenges.

The Transformation Mindset: Embrace the power of your mind to shape your reality. View each thought and visualization as a building block for your future success. Remember, your mind is the launchpad for your achievements, and your actions are the rocket fuel.

Mantra: "I visualize my success, and through my actions, I make it my reality."

Your mind is like a muscle; the more you train it to visualize success, the stronger it becomes at making those visions a reality. Consistently practice visualization, back it up with action, and watch as you overcome adversities and achieve your goals.

Transformation 9: The Habit of Hard!

Summary: Embracing the habit of doing hard things is crucial for personal growth, building resilience, and overcoming adversity. By consistently choosing the challenging path over the easy one, you forge yourself into a stronger, more capable individual. This Transformation step encourages you to actively seek out and conquer difficulties, transforming your life and preparing you for any obstacle. When you commit to doing hard things every day, you become above average by default.

Remember:
- Doing hard things builds mental and physical toughness.
- Growth lies beyond your comfort zone.
- Choosing difficult tasks prepares you for life's inevitable challenges.
- The easy path often leads to mediocrity and regret.
- Consistently doing hard things increases confidence and discipline.
- Your struggles today forge you into the person you need to be for tomorrow's challenges.
- Every transformation lesson in this book requires choosing the hard path.

Transformation Action Steps

Discovery: Take fifteen minutes to brainstorm a list of hard things you've been avoiding. Write down these tasks or challenges in various life areas.

Prioritize and Select: Arrange your list of hard things by priority. Choose the top item that would have the most significant impact on your life. Visualize the end result if you consistently tackled this challenge for an entire month.

Craft the Task: Write down tactical changes needed to commit to this task daily. Identify potential obstacles and plan to overcome them. Structure your day to accommodate this new challenge.

Commit: Commit to doing your chosen hard thing every day for thirty days. No excuses, no delays, start immediately. For weekly tasks, spend off-days educating yourself on the subject.

TRANSFORMATION STEPS QUICK REFERENCE

The Journey Never Ends: After thirty days, make the habit permanent, if applicable. Select the next hard thing from your list. Begin the process again, stacking new challenges on top of ingrained habits.

The Transformation Mindset: Embrace difficulty as an opportunity for growth. View each challenge as a chance to forge yourself into a stronger, more resilient individual. Remember, by consistently choosing the hard path, you're investing in your future self and preparing for any adversity life may throw your way.

Mantra: "I choose the hard path today to make my future self unstoppable."

Greatness isn't born in comfort, but in the relentless pursuit of challenge. By developing the habit of doing hard things, you're not just improving yourself, you're inspiring those around you and creating a life of purpose and achievement. The hard path may be difficult, but it's the only way to reach your true potential.

Transformation 10: Fuck Average!

Summary: In the face of adversity, we have a choice: to surrender to circumstances or to face them head-on, driven by a desire to be more than average. This final lesson ties together all previous transformations and challenges you to reject mediocrity in every area of your life. By adopting a "fuck average" mindset, you transform adversity into a catalyst for profound personal growth and extraordinary achievement. This isn't about competing with others, it's about refusing to accept mediocrity in yourself.

Remember:
- Every transformation lesson in this book requires choosing to be above average.
- True growth often emerges in our darkest hours.
- Being "average" means settling for less than your potential.
- "Fuck average" is about being better than YOUR OWN baseline, not competing with others.
- Adversity can be a powerful motivator to exceed your own expectations.
- Small, above-average efforts in multiple areas compound for extraordinary results.
- The path to extraordinary achievement is challenging but rewarding.
- You inspire others when you refuse to settle for mediocrity.

Transformation Action Steps

Mindset Shift: Commit to the habit of being more than average in all areas of life. Ask yourself if you're willing to:
- Take your adversities and learn from them, grow from them
- Refuse mediocrity, even when those around you have accepted it
- Go the extra mile in your work and rise to the top of your profession
- Become disciplined to do what you need to do to get where you want to go
- Take this life and make something special of it before your time runs out

Apply Above-Average Efforts:

- Your work or business
- Your health and wellness routines
- Pursuing your goals
- Your relationships
- Your mindset and personal development

Learn from Adversity: Use challenges as opportunities for growth and fuel to become extraordinary.

Make "Fuck Average" Your Mantra: Let it push you when you want to quit. Let it be the voice in your head when you're tempted to take the easy way out. Say it when you need strength.

Join the Movement: Share your wins, big or small—with #fuckaverage. Take a picture with this book and post it online. Show the world you're done with mediocrity.

The Transformation Mindset: Embrace adversity as an opportunity to prove your extraordinary capabilities. View each challenge as a chance to separate yourself from your own mediocre baseline and demonstrate your commitment to excellence. Remember, in times of greatest difficulty, your resolve to say "fuck average" can propel you to new heights.

Mantra: "Fuck average. I refuse to settle for mediocrity in any area of my life."

The path to being above average is not easy, but it's infinitely rewarding. By consistently applying an above-average mindset to all aspects of your life, you set yourself on a trajectory toward exceptional achievement and personal fulfillment. When life seems overwhelming, that's your cue to dig deeper and push harder, because that's where true growth and success are found.

A Quick Favor

Before you go, may I ask for a quick favor? If you enjoyed this book, would you please consider leaving a review on Amazon, Goodreads, or wherever you purchased it? Reviews are incredibly valuable for authors like me. They boost visibility and help other potential readers discover my work.

Your honest feedback, even just a few sentences about what you liked or who you'd recommend the book to, can make a significant difference. If you're not comfortable leaving a public review, recommending the book to a friend or following me on social media are also wonderful ways to show support.

Thank you so much for reading and being a part of this adventure. Your support means the world to me, and I'm truly grateful for every reader who takes the time to share their thoughts.

—Jono

Contact the Author

Thank you for reading *The Breaking Point*. I hope you enjoyed it and gained some value from it. Even if you learned just one thing, that's great.

I'm always grateful to connect with my readers and hear how this book has impacted their lives. So please don't hesitate to reach out to me! Here's how to connect with me and stay updated on future works:

Connect with Me

Website: www.jonogilardi.com
Facebook: facebook.com/jonogilardiauthor
Instagram: @jonogilardi

I'd love to hear from you! Whether you have questions about the concepts in this book, want to share your own insights, or are ready to take your transformation to the next level, please reach out. I read every message and do my best to respond personally.

Your journey is uniquely yours, and you are the ultimate authority on your own life. I'm here to offer guidance and support as you continue to move forward.

Trust yourself, stay curious, and keep exploring. I'm here if you need me.

Stay Updated

Join my newsletter for exclusive content, updates, and insights. Sign up at www.jonogilardi.com.

Book Me as a Speaker

I'm available for speaking engagements and events. To inquire about booking me for your next event, please check out my website for more information.

Wishing you all the best—Jono.

About Jono Gilardi

photo courtesy Elyss Studio Photography

Jono Gilardi is a man who once stood at the precipice of self-destruction. In his own words, he's "the guy who screwed up his life and almost threw it all away one dark night." But from that low point, Jono turned his life around, and is now thriving and married to the love of his life, and has two beautiful children. However, in dramatic fashion, adversity returned again and dragged him back down to the trenches as he battles and thrives against an incurable blood cancer. These experiences, while challenging, became the catalyst for a profound transformation in his life and worldview.

Today, Jono doesn't view his status as a cancer warrior as an accomplishment, but rather as a powerful teacher. The disease that threatens his life teaches him that life is precious and our time is limited. With this hard-won wisdom, he approaches each day as an opportunity to embrace each moment and to create the life he envisions, regardless of past mistakes or present challenges.

Jono's passion now lies in sharing his powerful stories through his writing and on stage. As a captivating speaker, he aims to inspire and empower others to overcome their own struggles with adversity. Through his writing he extends his reach, offering guidance and support to those who may not have the opportunity to hear him speak in person. His fundamental belief is that regardless of one's past, everyone deserves to live a fulfilling life.

www.ingramcontent.com/pod-product-compliance
Lightning Source LLC
Chambersburg PA
CBHW030452100526
44580CB00006B/96/J